Praise for *Bargaining for Advantage*

"Readers interested in developing or refining their negotiation skills should run, not walk, to the nearest bookstore for a copy of *Bargaining for Advantage*. . . . It belongs on any list of required reading for practitioners or educators in the field of negotiation and is also highly recommended to the general public."
    —*Alternative Dispute Resolution Report*

"Not only is Professor Shell's book one that no business man or woman should overlook, it is also very readable and enjoyable . . . regardless of what business you're in, this is one of those invaluable tools to make use of over and over again."
    —*The Update*

"Whether you're buying a car, trying to get the kids into bed, or brokering a major business deal, *Bargaining for Advantage* teaches you to think on your feet and discover imaginative ways to come to terms with anyone."
    —Laurie Calkhoven, editorial director, The Money Book Club

"Articulate, well-researched and tightly organized. . . . A smart, readable, helpful and nicely different take on negotiations."
    —*The Pennsylvania Gazette*

"A new book that could really shift your sensibilities about the art of negotiation—taking out the mystery and replacing it with a success 'toolbox' . . . A volume that gives direct and practical fundamentals to becoming an effective bargainer in any situation."
    —*Business Digest*

"When it comes to negotiation, Richard Shell at Wharton is the best. His book and workshop show how to play the game without giving up your self-respect or threatening the other party's self-esteem. *Bargaining for Advantage* is a must for everyone who wants to feel more comfortable and effective at the bargaining table."
    —Max J. Garelick, president and CEO, Perry Ellis International

"Packed with well-selected examples of negotiating strategies from the business world and fascinating cultural observations, *Bargaining for Advantage* details every aspect of the fine art of negotiating. Should be required reading for anyone who is about to make a deal."
    —Ann McLaughlin, chairman, The Aspen Institute

"Wise, persuasive, and entirely readable, *Bargaining for Advantage* provides practical step-by-step advice for negotiators who want to bargain effectively without compromising themselves or their values."
> —Michael Wheeler, Harvard Business School, coeditor of *The Negotiation Journal*

"Tightly written, entertaining, and smart, Richard Shell's *Bargaining for Advantage* is a must read for anyone seeking greater insight into the art and science of negotiation."
> —Judith Rodin, president, University of Pennsylvania, professor of psychology, psychiatry, and medicine

"Richard Shell's book is the first step toward going into a negotiation with confidence. His logical and specific advice is extremely helpful for any businesswoman trying to succeed in a negotiation with both skill and grace."
> —Hilary B. Rosen, president and CEO, Recording Industry Association of America

"*Bargaining for Advantage* delivers just the sort of real world tools we are constantly looking for at Compaq to help our managers negotiate and form alliances more effectively. Research-based but highly accessible, Richard Shell's work will become a cornerstone in our negotiation training efforts."
> —Myles A. Owens, director, Strategic Alliances and Partnership, Compaq Computer Corporation

"Richard Shell is known to be a star teacher of negotiation. His expertise comes through in this book . . . a wonderful integration of practical advice that will be useful to all readers."
> —Max H. Bazerman, Gerber professor of dispute resolution and organization, Kellogg School of Management at Northwestern University

"Shell's insights as a scholar, and his years of experience as a negotiation teacher at one of the world's leading business schools, come together on every page of this very readable book. The writing is clear; the ideas are sound; and the narrative is crisp and compelling. The book is rich in cogent observations and vivid examples that help connect academic bargaining concepts to the real-world arenas in which they play out."
> —Stanford University Professor Roderick M. Kramer in *The Negotiation Journal*

PENGUIN BOOKS
Published by the Penguin Group
Penguin Group (USA) Inc., 375 Hudson Street, New York, New York 10014, U.S.A.
Penguin Group (Canada), 90 Eglinton Avenue East, Suite 700, Toronto,
Ontario, Canada M4P 2Y3 (a division of Pearson Penguin Canada Inc.)
Penguin Books Ltd, 80 Strand, London WC2R 0RL, England
Penguin Ireland, 25 St Stephen's Green, Dublin 2, Ireland (a division of Penguin Books Ltd)
Penguin Group (Australia), 250 Camberwell Road, Camberwell,
Victoria 3124, Australia (a division of Pearson Australia Group Pty Ltd)
Penguin Books India Pvt Ltd, 11 Community Centre,
Panchsheel Park, New Delhi—110 017, India
Penguin Group (NZ), cnr Airborne and Rosedale Roads, Albany,
Auckland 1310, New Zealand (a division of Pearson New Zealand Ltd)
Penguin Books (South Africa) (Pty) Ltd, 24 Sturdee Avenue,
Rosebank, Johannesburg 2196, South Africa

Penguin Books Ltd, Registered Offices: 80 Strand, London WC2R 0RL, England

First published in the United States of America by Viking Penguin,
a member of Penguin Putnam Inc. 1999
Published in Penguin Books 2000
This edition published 2006

3   5   7   9   10   8   6   4

Grateful acknowledgment is made for permission to use the following selections, which have
been adapted for this book: "When Is It Legal to Lie in Negotiations?" by G. Richard Shell,
Sloan Management Review; "Bargaining Styles and Negotiation: The Thomas-Kilmann Conflict
Mode Instrument in Negotiation Training," by G. Richard Shell, *Negotiation Journal.*

PUBLISHER'S NOTE
This publication is designed to provide accurate and authoritative information in regard to
the subject matter covered. It is sold with the understanding that the publisher is not engaged
in rendering legal or other professional service. If legal advice or other expert assistance
is required, the service of a competent professional should be sought.

LIBRARY OF CONGRESS CATALOGING-IN-PUBLICATION DATA
Shell, G. Richard, 1949–
Bargaining for advantage : negotiation strategies for
reasonable people / G. Richard Shell.— [2nd ed.].
p. cm.
Includes bibliograpical references (p. 279) and index.
ISBN 0-14-303697-1
1. Negotiation.   2. Persuasion (Psychology).   I. Title.
BF637.N4S44 2006
302.3—dc22   2005056636

Printed in the United States of America
Set in New Baskerville
Designed by Kathryn Parise

PENGUIN BOOKS

BARGAINING FOR ADVANTAGE

G. Richard Shell is the Thomas Gerrity Professor at the Wharton School of the University of Pennsylvania, where he is academic director of the Wharton Executive Negotiation Workshop. *BusinessWeek*'s biannual "Guide to the Best Business Schools" named him three times as one of the nation's top business school professors. He consults widely and trains business executives, nonprofit leaders, and government officials from all over the world to be more effective negotiators. He lives with his wife and two sons near Philadelphia in Wynnewood, Pennsylvania.

BARGAINING

Negotiation Strategies for

Reasonable People

FOR ADVANTAGE

Second Edition

G. Richard Shell

PENGUIN BOOKS

Pour ma tendre
Véronica,

For Robbie, Ben, and Ned,
who have taught me so much.

Afin qu'elle
développe ses
qualités de
négociatrice, à
son avantage.
Tendres baisers.

Laurent

Preface to the Second Edition

<--->

I t is with real pleasure that I offer this second edition of *Bargaining for Advantage*. I wrote this book in the late 1990s because I was dissatisfied with the existing set of works for serious students and practitioners of this fascinating process we call negotiation. I wanted a book that would explore the immense variety of real-world negotiations, provide both historical context and a social science foundation for dealmaking, and be fun to read. The appearance of this new edition and the many foreign translations of this work (more than ten at last count) suggest the book hit its mark.

So why improve on something that works? Four reasons. First and foremost, a new edition gives me a chance to share with readers a new Bargaining Styles Assessment Tool, which can be found in Appendix A. I believe that many negotiators have distinctive talents, strengths, and weaknesses rooted in personality. These traits are not set in concrete, but they generate biases and preferences that strongly affect how they behave at the bargaining table. I designed this bargaining styles assessment instrument to probe such negotiation instincts. By including my new test here, along with a standardized grid for evaluating your results in comparison with those of more than 1,500 executives from all over the world, I hope readers can come away from the book with a deeper understanding of the kind of negotiator they are when they are at their best.

The second reason for a new edition has to do with advancing communication technology. At the time I was writing *Bargaining for Advantage*, the world had not yet become as dependent as it is now on Internet-enabled electronic communication systems such as e-mail and instant messaging. This second edition gives me a chance to directly address the perils and promise of electronic negotiations, which I do in Chapter 7. This same chapter also features a new section on using agents in the bargaining process, an important topic I neglected earlier.

Third, I have become more aware since publishing the first edition of the importance of gender and culture as negotiation variables. I therefore address these topics in Chapter 1 in more detail than before. The publication in 2003 of Linda Babcock's and Sara Laschever's *Women Don't Ask: Negotiation and the Gender Divide* helped clarify the gender issue in a particularly helpful way.

Finally, this edition gives me a chance to edit and supplement a variety of stories, research studies, and topics that will keep the work fresh. Close readers of the first edition will notice a number of such changes and updates. Throughout, however, my intention has been to leave what has worked well largely intact.

A number of readers and fellow negotiation teachers who use the book in classes kindly offered suggestions for this edition. Some of my colleagues at the Wharton School, especially professors Maurice Schweitzer, Rachel Croson, Ken Shropshire, and Jennifer Beer, offered ideas and perspectives. Professor Alice Stuhlmacher of DePaul University generously shared both her ideas and her research on the controversial issue of gender and negotiation. I am also grateful for suggestions from the negotiations teaching faculty at the Stanford Law School. Silicon Valley lawyer (and friend) Ralph Pais was especially helpful. Special thanks go to Chris Guthrie, a law professor at Northwestern University, whose influential book review of *Bargaining for Advantage* introduced it to law school audiences. I could not give legal negotiation the treatment it deserves without distorting the focus of this book, but I invite readers seeking more specialized knowledge in this area to consult the excellent *Beyond Winning: Negotiating to Create Value in Deals and Disputes* by law school professors Robert H. Mnookin, Scott R. Peppet, and Andrew S. Tulumello.

With that said, I present this new edition. I sincerely hope it guides you on one of the most interesting (and potentially profitable) journeys that life has to offer—the journey toward effectiveness in all of your negotiations.

—G. RICHARD SHELL

Acknowledgments

A book like this cannot be written without help from many people. Three in particular played key roles. First and foremost, I want to thank my wife, Robbie, for her patient and thorough job of editing. A journalist and editor by profession, she steered me reliably toward clarity and vividness—and away from academic jargon and dry explanation. Second, I am indebted to my agent, Michael Snell, for his encouragement, upbeat attitude, and careful tutoring as we moved this project from concept to finished product. He was a knowledgeable guide to the mysteries of trade book publishing. Finally, I want to recognize my editor at Viking Penguin, Jane von Mehren, for believing in *Bargaining for Advantage*, improving it with her editorial direction, and providing a cheerful, professional hand throughout. Her sense of humor reminded me to keep mine.

During the manuscript phase, a number of friends and colleagues gave generously of their time to read and comment in detail on drafts. Special thanks go to Simon Auster, Peter Cappelli, Eric Orts, Maurice Schweitzer, and Michael Wheeler. In addition, Larry Susskind, James J. White, Robert Cialdini, Tom Dunfee, Alan Strudler, Stuart Diamond, Howard Kunreuther, Bob Mittelstaedt, Michael Stein, Leslie Goode, and Tod Ibrahim also read all or parts of the manuscript and made useful suggestions. Wharton MBA students in my fall 1997 and spring 1998 negotiation courses, as well as executives in the Wharton Executive Negotiation Workshop during the same and earlier periods, gave me comments and provided memorable stories to include as illustrations. Jon A. Bjornson assisted on graphic design elements of the book.

Two members of the Wharton Legal Studies Department office team—our business administrator, Tamara English, and my administrative assistant, Andrea King—tirelessly and patiently typed, proofread, and assembled drafts as the manuscript took shape. My thanks for their cheerful help. Jeremy Bagai, Bernadette Spina, Tracy Denton, and Brian Okay contributed outstanding research assistance.

Bargaining for Advantage reflects an intellectual journey as well as a writing project. I owe a particular debt to Professor Robert B. Cialdini, whose book *Influence: The Psychology of Persuasion* opened my eyes to lines of social psychological research that turned out to be especially relevant to negotiation. Cialdini's book also provided a model for making social science research both readable and entertaining. In addition, my colleague Stuart Diamond, with whom I teach in the Wharton Executive Negotiation Workshop, is always challenging my perspectives on the subject. His insistence on the importance of daily practice, personality styles, and standards led me to investigate these aspects of negotiation training and effectiveness more deeply than I might otherwise have done.

Finally, I have benefited over the past decade from many professional associations with leaders in the negotiation and conflict resolution fields. I had a particularly interesting academic experience as a Visiting Scholar at the Harvard Program on Negotiation in the 1993–1994 academic year. I also want to give special thanks to Larry Susskind (MIT), Len Greenhalgh (Dartmouth), Howard Raiffa (Harvard Business School), Max Bazerman (Kellogg School at Northwestern University), and Roy Lewicki (Ohio State University). These scholars introduced me to the subject of negotiation in its academic setting, generously shared teaching materials with me in the early going, and pointed me toward the intellectual and practical questions that make the field so interesting.

—G. Richard Shell

Contents

Introduction:
It's Your Move

At the Wharton School, I teach negotiation to some of the best and brightest business people in the world—both students and executives. I also serve as the academic director for a week-long negotiation program for senior managers called the "Wharton Executive Negotiation Workshop: Bargaining for Advantage." But despite these credentials, I have to admit that bargaining can make me a little anxious. In fact, sometimes I do not even realize I am negotiating at all—until it is too late.

For example, not long ago, I was sitting at the dinner table with my family when the telephone rang. I answered. It was a neighbor's teenage daughter, Emily.

"I'm raising money for our school softball team so we can take a trip this winter to play in a tournament," she explained. "We're selling citrus fruits like oranges and grapefruits. Would you like to buy some?"

We are friends with Emily's family and have known her since she was four. Naturally, I wanted to help out.

"Tell me about it," I said.

She explained the various packages and prices: $11 for the small sampler, $20 for a package with more grapefruit, $35 for the grand collection. I found myself wondering where we were going to store $35 worth of citrus fruit.

"OK," I said at the end of the pitch. "I'll take the eleven-dollar package."

Just then my wife, Robbie, got my attention. "Ask Emily about the guinea pig!" she said. I looked puzzled.

My older son, Ben, joined in a little more loudly: "*Ned's* guinea pig," he explained. "See if she can take care of Ned's guinea pig this weekend while we're away." Our eight-year-old had recently acquired a pet guinea pig that needed a sitter for the fast-approaching Thanksgiving weekend.

"Ah!" I said. I got back onto the phone. "Are you going to be here this weekend?" I asked.

"Yes," came the reply.

"Could you take care of Ned's new guinea pig for us? We'll be in New York and need to find her a home."

"No problem," she replied brightly. Then she went on without missing a beat: "In that case, do you think you could buy the twenty-dollar package?"

It was my move. "Sure," I said with a laugh. "We'll take the twenty-dollar package."

Negotiations—from the megamergers on Wall Street to budget meetings at work to everyday encounters at home—take unexpected turns and involve high stakes so often that many graduate professional schools in the United States now offer semester-long courses on the subject. In fact, they are some of the most sought-after courses in the entire curriculum. Why? Because students entering professional life—whether in business, law, medicine, education, politics, or public administration—are anxious about negotiation and want to improve their skills. They know they will face all sorts of negotiation challenges in their future roles as business and professional leaders, and they want to replace their anxiety with greater confidence.

These students are acting wisely because anxiety hampers negotiation performance in predictable ways. It interferes with our ability to think on our feet and narrows our perspective about the problem we are solving. Most critically, anxiety leads many reasonable people to seek simplistic answers to the question "How should I negotiate?" They grasp at phrases like "win-win" and "win-lose," hoping these formulas will explain what negotiation is about. Anxious negotiators search for single, one-size-fits-all strategies that will give them a feeling of control over the process.

But these attempts to simplify negotiations just don't work. First, *all deals that close are win-win deals.* The two sides would not agree to a proposal unless they thought agreement was better for them than no deal. Second, "win-lose" is often just a label we give a deal when we don't like the way the other side treated us. Finally, all-purpose strategies are an illusion. Experienced negotiators know that there are too many situational and personal variables for a single strategy to work in all cases.

To become more effective, you need to get beyond simple negotiation ideas such as these. You need to confront your anxieties, accept the fact that no two negotiators and situations are the same, and learn to adapt to these differences realistically and intelligently—while maintaining your ethics and self-respect. And to achieve these goals you need something more than simple phrases; you need a confident attitude based on tested and reliable *knowledge* about the negotiation process.

Such knowledge is at hand—the last twenty-five years has seen a veritable explosion of negotiation research and writing—but it is relatively inaccessible. Negotiation scholars publish their findings on negotiation in academic journals and books that most real-world negotiators do not read. And it is hard for reasonable people to sift the good advice from the bad in the popular writing on bargaining. Just because a technique works well for a sports celebrity or Hollywood agent does not mean it will work for you.

◄ Look Inside Your Toolbox: It's Your Move ►

This is why I wrote *Bargaining for Advantage*. In my work at the Wharton School, I have canvassed both the academic and popular literatures on bargaining in search of ideas and approaches that dependably help people achieve superior results at the bargaining table. And I have organized this knowledge in a straightforward way so busy people can use it.

My approach to negotiation starts with you. My own experience and a lot of research tell me that you already have what it takes to be a competent negotiator. You have a set of tools in your own personal negotiation "toolbox." The same basic communication and cognitive skills that got you where you are today—advancing toward your personal and professional goals—are the ones needed to negotiate effectively. And everyone—regardless of their current skill level—can improve their performance by identifying their strengths and weaknesses, planning more carefully and sharpening their tools through practice.

Many people are naturally accommodating and cooperative; others are basically competitive; some are equally effective using either approach. But there is only one truth about a successful bargaining style: To be good, you must learn to *be yourself* at the bargaining table. Tricks and stratagems that don't feel comfortable won't work. Besides, while you are worrying about your next tactic, the other party is giving away vital clues and information that you are missing. To negotiate well, you do not need to be tricky. But it helps to be alert and prudent. The best negotiators play it straight, ask a lot of questions, listen carefully, and concentrate on what they and the other party are trying to accomplish at the bargaining table.

Negotiation is not rocket science, but it is not simple intuition either. No matter who you are, your intuition will fail you in important bargaining situations. To improve, you need to shed your assumptions about the process and open yourself to new ideas. Most of all, you must learn to recognize the hidden psychological strategies that play such important roles in the process.

For example, as this book will show you, skilled negotiators see more than just opening offers, counteroffers, and closing moves when they look at what happens at the bargaining table. They see psychological and strategic currents that are running just below the surface. They notice where the parties stand in terms of the reciprocity norm. They look for opportunities to use what psychologists call the consistency principle to commit other parties to standards and then hold them to their prior statements or positions, and they know that the timing of a proposal is almost as important as its content. People need to feel they have "earned" concessions even when you are willing to give them away for free.

Knowledge of these and other patterns embedded in the negotiation process help experienced negotiators structure their proposals and predict what the other party will do next. Once you learn to see these and similar features of the bargaining landscape, you too will be able to "read" bargaining situations more accurately and make your moves with more confidence.

◄ The Approach: ►
Information-Based Bargaining

I call my approach to negotiation Information-Based Bargaining. This approach focuses on three main aspects of negotiation: solid planning and preparation before you start, careful listening so you can find out what the other side really wants, and attending to the "signals" the other party sends through his or her conduct once bargaining gets under way. As the name suggests, Information-Based Bargaining involves getting as much reliable knowledge about the situation and other party as possible.

My approach focuses on six factors or, as I call them, Foundations, of effective negotiation. These Six Foundations, which make up Part I of the book, are: your personal bargaining styles, your goals and expectations, authoritative standards and norms, relationships, the other party's interests, and the diverse ingredients that go into that most important of all bargaining assets: leverage (this idea is explained in detail in Chapter 6). With information on these foundations in hand, you are ready to move down the predictable path that negotiations follow, from the creation of a bargaining plan to preliminary exchanges of information to explicit, back-and-forth bargaining, and finally to the closing and commitment stage. Part II of the book will walk you through this four-stage process step by step.

Information-Based Bargaining is a "skeptical school" of negotiation. It treats each situation and person you face as unique. It cautions against making overly confident assumptions about what others want or what might be motivating them. And it emphasizes "situational strategies" tailored to the facts of each case rather than a single, one-size-fits-all formula.

To help you learn, the book illustrates the principles of Information-Based Bargaining with stories from the lives of some of the best negotiators who ever lived. You will study bargaining strategies used by successful people from many cultures and eras, including Sony Corporation's legendary founder Akio Morita, American tycoons such as J. P. Morgan, John D. Rockefeller, Sr., and Andrew Carnegie; modern deal makers H. Wayne Huizenga, and Donald Trump; historical figures such as Mahatma Gandhi and Benjamin Franklin; and a variety of less well-known but equally talented businesspeople and community leaders. You will see how these experts succeeded and, just as important, learn how they sometimes failed.

Such role models can teach us a lot, but even more important than their experiences are their attitudes about negotiation. The best negotiators treat bargaining seriously, but they also keep a professional perspective. They can always walk away. They maintain their balance no matter what the other side does, respond promptly to the other party's maneuvers, and keep moving patiently and persistently toward their goals.

The best negotiators also have explicit ethical guidelines for their own conduct at the table, regardless of what others may do. They know which moves are within the "rules of the game" and which ones lie outside ethical boundaries. To be truly effective, you will need to develop your own ideas about bargaining ethics; Chapter 11 provides a framework for you to begin thinking about this important topic.

➤ You Can Learn Only by Doing ➤

At the Wharton Executive Negotiation Workshop, I am fond of quoting a New York lawyer and deal maker named James C. Freund. Freund has written a number of books on business mergers as well as negotiations. He once stated that "in the last analysis, you cannot learn negotiation from a book. You must actually negotiate."

I agree. This book is a guide to better negotiation practice—not a substitute for it. So take the knowledge you find here and build your own foundations for an effective style. Consider every bargaining opportunity a "laboratory" to improve your skills. As you gain experience and confidence, you will discover that negotiations will cease being anxiety-filled encounters. Instead, they will become enjoyable—and profitable—challenges.

BARGAINING
FOR ADVANTAGE

PART I

THE SIX FOUNDATIONS OF EFFECTIVE NEGOTIATION

The First Foundation:
Your Bargaining Style

You must bake with the flour you have.

—Danish folk saying

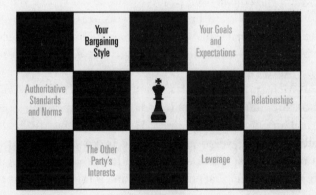

Two men entered a conference room in an office tower high above Lexington Avenue in New York City. It was a cold, wintry day in January. They greeted each other cordially but with noticeable restraint. Taking seats on opposite sides of a large conference table, they settled down to begin discussions over the possible merger of their two giant companies.

On one side of the table sat Peter Jovanovich, the proud chief executive of an esteemed American publishing house called Harcourt Brace Jovanovich (HBJ), which was now teetering on the edge of financial ruin. As the son of one of the firm's founders, Jovanovich was deeply committed to preserving his family's legacy. Across the table sat Dick Smith, the aggressive, entrepreneurial leader of General Cinema, a large, well-funded conglomerate probing for a corporate foothold in the publishing business. Flanking the two men and waiting expectantly were assorted legal and financial advisers.

Both sides had carefully prepared their "scripts" for the opening of the negotiation. Smith was to be the suitor. After months of analysis, he had concluded that HBJ was a perfect fit for General Cinema. But he was not sure that Jovanovich shared his vision of the opportunities that lay ahead. Smith planned a detailed presentation on General Cinema's financial strength and reputation. He would indicate that he sympathized with HBJ's woes and was willing to offer hope. But he would be cautious, not wanting to raise expectations about his price.

Jovanovich's team, also very positive about the deal, had prepared Jovanovich for the role of "listener." They had determined that General Cinema offered HBJ its best chance of corporate survival, but they, too, advised caution: Jovanovich's attitude would be interested but noncommittal. He would not tip his hand or show his urgency.

On cue, Smith began his opening speech, but within seconds Jovanovich interrupted—and the HBJ advisers stirred. This was not in the script. What was Peter up to?

As Jovanovich spoke, he took a small box from his coat pocket and placed it on the table between him and Smith. Jovanovich opened the box to reveal an engraved HBJ watch. He pushed it over to Smith.

"My father always gave a watch like this to his partners at the beginning of a new business relationship," said Jovanovich. "This is meant to signify my sincere belief that General Cinema is the right buyer for HBJ."

It was a risky admission, and both men knew it. The anxiety in the room eased. The two men, joined by their teams, began to talk in earnest about how a deal might be done. They kept talking into the night.

◄ Talking to the Mountain ►

Many years earlier and thousands of miles away, in a valley in Tanzania, East Africa, two elders representing separate lineages of the Arusha people were meeting in the late morning under a stand of large, shady trees. Beyond the elders in the distance loomed a 14,000-foot mountain: Mount Meru. Two groups of men flanked the elders, standing on opposite sides of the open area under the trees.

Shade trees are the conference rooms of rural Africa. Like thousands of similar trees near similar villages, these trees near the Arusha village provided a focal point where people could discuss important business at leisure. Today, the trees sheltered a negotiation.

The two elders addressed each other formally, describing a dispute between two neighboring farmers. Each elder described a list of grievances and demanded compensation for various wrongs. Each farmer, echoed by his group, loudly rejected the other's demands and elaborated further on his own elder's arguments.

Each man lay claim to a vacant area of land between their farms that had once been occupied by a family whose lineage had died out. The farmers' dispute had led to a series of incidents: One farmer's son had damaged an irrigation gate on the other's land; the owner of the irrigation gate had beaten the farmer's son for trespassing. The father of the beaten boy had gone to the elders, demanding a formal meeting to settle the issues.

The process they were engaged in reflected their African landscape like a mirror. They were, to use the Arusha word for the opening stage of negotiations, "talking to the mountain." And it was going well. A full day of discussions lay ahead. Everyone had brought lunch.

◄ The Path of Negotiation ►

Two groups. Two problems. Two cultures. Yet in both situations people were engaged in a single, familiar process called "negotiation"—an instantly recognizable human activity that helps people achieve goals and resolve problems. In both cases described above, as we shall see later, the process ended in a successful agreement. Exactly how and why negotiation achieves such results is the subject of this book.

People negotiate in generally similar ways in virtually every culture in the world and have done so since time began. An Arusha elder sitting in the New York conference room where Jovanovich and Smith met might not have understood the words being said, but he would have recognized the purpose and value of Jovanovich's gift to Smith. The Arusha negotiation involved a dispute rather than a deal. But, as we shall see, it concluded with an exchange of gifts. Gifts are part of a universal language of human relationships. And negotiations are fundamentally about the reciprocity norms underlying such relationships.

Negotiations proceed through a form of prudently cooperative communication. And negotiations commonly follow a recognizable four-step path: preparation, information exchange, explicit bargaining, and commitment. In the world of sophisticated big-city business deals, lawyers and investment advisers gather in their conference rooms and run through their carefully scripted openings. They discuss the issues, then usually ask for more and offer less than they expect to settle for in the end. In Tanzania, the Arusha people establish their agenda, list their demands, and "talk to the mountain," making exaggerated offers and counteroffers. They, too, are staking out the boundaries of possible agreement and watching for signals from the other side about what may or may not be acceptable. From here, people get down to the business of making concessions and establishing commitments. Negotiation is, in short, a kind of universal dance with four stages or steps. And it works best when both parties are experienced dancers.

➤ We Are All Negotiators ➤

All of us negotiate many times a day. We negotiated as children for things we wanted: attention, special treats, and raises to our weekly allowance of spending money. We negotiate as adults for much more complex sets of desires that, when you examine them closely, often come down to the same things we negotiated for as children. Negotiation is a basic, special form of human communication, but we are not always aware that we are doing it. A single definition that can help us recognize negotiation when it happens is the following:

A negotiation is an interactive communication process that may take place whenever we want something from someone else or another person wants something from us. We negotiate at kitchen tables as often as we do at bargaining tables. But our personal relationships and professional roles sometimes make complete cooperation and even sacrifice, rather than negotiation, the "right" answer to many requests. When a winter storm knocks out the electric power in our community and a neighbor calls asking for help, we do not stop to haggle with him—we respond. If our work calls on us to deliver uncompromising customer service and a customer needs something, we accommodate.

But notice something. Even these obvious examples of situations that do not seem to involve negotiation arise within the context of ongoing relationships that are characterized by deeply embedded norms of reciprocity. If our neighbor is known for his loud, late-night parties and never responds when we ask him to quiet down, his appeal for help in the storm may have to wait until we have taken care of others. And the customers we serve give us more business the better we serve them. There is a quid pro quo. So situations that involve pure cooperation and sacrifice with no thought of reciprocal accommodation are, in fact, relatively rare occasions. The rest of the time, we are involved in some sort of negotiation, broadly defined.

Not all negotiations are alike. Bargaining with family members and friends over such things as schedules, meals, obligations, and duties is more in the nature of problem-solving sessions than deal making. That is because we usually negotiate differently with those we love than we do with strangers.

Pushing past the protective envelope of our closest relationships, we confront a complex world of negotiations with banks, stores, hotels, airlines, credit card companies, health care institutions, and the other services that govern our day-to-day lives. In the industrialized countries, many of these consumer negotiations are mediated by markets and we pay prices that are marked or printed on tags. As American consumers are rapidly learning, however, there is often a lot more room to negotiate with hospitals, department stores, and other service providers than we once thought. The norm of "customer satisfaction" often means there is one price marked on a price tag for those who wish to pay it—and another, lower one for those who wish to negotiate.

Other parts of the world use an explicit ritual of haggling as the expected way of conducting consumer sales. A visit to the open markets of India or Egypt shows how merchants rely on bargaining to accomplish even the simplest consumer transaction. In these societies negotiation is an important form of personal expression and even entertainment, not just a business event.

Finally, in our jobs and professions, we depend on negotiation skills to get things done with coworkers, bosses, suppliers, and, at the highest levels, CEOs and boards of directors. Indeed, negotiations within companies and institutions to solve in-house problems are among the most common and troubling negotiation situations many people face on a daily basis.

Through all of this, as I pointed out in the introduction, many reasonable people have a nagging, uneasy feeling about negotiation. They are anxious about it. The interpersonal conflicts, the possibility of leaving "money on the table," the chance they could be "taken," and even the thought that they have done "too well" are all unsettling.

Knowledge about the negotiation process and bargaining strategy helps reduce this anxiety and puts you on the road to improved negotiation results. And the place to begin building this knowledge is the same place that all negotiations begin: with the First Foundation of Effective Negotiation—your own style and personality as a negotiator. That is where our study starts.

◄ What's Your Style? ►

Your personal negotiation style is a critical variable in bargaining. If you don't know what your instincts and intuitions will tell you to do under different conditions, you will have a great deal of trouble planning effective strategies and responses.

Steve Ross, the supercompetitive founder of Warner Communications and later CEO of Time Warner Inc., was once playing canasta with his wife and another couple on a trip in a Warner corporate jet. He lost the last game just before the plane was preparing to land—and ordered the pilot to circle the airport until he finally won a hand. This was typical of the way Ross played the "game" of business, and people who negotiated against him were wise to take this personality trait into account.

By contrast, Larry King, the popular host of CNN's interview program *Larry King Live*, has a reputation as one of the nicest men in the world of big-time entertainment. In the middle of King's career, his agent decided to shop Larry to various other television networks. The idea was to gather some competing offers, then demand a multimillion-dollar raise from CNN's owner, Ted Turner.

The agent's plan was working fine, with seven-figure offers coming in from various networks, but Turner would not budge. The agent then played his "other offer" card and said that King might move to a major television network if Turner would not match the competing bids.

Turner had known King for years and knew him to be a loyal and cooperative guy, not a "hardball" negotiator. With the agent sitting right there in Turner's office, Turner picked up the telephone and called King directly. After a little chat about old times and how much he liked King as a person, Turner laid his request on the line: "Stay with me," he said.

"OK," said King simply, "I'll stay."

The agent was flabbergasted. But King was happy. He liked the money he was making, he liked Ted Turner, and he liked the fact that Turner liked him. Ted gave Larry a modest raise. Score one for Ted.

Lesson: If you are basically a nice person, it will be a real stretch to act like Steve Ross at the bargaining table. You can do it, but not for long and not with a lot of credibility. And if you are basically a competitive negotiator, your go-for-it instincts will very likely shine through no matter how hard you try to suppress this aspect of your personality. In fact, even if you genuinely hate to negotiate, you can do just fine, provided you accept this about yourself and learn to work with it.

I once led a workshop for a number of high-level business luminaries—including a man who founded and serves as chairman of the board at one of the world's most successful Internet companies. After the workshop, he confided to me that most negotiations make him quite uncomfortable. As a result, he avoids the process whenever possible and considers himself a poor negotiator. I responded that he had made several billion dollars, so he could not be *that* bad. Not true, he replied. He had succeeded by focusing on his innovation skills—designing an Internet auction system that completely eliminates all haggling from the selling process—and by delegating the really tough negotiations at his company to other executives who excel at (and enjoy) bargaining. Instead of negotiating, he specializes in collaborative aspects of his business such as strategic planning, managing the board of directors, and enhancing the experience of his company's unique online community. He became successful not by overcoming his negotiation weaknesses, but by accepting them.

So my advice is to begin your study of negotiation by taking a good look in the mirror. Which moves come most naturally and comfortably to you? And how can you use those instincts as a solid foundation to build a set of effective skills and strategies for achieving your goals? You will become the best negotiator you can be by identifying and then building on your genuine strengths and talents.

◄ Five Strategies and Negotiation Styles: ►
A Thought Experiment

To begin our exploration of your bargaining strengths, try the following thought experiment. Imagine you are one of ten people, all of whom are strangers, sitting at a big round table in a conference room. Someone comes into the room and makes the following offer: "I will give a prize of one thousand dollars to each of the first two people who can persuade the person sitting opposite to get up, come around the table, and stand behind his or her chair."

Do you have that picture in mind? You are one of the ten strangers at the table. You can see the person sitting opposite you, and that person is looking at you. The first two people who can persuade the person sitting opposite to get up, come around the table, and stand behind his or her chair gets $1,000. Everyone else gets nothing.

What strategy would you use to respond to this strange offer? You will need to move quickly because everyone else is also thinking about what to do.

Before reading on, close your eyes and think of your response. Note what strategy comes to your mind first and write it down. Then see what other responses you can think of. The possibilities will help me introduce five generic negotiating strategies, which will, in turn, lead us to a deeper look at your personality as a negotiation variable.

One reaction is to sit tight and do nothing, suspecting a trick or worrying that you might look like a fool running around a table in response to a stranger's offer. "I don't like to negotiate, so I don't do it unless I have to," you might say. This is the **avoiding** response favored by the Internet entrepreneur I mentioned above. Some people might say that avoiding a negotiation is a cop-out, not a bargaining strategy. But you do not have to look very far to notice that many important negotiations are marked by one side or the other studiously avoiding coming to the table. The North Koreans successfully avoided negotiating over their nuclear weapons programs for years—and built up bargaining leverage in the meantime. Presidential candidates in the United States who find themselves ahead in the polls frequently decline to negotiate when their opponents want to increase the number of presidential debates. In general, avoiding is a good strategy when you are happy with the status quo—but it may not be the best approach to the table problem.

Perhaps the most obvious response is to offer the person sitting opposite you $500 if he or she will race around and stand behind your chair. This is the **compromise** solution. Each person agrees to share the gains equally between them. Compromise is a simple, fair, fast strategy that resolves many negotiations amicably. But is it a good strategy for the table problem? You and your partner may arrive at a quick agreement to split the money evenly, but which of you should run and who should sit? During the few seconds it takes to address this issue, other people are already racing around the table. There is no compromise solution to the question of which of you should run—so a simple compromise does not fully solve the problem. An additional strategy is needed.

That strategy is our third candidate—**accommodation**. You could simply get up and run behind your opposite's chair. If you do this in response to your partner's offer to split the money, you can refer to that promise as a bargaining standard in any subsequent negotiation over the money. But there may be no money to split. The people who implemented the 100 percent accommodating strategy took off as soon as they heard the stranger's offer and got to their partners' chairs before you did. But they face a problem, too. The lucky people who were the beneficiaries of the accommodating strategy now have $1,000 and the people who ran have nothing. These helpful negotiators must trust the people for whom they earned the money to share it—without the benefit of a prior commitment on how it will be shared. And remember—everyone at the table is a stranger who never expects to see their counterpart again.

The fourth response embodies the **competitive** strategy. The idea here is to obtain the entire $1,000 as well as the power to decide how it will be shared. One way might be to offer to split the money 50-50 and then later refuse to do so—to renege on your promise. That would obviously be unethical, but some people might do it. After all, there was no mention of a court system to litigate disputes about who said what. An even more aggressive stance would be to lie and say you have a broken leg so you can't move, begging your partner to run as quickly as possible. Are all competitive strategies as ethically dubious as these two? No. We will see examples of many competitive strategies in the pages ahead that are perfectly ethical under any system of morals. But the table problem is not structured well for a strategy that is both ethical and competitive. Moreover, this strategy, like the compromise approach, may take too long to implement.

The final strategy is the most imaginative, given the terms of the offer. You get out of your chair, start running, and scream: "Let's both get behind each other's chairs! We can each make a thousand dollars!" This can work—if you are quick enough. This is the **collaborative** or **problem-solving** strategy. Instead of trying to figure out how to divide $1,000 two ways, the person using this approach has the insight to see that there is a way for *both parties* to get $1,000 out of the situation.

The collaborative strategy is often the hardest to implement. It seeks to discover the underlying problem through good analysis and candid disclosure of interests, find the most elegant solution by brainstorming many options, and resolve tough issues using fair standards and criteria.

In many ways, it represents an ideal. As we shall see, problem-solving strategies are especially useful in complex negotiations, such as those faced by international diplomats or corporate negotiators doing mergers or acquisitions. They can also play a useful role in family negotiations, where it is vitally important to avoid having "winners" and "losers." But many obstacles stand in the way of collaborative approaches, such as lack of trust between the parties, greed, personality, cultural differences, and simple lack of imagination.

How many of these five strategies did you think of? And, just as important, which of the five would you feel most comfortable and natural implementing? We can now use our knowledge of these five strategies to probe your personal inclinations and styles as a negotiator.

In Appendix A, I have provided you with the self-assessment test we give our participants at the Wharton Executive Negotiation Workshop to help them determine their preferred bargaining styles. It takes only about five minutes to complete and score, so I suggest you turn to Appendix A now and complete your Bargaining Styles Assessment. Once you obtain your results, you can jump back to this chapter and read on. Later, if you want to learn more about the various styles and how they interact with one another, you can go back to Appendix A for further study.

Your personal bargaining styles are nothing more (or less) than your inclinations or predispositions to make certain moves when you are negotiating. These inclinations can come from many sources—childhood, family, early professional experiences, mentors, ethical systems or beliefs, and so on. And your inclinations can change over time as your knowledge of negotiation grows and you gain more confidence in a wider range of skills. But I genuinely believe that most of us have a set of core personality traits that make radical changes in our basic bargaining preferences difficult. For example, I was raised in a household by two loving parents who were very strongly inclined to avoid interpersonal confrontations between themselves and between them and their three children (my two sisters and me). On the Bargaining Styles Assessment, they each would have scored very high in the "avoiding" category. This rubbed off on me more or less permanently. To this day, I instinctively and automatically try to deflect conflict in my interactions with others, although I have become much more capable of handling conflict through a lifetime of professional and personal experiences. My diplomatic trait is just part of the bargaining personality I bring with me to negotiation interactions. I have other instincts that come into play in different situations and with different people, but my diplomatic trait is never far from the surface.

Each style or combination of styles brings a set of associated talents with it. Someone dominated by a strong inclination to compete has a talent for seeing more quickly than others how power and leverage can be gained in a given situation. And he or she derives more satisfaction from getting a great price in a haggling situation than do people who are only weakly inclined to measure their success in these terms. This person will also see the potential for using a competitive approach in more situations than will the rest of us.

Someone who is strongly inclined to accommodate will have a talent for being a team player and helping other people, even when there is a conflict of interest. He or she will be focused on the interpersonal relationship aspect of an interaction when the rest of us are focused on the money. A person dominated by a preference for compromising will automatically seek simple, fair methods of taking turns or splitting the difference to resolve negotiation differences quickly and fairly much more often and much sooner in the process than will people who lack this inclination. And, finally, people who bring to the table very strong inclinations to collaborate will find themselves facilitating the process, asking lots of questions and developing different ways of looking at the issues to meet as many needs as possible—including their own. They will genuinely enjoy complex, prolonged negotiations in a way that someone predominantly inclined toward simple compromises will not.

The Bargaining Styles Assessment is a good place to start in understanding your styles, but it is only one data point in your quest to learn about yourself as a negotiator. As you read about different negotiations in this book and encounter various situations in your life, note which experiences you enjoy and which ones cause you stress. Those that feel good are the ones for which you have natural talents. Build on the insights you gain from these experiences, and, in the words of the Danish folk saying that led this chapter, "bake with the flour you have."

◄ Cooperative Versus Competitive Styles ►

Beneath the five personal inclinations discussed above reside two even more basic types: cooperative and competitive. Much research on the personality variable in negotiation has centered around these two basic categories. Depending on the situation, each style can be effective and each exposes its possessor to certain dangers. In Chapter 12, I give some specific advice on how to compensate for the weaknesses inherent in each approach.

Many researchers have wondered whether people are, in general, more competitive or cooperative in their basic orientation toward bargaining. The stereotype negotiator depicted in the press, movies, and mass media is a competitive person who is adept at using hardball tactics such as ultimatums, walkouts, public posturing, and table pounding. This is not surprising, given the mass media's attention to drama and entertainment, but it is not an accurate reflection of how the average professional negotiator—or even the average professional person—actually behaves.

Two studies of negotiator behavior have revealed a more complex and accurate profile of how the average professional conducts himself or herself at the bargaining table. The first study covered American lawyers; the second looked at English labor negotiators and contract managers.

A study of American lawyer-negotiators reported by Professor Gerald R. Williams revealed that roughly 65 percent of a sample of attorneys from two major U.S. cities exhibited a consistently cooperative style of negotiation, whereas only 24 percent were truly competitive in their orientation (11 percent defied categorization using these two labels). Roughly half of the sample was rated as "effective" negotiators by their peers. Most interesting, more than 75 percent of the "effective" group were cooperative types and only 12 percent were competitive. The remaining effective negotiators came from the pool of mixed strategy negotiators.

In contrast to the stereotypes, this study suggests that a cooperative orientation is more common than a competitive orientation within at least one sample of professional negotiators in the United States. Moreover, it appears to be easier to gain a reputation for being effective (at least as rated by peers) by using a cooperative approach rather than using a competitive one.

The second study was conducted over a period of nine years by Neil Rackham and John Carlisle in England. Rackham and Carlisle observed the behavior of forty-nine professional labor and contract negotiators in real transactions. Some of the results of their work will be discussed in Chapters 5 and 8 later in this book. The point I want to make here relates to the styles exhibited by these professionals. The most effective of them displayed distinctly cooperative traits.

For example, the study examined the use of what the researchers called irritators at the negotiating table. Irritators are such things as self-serving descriptions of one's offer, gratuitous insults, and direct attacks on the other side's proposal—typical competitive tactics. The average negotiator used 10.8 irritators per hour of negotiating time; the more skilled negotiators used an average of only 2.3 irritators per hour.

In addition, skilled negotiators avoided what the researchers called defend/attack spirals, cycles of emotion-laden comments assigning blame or disclaiming fault. Only 1.9 percent of the skilled negotiators' comments at the table fell into this category, whereas the average negotiators triggered or gave momentum to defend/attack spirals with 6.3 percent of their comments. The profile of the effective negotiator that emerges from this study seems to reflect a distinct set of cooperative, as opposed to stereotypically competitive, traits.

The conclusion from both studies? Contrary to popular belief, perfectly reasonable, cooperative people appear to have a strong potential to become extremely effective negotiators.

◄ Gender and Culture ►

Bargaining style preferences originate from deep psychological sources, including conflict resolution patterns with parents, early experiences with siblings and playmates, and lessons we learn at the outset of our careers. And these early, formative experiences sometimes derive from two even more basic aspects of our social identities: our gender and culture. These two topics are controversial because intelligent discussion can rapidly slip into destructive (and misleading) stereotypes. But researchers have identified some reliable truths about these variables, so they are well worth addressing.

THE GENDER DIFFERENCE IN NEGOTIATION

Studies indicate that men and women can differ in the ways they communicate—especially in work settings. Georgetown linguistics professor Deborah Tannen has demonstrated in books such as *You Just Don't Understand: Men and Women in Conversation* and *Talking from 9 to 5: Women and Men at Work* that men tend to be more assertive, more likely to interrupt their counterpart, and more oriented toward affirming their status. Women, meanwhile, listen more than men do and pay greater attention to emotional rapport and taking turns when speaking. Although you probably know plenty of emotionally oriented men and status-oriented women, the statistics support Tannen's overall findings. The question then becomes how these various behavioral tendencies can be used or adapted so they are sources of strength rather than weakness in particular professional contexts.

Research on American women suggests that there are two main ways that gender differences affect negotiations. First, there is solid empirical evidence that women—including professionals in high-stakes business careers—choose to negotiate somewhat less often than do men in such important areas as salary and promotion. In negotiation style terms, women behave, on average, a bit more cooperatively than men. In a study conducted at Carnegie Mellon University's business school, Professor Linda Babcock discovered that the difference between the starting salaries women MBA graduates were getting and the salaries men were offered (roughly a $4,000 difference in favor of the men) could be accounted for by one single behavioral fact: 57 percent of the men asked for more money after receiving an initial offer whereas only 7 percent of women asked for more. Those who negotiated—both women and men— received an average of $4,053 more than those who did not. Babcock's research, summarized in her book, *Women Don't Ask*, confirms this tendency across a number of studies and contexts. Students in my negotiation classes have added another item to the list of practices women tend to follow more than men: they rely heavily on "fairness" arguments, assuming their counterparts will be responsive to their reasoned, relationship-friendly methods. These tactics can pay off, of course, but only when other parties are tuned to the same relationship wavelength.

The experience of one of my students, Marci, vividly illustrates exactly how the gender factor can subtly work its way into the bargaining process. Prior to starting her MBA studies, Marci worked for a midsized computer services firm and was the only female in her unit. Consistent with Babcock's research, Marci had not negotiated her offer when she received it from her new employer. In fact, she was simply delighted to get the job. After a couple of years of exemplary work, she gradually became responsible for business representing 30 percent of the company's revenue—while two better-paid male counterparts who started work with her were handling projects worth only 1 percent of revenues each. She thought she deserved a raise.

Her method of introducing the raise issue was characteristically indirect, however. She went to her boss and requested a performance review. "I thought it was a great way to get my superiors to notice my success without blowing my own horn," she told me during class. "I did not want to appear pushy." Her tactic did not work. The boss could not find the time to review her.

Many women might stop here, but Marci was persistent. She went to the president of the company and boldly asked for a 20 percent raise, arguing that her male coworkers were getting 20 percent more pay but managing fewer people and projects. Thus, a 20 percent raise was "fair." This, too, failed. As she described it, "I kept repeating, 'This is not fair.' In retrospect, fairness required even more than a 20 percent salary increase based on my contribution, but I was not confident enough to ask. No doubt, this insecurity shined forth." In addition, as she put it, "given that I was working such late hours, seemed so committed to my position, and appeared to have no inclination to look for another job, there was no urgent necessity to listen to me."

In the end, Marci got her raise—just in time for her to turn it down. When the company discovered that she had been accepted into Wharton's MBA program and intended to go, it offered her a 35 percent raise. But by this time, Marci was already out the door. As she told her fellow students, "Being afraid to ask is the most self-defeating trait a woman can have. Don't be afraid to look pushy."

The second gender-based research finding I find persuasive has to do with stereotypes. Because women appear, on average, to be somewhat more cooperative than men, both men and women bring stereotypes to the bargaining table that exaggerate this difference, creating self-fulfilling prophecies and blinding them to what is really going on. This can work either to women's disadvantage or advantage, depending on the experience of the negotiator.

For example, studies have shown that women bargain less effectively when they are reminded of a negative, women-are-wimps gender stereotype just prior to a transaction. It seems that fear of being stereotyped as a passive female can sabotage a woman's confidence and hence her ability to effectively use her own style, whatever that style may be. Even attempts to prove the stereotype wrong seem to backfire, leading to overly aggressive behavior and less-than-stellar results. This psychological process is reversed if women are given a positive, women-are-collaborative stereotype just prior to negotiating. Now the self-fulfilling prophecy creates a good bargaining experience and better results. But because the actual stereotype in the world is more often negative than positive, women sometimes suffer from what scholars call "stereotype threat."

On the other hand, skilled manipulation of others' stereotypes regarding women can give a female negotiator a significant *advantage* if she plays her cards right. This ability to turn the tables on opponents seems to come with experience. A top-ranked woman negotiator once spoke to our class about her adventures representing distressed companies in "work-out" situations. These hard-nosed negotiations take place between creditors and companies that cannot pay their bills. Potential bankruptcy forms the backdrop to the bargaining. Few women make this their professional calling, and our speaker reported that her femininity was almost always an asset in this tough arena. "For example," she said, "whenever a guy on the other side of the table attacks me personally, I never speak up to defend myself. I wait for a man on the other team to come to my defense—one always does—and then I have gained an ally and divided their group. It's an advantage." Another speaker, a petite woman who was head of mergers and acquisitions for a major pharmaceutical company, reported that she liked to play with stereotypes of all kinds. She was born in Poland but moved to Israel as a child. "Before a negotiation," she explained, "I always find a way to make it known that I was once an Israeli military officer. I create the impression that I am going to be tough as nails, and then I go in and melt their hearts. They are so relieved—and they work with me. Of course, I can always fall back on that first impression if I need to."

Gender does not have to become an issue in negotiations. But smart negotiators try to anticipate every aspect of their own and their counterparts' behavior as part of a good preparation. They also need to be aware of their own assumptions. Gender differences are therefore well worth considering as part of a complete style analysis.

A WORLD OF DIFFERENT CULTURES

If gender can complicate the negotiation process, cross-cultural issues can be showstoppers. At the Wharton School, we used to have a small, specialized program in "international business." Now the entire MBA program focuses on global business problems. And in doing global deals, sensitivity to issues of language, customs, social expectations, and religion can mean the difference between a successful long-term business relationship and a short-lived, unprofitable transaction.

Consider the following examples:

A British CEO once told me about his first negotiation in Lebanon. He started the negotiation well, but every time he made a concession, the other parties escalated rather than reduced their demands. After several rounds of this over a couple of months, he quit, telling his counterparts that he was thoroughly disgusted with their tactics and that he wanted nothing to do with them. A few days later, they called, saying that they now had "serious" proposals to put to him. He rejected the overture. A week later, they called again, making several concessions they had previously said were absolutely impossible. He reiterated that he had no interest in further dealings. At this point in his story, he looked at me ruefully. "The whole thing was really my own fault," he said. "I later learned that walking away from the table is a very common way to show you are serious in that part of the world. If I had walked out two months sooner, they would have behaved better and I probably could have closed the deal."

Culture can also affect decisions about who should be at the table. For example, different cultures have different sensitivities regarding the status of people at the bargaining table. Some formal cultures require participation by people of equal rank. Other, less formal cultures use functional knowledge and decision authority as criteria for picking negotiators. Such differences can lead to serious breakdowns and misunderstandings.

A female attorney working for a prestigious New York law firm once accompanied the male CEO of a major client to Latin America to negotiate a complex deal. Soon after they arrived, the head of the prospective Latin American partner suggested that he and the CEO go off together to discuss business—while his wife and the lawyer go shopping. The lawyer was outraged, assuming this to be a blatant example of Latin American gender bias. Before voicing her objections, however, she called a colleague back in New York, who told her that he, too, had been excluded from preliminary talks during his last negotiation in that country. The Latin American executive was just looking for a diplomatic way to get her out of the picture *as a lawyer*, not as a woman. It was the local practice, the colleague suggested, for lawyers to negotiate only with other lawyers, not with the businesspeople. Had the woman attorney insisted on participating, she would have soured the deal and destroyed her credibility.

These and countless examples like them confirm that culture presents a veritable minefield of stylistic differences in negotiation. The Arusha people gathering under their shade trees in Africa may engage in a process similar to the one business moguls use in New York, but the tone, pacing, signals, cues, and underlying assumptions about relationships can be radically different. Because our global economy depends on bridging these cultural divides, entire books (some of which I list in the bibliography) detail the pitfalls, opportunities, and customs that characterize negotiating in every commercially important region in the world.

I will be referring to a variety of different cultural practices throughout the book, especially in the chapters dealing with relationships, exchanging information, and bargaining. For now, I simply want to flag two important points.

First, cultural issues usually have more to do with form than substance. That is, they add complexity and potential misunderstanding to the way people communicate with one another, but money, control, and risk are still likely to be the most important issues on the table regardless of what country you are in. And the best way to avoid miscommunication is to do your homework on the culture in question, hire skilled interpreters, and use cultural liaisons to help you avoid cross-cultural meltdowns.

Second, the single most important difference in cross-cultural negotiations—other than the obvious problems of language and custom—is the way the parties perceive the relationship factor. As I will detail in the chapter on information exchange, North Americans and northern Europeans tend to focus more quickly on the transactional aspects of the deal, whereas most Asian, Indian, Middle Eastern, African, and Latin American cultures focus more intently on social, relational aspects. As a Japanese MBA student of mine once put it, "Japanese people tend to think of negotiation as a process leading up to an 'arranged marriage.' And they behave as if they really are in such a situation." Western negotiators doing business in Japan or other relationship-based cultures do well to approach preliminary social events in this spirit. Cultures may vary in the degree of formality they associate with prewedding festivities, but families in all cultures use these events to thoroughly size up and woo their new, would-be relations. If you want to be successful negotiating in a relationship culture, therefore, be patient and realize that the contract (if one comes) is just one part of a much bigger picture.

◂ Beyond Style—to Effectiveness ▸

People bring many personal differences to the bargaining table, but the overriding goal for each of us remains constant: How can we become as effective as possible using our unique combination of traits and talents? Many attributes go into making a skillful negotiator, including such things as having a good memory, being "quick" verbally, and handling stress well. But effectiveness is as much a matter of *attitude* as it is of ability. The best negotiators exhibit four key habits of thought that everyone, regardless of their style, gender, or culture, can adopt to improve their negotiation results. They are:

- A willingness to prepare
- High expectations
- The patience to listen
- A commitment to personal integrity

These practices will serve as themes throughout the book. Let's look briefly at each of them.

A WILLINGNESS TO PREPARE

The research on the importance of preparation is extensive. Nearly every research study on negotiation has confirmed its importance. Here is an illustration.

Several years ago, a colleague and I were investigating the use of computer networks as a method for negotiation. We designed a network computer system to help parties reach better agreements and then set out to test it. We gave the same four-issue, buy-sell exercise to hundreds of MBA students. Students playing the "buyer" role were paired with others playing the "seller" role. We instructed half the pairs to read the problem and negotiate whenever they thought they were ready—some face-to-face, others using e-mail. They usually took about ten to fifteen minutes to prepare, then they negotiated.

We required the other groups to go through a structured, individual preparation process on the computer that usually took about thirty to forty minutes. Some students then negotiated the buy-sell exercise using our computer network system while others bargained face-to-face.

We were surprised by the results. Our fancy, computerized method of negotiation did not matter much. But the preparation process did. The students who used the formal preparation system reached better agreements in *both* the face-to-face and the computer network conditions—not just for themselves, but for both sides.

HIGH EXPECTATIONS

Research on negotiation reveals a striking fact: People who expect more generally get more. I will discuss the best way to set goals in Chapter 2. To acquire high expectations, you must combine specific goal setting with a personal commitment to performance. Expectations come from your overall attitude about what you are trying to achieve and derive from unstated, sometimes unidentified, beliefs about what is fair and reasonable. Failure to develop explicit expectations is an important over-sight in many people's preparation.

To improve your negotiation results, you need to get into the habit of thinking carefully about the full range of "fair and reasonable" outcomes for a given problem, then developing an expectation that you should achieve results in the high end of that range. You can always tell, when a negotiation is over, where your expectations were really set. If you feel genuine disappointment that you fell below a certain level, that is where your expectation was set. If you feel genuinely satisfied, you met or exceeded your expectation. The goal of an effective negotiator is to have expectations that are high enough to present a real challenge but realistic enough to promote good working relationships.

THE PATIENCE TO LISTEN

It is hard to overstate the importance of listening skills in bargaining. Information-Based Bargaining begins with the idea that information is power. Listening enables you to get information.

If having high expectations is sometimes a problem for cooperative people, listening requires special effort for competitive types. Aggressive bargainers spend most of their time at the bargaining table either talking about what they want or thinking of something clever to say next that will put the other side on the defensive. As we shall see, the best negotiators follow a different practice: They ask questions, test for understanding, summarize discussions, and listen, listen, listen.

A COMMITMENT TO PERSONAL INTEGRITY

Effective negotiators are reliable. They keep their promises, avoid lying, and do not raise hopes they have no intention of fulfilling.

The research on this is reassuring. Skilled negotiators prize their reputations for straightforward dealing very highly. That makes sense. Given a choice, would you want to do business with someone you could trust or someone who might be trying to cheat you?

This sounds good, but does it really pay to be honest in bargaining? After all, most people do not candidly disclose all of their information in a negotiation. Does personal integrity require you to reveal your bargaining position? What if the other side fails to ask an important question? Do you have a duty to volunteer an answer? Finally, can you exaggerate the attractiveness of your own alternatives and downplay the other side's current offer, regardless of your true feelings?

I will address these and similar issues in Chapter 11. For now, I will simply say, "It depends." Integrity in bargaining is more than a set of rules. It is, like high expectations, an attitude. Relationships, social norms, culture, and bargaining etiquette all make a difference. Therefore, when I speak of a commitment to personal integrity in negotiation, I mean that effective negotiators can be counted on to negotiate consistently, using a thoughtful set of personal values that they could, if necessary, explain and defend to others. This approach obviously leaves a lot of room for individual interpretation about what is right and wrong. But such differences are an inevitable part of human interaction. The main thing is to attend to your reputation and self-regard. Be reliable.

◄ From Manhattan to Mount Meru ►

Before we leave this chapter, let's look again at the two deals described at the beginning. Both worked out. We left each story as the parties began to share information with each other.

Jovanovich's symbolic gift-giving gesture and welcoming statement sent a clear message to Smith that Jovanovich wanted to act cooperatively to make the deal happen. Smith gracefully accepted both the watch and the tacit admission that Smith had most of the bargaining leverage with reciprocal signals of cooperation. The initial meeting between the two men and their advisers went on through the evening and into the night. Building on the rapport established by Jovanovich's opening moves and fueled by careful listening, progress was rapid. Jovanovich's and Smith's problem-solving styles matched well. Within days, they created an outline of a merger agreement to create a new company: Harcourt General Inc.

Back in the shadow of Mount Meru, the two farmers went back and forth all day. At length, one of the elders proposed dividing the disputed land along a prominent footpath that formed a natural boundary. Then someone in the crowd called out: "Perhaps someone could find a goat!" There was a murmur of agreement from both groups of supporters. The farmers huddled with their bargaining teams. The social pressure for an agreement intensified.

The farmer who had demanded the meeting in the first place (the one whose son had been beaten) then stepped into the center of the circle. "For the sake of friendship," he said, he would offer the gift of a small goat to his neighbor. He added that he would also help pay for his neighbor's broken irrigation gate and abide by the new boundary.

The owner of the damaged gate then replied that he would make a gift of "some beer" to his neighbor. He, too, would honor the new arrangement. They had a deal. These public declarations and a ritual feast that followed served to commit the parties. Everyone in the community would remember the agreement and help enforce it if necessary.

◄ Summary ►

All negotiations begin with you. The First Foundation of Effective Negotiation is therefore your preferred bargaining styles—the ways you communicate most confidently when you face a negotiation. Your success depends on candidly assessing your strengths and weaknesses as a communicator.

Some people have a wide "bandwidth" when it comes to bargaining. They can adapt easily to many different situations and opponents. Others are more limited in their range of effective action. They may be quite strong in situations requiring competitive instincts but weak when it comes to accommodation or compromise. Or they may be strong in cooperative skills and weak if the situation calls for hardball tactics.

Many negotiation experts try to teach people a single, all-purpose menu of bargaining moves. I do not believe this is either helpful or realistic. People and situations are too varied for such mechanical advice to work.

Rather, your job as a negotiator is to understand your style preferences, see how they match up with the situation (more on this in Chapter 7), plan your path through the four steps that negotiations follow, and try your best to be effective by preparing, forming high expectations, listening to the other party, and acting with integrity in the process.

Information-Based Bargaining proceeds from the assumption that you will get better results for yourself and achieve more for others who depend on you by tirelessly searching for key information about the parties and the situation. Your success then turns on using this information skillfully as bargaining goes forward. Now that we have examined the issue of personal styles, let's move to the critical issue of what you hope to achieve in bargaining. It is time to explore the Second Foundation, your goals and expectations.

◄ YOUR BARGAINING STYLE: ► A CHECKLIST

✓ Understand your bargaining instincts, including how family, gender, and culture have shaped your preferred styles.

✓ Acquire a willingness to prepare.

✓ Set high expectations.

✓ Have the patience to listen.

✓ Make a commitment to personal integrity.

2

The Second Foundation:
Your Goals and
Expectations

High achievement comes from high aims.
—KING CHING OF CHOU (1100 B.C.)

I believe in always having goals, and always setting them
high.

—SAM WALTON, FOUNDER OF WAL-MART

In 1955, a small Japanese company called Sony Corporation had a new
product: a $29.95 miniature transistor radio. The radio was selling well
in Japan, but Sony's energetic leader, Akio Morita, was not satisfied. He
wanted to introduce Sony's radio to the world's biggest consumer mar-

ket: the United States. Morita went to New York City to see if he could interest American retailers in selling Sony's new radio. He quickly ran into a problem: The tiny radio was unlike anything Americans had ever seen. As Morita would later write, many U.S. companies said, "Why are you making such a tiny radio? Everybody in America wants big radios."

Morita was persistent, however, and he soon attracted the interest of Bulova, one of the most respected names in electronics of its day. Bulova offered to buy 100,000 of the radios for distribution through its strong U.S. retail network.

Morita was stunned by the size of the order. At the price that Bulova was willing to pay, the order was worth several times Sony's total working capital. This was the deal of a lifetime.

There was just one condition to the offer: Sony would have to act as an "original equipment manufacturer" in the deal; that is, Sony would make the radios but Bulova would sell them under its own brand name. This condition conflicted directly with an important long-range goal Morita had set for his firm: to establish Sony as an independent, global brand name based on its innovative, quality products.

Morita cabled his executive board at Sony headquarters in Japan for instructions. The board enthusiastically cabled back its response: Forget about the problem with the brand name and take the order.

Morita thought it over carefully for a week, then returned to Bulova to continue the negotiations. He told Bulova he would like to make a deal, but he could not accept the condition.

Now it was the Bulova purchasing officer's turn to be stunned. Bulova's condition was standard in this sort of transaction.

"Our company name is a famous brand that has taken over fifty years to establish," the purchasing officer urged. "Nobody has ever heard of your brand name. Why not take advantage of ours?"

"Fifty years ago," Morita calmly replied, "your brand name must have been just as unknown as our name is today. I am here with a new product, and I am now taking the first step for the next fifty years of my company. Fifty years from now I promise you that our name will be just as famous as your company name is today." Morita walked away from the biggest deal in his company's history. Indeed, his board was shocked when he reported his decision and told Morita that he was being foolish.

Shortly thereafter, Morita received a more modest order from another American distributor, but this one let Morita keep the Sony name on the radio. He quickly agreed, and the miniature radio caught the American public's eye—along with the name Sony. Of his negotiations with Bulova,

Morita later wrote, "I said then and I have said it often since: It was the best decision I ever made."

Morita's decision to reject Bulova's lucrative offer was risky. But his bargaining stance reflected the strength of his vision for Sony. Morita had a goal: to make the name Sony a household word for quality electronics throughout the world within fifty years. He achieved that goal with time to spare—and made himself a business legend in the process.

The Second Foundation of Effective Negotiation focuses on your goals and expectations. You cannot know when to say "yes" and when to say "no" without first knowing what you are trying to achieve. And research on setting goals discloses a simple but powerful fact: The more specific your vision of what you want and the more committed you are to that vision, the more likely you are to obtain it.

As Morita's story illustrates, goals often dictate the path that negotiations take. Bulova's purchasing officer faced an unusual man that day in New York, a man whose depth of feeling about, and strength of commitment to, his ambitious goals distinguished him from the average businessperson. But you do not need to be the next Akio Morita to draw a lesson from his story. Research on negotiation confirms that anyone who is willing to take the time to develop higher expectations will do significantly better and do so without putting his relationship or reputation with others at risk.

➤ Goals: You'll Never Hit the Target ➤ if You Don't Aim

In Lewis Carroll's *Alice's Adventures in Wonderland*, Alice finds herself at a crossroads where a Cheshire Cat materializes. Alice asks the Cat, "Would you tell me please, which way I ought to go from here?" The Cat replies, "That depends a good deal on where you want to get to." "I don't much care where," says Alice. "Then it doesn't matter which way you go," the Cat replies, cutting her off.

To become an effective negotiator, you must find out where you want to go—and why. That means committing yourself to specific, justifiable goals. It also means taking the time to transform your goals from simple targets into genuine—and appropriately high—*expectations.*

What is the difference between a simple goal and something that has matured into a genuine expectation? Basically one thing: your attitude. Goals are things we strive toward that are usually beyond the range of our past achievements. Such things as investment goals, weight loss goals, and athletic goals are typical. We set goals to give ourselves direction but we are not greatly surprised or disappointed if we fall short.

An expectation, by contrast, is a considered judgment about what we can and ought reasonably to accomplish. If we fall short of our expectations, we will feel sincere loss and disappointment. It will hurt. We may set a goal of having our children attend an Ivy League college, but we have an expectation that they will attend college *somewhere*. Our expectation about college affects the way we communicate about the subject with others, including our children. They begin to share our assumption that college is in their future, and their behavior reflects that assumption. And guess who in fact expects to go to college? Kids of parents who went to college. The same pattern holds all the way up to the children who expect to obtain doctoral degrees.

So it is with negotiation. Our goals give us direction, but our expectations are what give weight and conviction to our statements at the bargaining table. We are most animated when we are striving to achieve what we feel we justly deserve.

The more time we spend preparing for a particular negotiation, researching what others have achieved in similar circumstances, and gathering information that reinforces our belief that our goal is legitimate and achievable, the firmer our expectations grow. Morita had two important goals for Sony when he headed for America in 1955: to sell a lot of radios and sell them using Sony's name. Partly as a result of his experience with Bulova, he learned that the "using Sony's name" goal was more important than the "sell a lot of radios" part. As his goal matured into a solid expectation, he was able to communicate this vision more clearly to his own board of directors and to potential customers.

What you aim for in negotiations often determines what you get. Why? The first reason is obvious: Your goals set the upper limit of what you will ask for. You mentally concede everything beyond your goal, so you seldom do better than that benchmark.

Second, research on goals reveals that they trigger powerful psychological "striving" mechanisms. Sports psychologists, salespeople, and educators alike confirm that setting specific goals motivates people, focusing and concentrating their attention and psychological powers.

Third, we are more persuasive when we are committed to achieving some specific purpose, in contrast to the occasions when we ask for things half-heartedly or merely react to initiatives proposed by others. Our commitment is infectious. People around us feel drawn toward our goals.

President Lyndon Johnson once said, "What convinces is conviction." And H. Wayne Huizenga, an energetic American entrepreneur, maintains that one of the secrets of success in business negotiations is having a passionate commitment to ambitious goals. This trait enables effective negotiators to communicate enthusiasm and direction at the bargaining table. Huizenga should know, having built three successful megacorporations from scratch at the same time he was buying or founding three professional sports teams—the Miami Dolphins (football), the Florida Marlins (baseball), and the Florida Panthers (ice hockey). We will encounter some interesting stories about Huizenga's negotiation practices later in the book.

I have personally observed this "goal effect" in watching some of the best negotiators in the business both at the bargaining table and in executive training sessions. Negotiators striving to achieve concrete goals are more animated, committed, prepared, and persistent. Nor is this effect limited to experienced deal makers. Everyone gains a significant psychological edge when he or she is working to achieve a specific target in bargaining.

◄ Goals Versus "Bottom Lines" ►

Most negotiation books and experts emphasize the importance of having a "bottom line," "walkaway," or "reservation price" for negotiation. Indeed, the bottom line is a fundamental bargaining concept on which much of modern negotiation theory is built. It is the *minimum acceptable level* you require to say "yes" in a negotiation. By definition, if you cannot achieve your bottom line, you would rather seek another solution to your problem or wait until another opportunity comes your way. When two parties have bottom lines that permit an agreement at some point between them, theorists speak of there being a "positive bargaining zone." When the two bottom lines do not overlap, they speak of a "negative bargaining zone." This is what happens when a buyer does not have enough money in his or her budget to meet a seller's minimum acceptable price.

A well-framed goal is quite different from a bottom line. As I use the word, "goal" is your *highest legitimate expectation* of what you should achieve. For example, in the case of the used CD player illustrated in Figure 2.1, the seller has a bottom line of getting at least $100, but the seller might set a *goal* of $130 based on the prices paid for similar CD players in used equipment stores. Bottom lines are vitally important to negotiation theory,

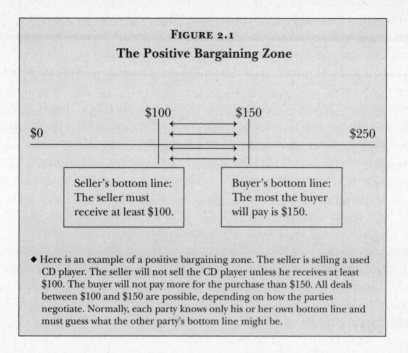

FIGURE 2.1

The Positive Bargaining Zone

$100 $150

$0 $250

Seller's bottom line:
The seller must
receive at least $100.

Buyer's bottom line:
The most the buyer
will pay is $150.

◆ Here is an example of a positive bargaining zone. The seller is selling a used
CD player. The seller will not sell the CD player unless he receives at least
$100. The buyer will not pay more for the purchase than $150. All deals
between $100 and $150 are possible, depending on how the parties
negotiate. Normally, each party knows only his or her own bottom line and
must guess what the other party's bottom line might be.

but setting and negotiating toward a legitimate goal is the key factor in
most bargaining success stories. Let me explain why.

Researchers have discovered that humans have a limited capacity for
maintaining focus in complex, stressful situations such as negotiations.
Consequently, once a negotiation is under way, we gravitate toward the
single focal point that has the most psychological significance for us.
Once most people set a firm bottom line in a negotiation, that becomes
their dominant reference point as discussions proceed. They measure
success or failure with reference to their bottom line. Having a goal as
your reference point, by contrast, prompts you to think you are facing a
potential "loss" for any offer you receive below your goal. And we know
that avoiding losses is a powerful motivating force. This power is not
working as strongly for you when you focus solely on your bottom line.

Thus, if you are selling your used CD player and have focused on getting at least $100 in order to buy some other item that costs about that
much, you will tend to relax once the buyer makes an offer above $100.
You can now end your search for a buyer and begin mentally possessing
the other item you want. If the buyer is alert (and most are when it comes
to money), he will sense your relaxation and stop the bidding. If, instead
of focusing on your bottom line, you orient toward your goal of getting

$130 based on comparable store prices, you don't stop striving quite so soon. And if the buyer is focused on *his* bottom line of $150, chances are you will end up with a higher price than you otherwise would receive.

What is the practical effect of having your bottom line become your dominant reference point in negotiations? Over a lifetime of negotiating, your results will tend to hover at a point just above this minimum acceptable level. For most reasonable people, the bottom line is the most natural focal point. Disappointment arises if we cannot get the other side to agree to meet our minimum requirements (usually established by our available alternatives or our needs away from the table), and satisfaction arises just above that level. Meanwhile, someone else who is more skilled at orienting himself toward ambitious goals will do much better. Not surprisingly, research shows that parties with higher (but still realistic) goals outperform those with more modest ones, all else being equal.

To avoid falling into the trap of letting your bottom line become your reference point, be aware of your absolute limits, but do not dwell on them. Instead, prepare your bottom line, then set it aside while you work energetically on formulating your goals. Like Akio Morita, test the other side's reaction to your goal. Then, if you must, gradually reorient toward your bottom line as that becomes necessary to close the deal. With experience, you should be able to keep both your goal and your bottom line in view at the same time without losing your goal focus. Research suggests that the best negotiators have this ability.

If setting goals is so vital to effective preparation, how should you do it? Use the following simple steps:

1. Think carefully about what you really want—and remember that money is often a means, not an end.
2. Set an optimistic—but justifiable—target.
3. Be specific.
4. Get committed. Write down your goal and, if possible, discuss the goal with someone else.
5. Carry your goal with you into the negotiation.

◄ What Do You Really Want? ►

Begin your preparation for negotiation by considering your own underlying needs and interests. In business or consumer negotiations, a good price is usually an important goal because it is precise and quantifiable; it helps you "keep score" and measure success. But it is easy to forget that price is often a means to an end, not an end in itself. The goal is to achieve more value or profit, not a victory on the price term.

This is not as paradoxical as it sounds. If you are on the buy side, you want to make sure that you get a specified level of quality for the money you spend, not just a low price. And sellers need to be careful that their sales create the conditions for future business. Canceled orders and one-time sales do not make for a profitable enterprise, even if the price achieved on any given sale looks good.

The founder of CBS, William Paley, was having a hard time making money in the radio broadcast marketplace in its early days. He was negotiating with local stations over prices for CBS shows the local stations would run, and the stations had all the power. They did not have to buy and often did not. Paley revolutionized radio and created the modern network by realizing that the price for his shows was a means, not an end in itself. In the late 1920s, he started *giving away* CBS's radio programming in exchange for the right to run advertisements on local stations during prime-time slots. The strategy earned him millions. Later, in the 1940s, Paley took the U.S. recording industry by storm with a similar move: cutting the prevailing price of records in half.

Experienced negotiators often report that price can be a relatively easy term to resolve compared with less obvious but more explosive issues such as control, turf, ego, and reputation. In the legendary fight over RJR Nabisco chronicled in *Barbarians at the Gate* and discussed in Chapter 10, a multibillion-dollar bid from one of Henry Kravis's rivals for RJR collapsed when two major investment banking firms—Drexel Burnham Lambert and Salomon Brothers—could not agree on which firm's name would appear on the left-hand side of the *Wall Street Journal* ad announcing the financing of the transaction. The position of the firm's name in the ad would signal to the financial community which of the two banks was the "lead bank" in the deal and neither would accept second-place status.

So when you formulate your goals, consider carefully what really matters to you. Sure, money is important. But identify your underlying interests and needs clearly. Once negotiations start, it is all too easy to become preoccupied with competitive issues such as price and forget what you are really trying to accomplish.

◄ Set an Optimistic, Justifiable Target ►

When you set goals, think boldly and optimistically about what you would like to see happen. Research has repeatedly shown that people who have higher aspirations in negotiations perform better and get more than people who have modest or "I'll do my best" goals, provided they really believe in their targets.

In one classic study, psychologists Sydney Siegel and Lawrence Fouraker set up a simple buy-sell negotiation experiment. They allowed the negotiators to keep all the profits they achieved but told the subjects they could qualify for a second, "double-their-money" round if they met or exceeded certain specified bargaining goals. In other words, Siegel and Fouraker gave their subjects both concrete *incentives* for hitting a certain specified level of performance and, perhaps unintentionally, a hint that the assigned target levels were realistically attainable (why else would subjects be told about the bonus round?). One set of negotiators was told they would have to hit a modest $2.10 target to qualify for the bonus round. Another set of negotiators was told they would have to hit a much more ambitious target of $6.10. Both sides had the same bottom line: They could not accept any deal that involved a loss. The negotiators with the more ambitious $6.10 goal achieved a mean profit of $6.25, far outperforming the median profit of $3.35 achieved by those with the modest $2.10 goal.

My own research has confirmed Siegel's and Fouraker's findings. In our experiment, unlike the one Siegel and Fouraker conducted, negotiation subjects set their own bargaining goals. And instead of letting everyone keep whatever profits they earned, we gave separate $100 prizes to the buyer and the seller with the best individual outcomes. The result was the same, however. Negotiators who reported higher prenegotiation expectations achieved more than those who entered the negotiation with more modest goals.

Why are we tempted to set modest bargaining goals when we can achieve more by raising our sights? There are several possible reasons. First, many people set modest goals to protect their self-esteem. We are less likely to fail if we set our goals low, so we "wing it," telling ourselves that we are doing fine as long as we beat our bottom line. Modest goals thus help us avoid unpleasant feelings of failure and regret.

Second, we may not have enough information about the negotiation to see the full potential for gain; that is, we may fail to appreciate the true worth of what we are selling, not do the research on applicable standards, or fail to note how eager the buyer is for what we have to offer. This usually means we have failed to prepare well enough.

Third, we may lack desire. If the other person wants money, control, or power more urgently than we do, we are unlikely to set a high goal for ourselves. Why look for conflict and trouble over things we care little about?

Research suggests that the self-esteem factor plays a more important role in low goal setting than many of us would care to admit. We once had a negotiation speaker who said that the problem with many reasonable people is that they confuse "win-win" with what he called a "wimp-win" attitude. The "wimp-win" negotiator focuses only on his or her bottom line; the "win-win" negotiator has ambitious goals.

I see further evidence of this in negotiation classes. As students and executives in negotiation workshops start setting more ambitious goals for themselves and strive to improve, they often report feeling more *dissatisfied and discouraged* regarding their performance—even as their objective results get better and better. For this reason, I suggest raising one's goals incrementally, adding risk and difficulty in small steps over a series of negotiations. That way you can maintain your enthusiasm for negotiation as you learn. Research shows that people who succeed in achieving new goals are more likely to raise their goals the next time. Those who fail, however, tend to become discouraged and lower their targets.

Once you have thought about what an optimistic, challenging goal would look like, spend a few minutes permitting realism to dampen your expectations. *Optimistic goals are effective only if they are feasible; that is, only if you believe in them and they can be justified according to some standard or norm.* As I discuss more fully in Chapter 3, negotiation positions must usually be supported by some standard, benchmark, or precedent, or they lose their credibility. No amount of mental goal setting will make your five-year-old car worth more than a brand-new version of the same model. You should also adjust your goal to reflect appropriate relationship concerns, a subject I address in Chapter 4.

With the preliminary work done, you are ready to enter the negotiation process and encounter the values and priorities the other side is bringing to the deal. Until you know for sure what *the other side* has for goals and what *the other side* thinks is realistic, you should keep your eyes firmly on your own defendable target. The other party will tell you if your optimistic deal isn't possible, and you will not offend him or her by asking for your goal so long as you have some justification to support it, you advance your ideas with courtesy, and you show a concern for his or her perspective.

◄ Be Specific ►

The literature on negotiation goal setting counsels us to be as specific as possible. Clarity drives out fuzziness in negotiations as in many other endeavors. With a definite target, you will begin working on a host of psychological levels to get the job done. For example, when you land your new job, don't just set a goal to "negotiate a fair salary." Push yourself to take aim at a specific target—go for a 10 percent raise over what you made at your last job. Your specific goal will start you thinking about other, comparable jobs that pay your target salary, and you will begin to notice a variety of market standards that support a salary of that amount.

Be especially wary of goals such as "I'll do the best I can" or, worst of all, "I'll just go in and see what I can get." What we are really saying when we enter a negotiation with goals such as these is, "I do not want to take a chance on failing in this negotiation." Fear of failure and our natural desire to avoid feelings of disappointment and regret are legitimate psychological self-protection devices. But effective negotiators do not let these feelings get in the way of setting specific goals.

◄ Commit to Your Goal: ► Write It Down and Talk About It

Your goal is only as effective as your commitment to it. There are several simple things you can do that will increase your level of psychological attachment to your goal. First, as I suggested above, you should make sure it is justified and supported by solid arguments. You must believe in your goal to be committed to it.

Second, it helps if you spend just a few moments vividly imagining the way it would look or feel to achieve your goal. Visualization helps engage our mind more fully in the achievement process and also raises our level of self-confidence and commitment. One of my better MBA students, a young man from India who came to the United States via a career in Hong Kong, once confided to me that before he had applied to the Wharton School he had come to Philadelphia and had his picture taken in the school's main building. He then kept that picture over his desk for several years as he directed all his professional energies toward gaining admission. After being turned down once, he was finally admitted. When he arrived on campus, he had another picture taken of himself in the same building, and he now displays the two pictures together with great satisfaction. He credits the visual image of his goal with keeping him on track toward its achievement. The same visualization techniques work for negotiation goals.

Third, psychologists and marketing professionals report that the act of *writing a goal down* engages our sense of commitment much more effectively than does the mere act of thinking about it. The act of writing makes a thought more "real" and objective, obligating us to follow up on it—at least in our own eyes. According to psychologist Robert Cialdini, successful door-to-door sales companies sometimes ask all their sales representatives to write down their sales goals, declaring in their training manuals that "there is something magical about writing things down" that improves salespeople's performance.

You can begin your practice of writing down negotiation goals by referring to Appendix B, the "Information-Based Bargaining Plan." Note the space provided for recording your "specific, optimistic goal." I discuss the use of this plan in more detail in Chapter 7.

To commit yourself even further to your goal, tell another person about it and show him or her your written goal. If other people know about the goal, you begin to feel subtly accountable to them, and research indicates that negotiators bargain harder when they must explain to someone why they failed to achieve a goal. Labor, sports, and political negotiators go to extreme lengths to mobilize this power: They sometimes announce their bargaining goals to the press, thereby putting everyone (including their constituents and the other side) on notice as to what they want to achieve. This sort of public commitment is a powerful way of binding yourself to your goals.

Of course, as in all other aspects of negotiation, one should use judgment in committing to goals. If both parties engage in dramatic forms of public commitment, with press conferences and do-or-die statements to their respective audiences, they can paint themselves into a corner from which it is impossible to escape. Labor strikes, political showdowns, and wars are examples of failed negotiations, not successes.

Finally, any type of material investment you can make in the goal that would be lost if you fail to achieve it will add greatly to your commitment. A major airline recently announced that it had signed a deal to acquire as many as four hundred new planes to expand and upgrade its fleet. It went on to state that the airline would be forced to cancel that order if it failed to reach a favorable wage agreement with its pilots before the deadline for closing the purchase. With that one move, the airline secured three negotiation advantages: a public commitment to its stated wage target, a credible deadline for concluding negotiations with its pilots, and, most important, a vision of what it (and the pilots) would lose if the airline failed to achieve its wage goals. The negotiations ultimately closed by the deadline and within the wage constraints the airline had set.

◄ Carry Your Goals with You ►
into the Negotiation

It is sometimes easy to get knocked off your target by the other party during a negotiation. It therefore pays to carry your goals with you and, if you feel yourself getting swept away, take a break and review them before going forward. I find it sometimes helps to literally carry a short summary of my goals in my pocket or wallet. Even if you just carry it in your head, however, the point is not to lose sight of your goals in the confusion of actual negotiation.

Barry Diller, the successful television executive and entrepreneur, learned this lesson the hard way when he got caught up in bidding for the rights to the first television showing of the movie *The Poseidon Adventure* in the early 1970s. Representing ABC, Diller ended up bidding $3.3 million—by far the highest amount ever paid for such a property at the time—and losing money for his network. The reason Diller paid so much? He agreed to participate in the first (and, for him, the last) open-bid auction for TV rights to a movie. In the frantic bidding that followed, he forgot about his primary goal—making a profit—and got caught up in what one CBS executive who bid against him called the "fever" of winning a competition.

Negotiation scholars have observed this phenomenon so often both in experiments and in real life that they have a name for it: "escalation of commitment." People lose sight of their real goals in competitive situations and pay far too much money, spend too much time, or sacrifice too many other interests for the privilege of saying they have won. It usually does not take long for regret to set in after such a victory, teaching the winners that it is not enough to prepare goals—you must remember them during the negotiation. In auction situations, the final bidder overpays so often that economists call the accompanying feel[ ] "winner's curse."

◄ Summary ►

The first important step in preparation is to commit to specific, justifiable goals. Clarity of purpose and optimism are key attitudes to bring to the goal-setting process.

First, a concrete, challenging goal will motivate you. You will tend to see proposals below your goal as a "loss." In addition, the intuitive part of your mind—the part that works and learns "below the surface" while you are getting ordinary things done during the day—will become a powerful ally and problem solver. You will become more focused, persistent, and achievement-oriented, and you will be more likely to come up with good arguments and new ideas about how to get what you want. You will also avoid the common trap of becoming focused on your bottom line too early. This "goal focus" gains you a significant advantage over the average person, who is inclined to pay more attention to his or her bottom line than to any other single bargaining point.

Second, your clarity will communicate confidence and resolve to the other party. You will convey the message that you have high expectations for both yourself and the deal. And perhaps no other personal variable makes such a difference in negotiation as the quiet feeling of confidence, self-esteem, and commitment that emanates from people who know what they want and why they ought to get it.

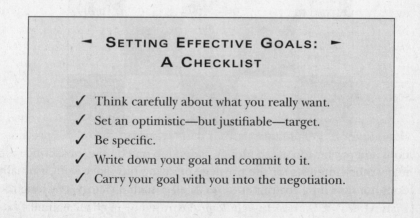

◄ SETTING EFFECTIVE GOALS: ► A CHECKLIST

✓ Think carefully about what you really want.
✓ Set an optimistic—but justifiable—target.
✓ Be specific.
✓ Write down your goal and commit to it.
✓ Carry your goal with you into the negotiation.

3

The Third Foundation:
Authoritative Standards
and Norms

The first duty of a wise advocate is to convince his opponents that he understands their arguments . . .

—SAMUEL TAYLOR COLERIDGE

A man always has two reasons for the things he does—a good one and the real one.

—J. P. MORGAN

In addition to the power of clear goals, negotiations harness one of human nature's most basic psychological drives: our need to maintain (at least in our own eyes) an appearance of consistency and fairness in our words and deeds. The Third Foundation of Effective Negotiation directs attention to this psychological drive. Let's begin with an example that shows how the need to maintain consistency with established standards influences virtually all negotiations.

◄ The Story of the Two Pigs ►

In his 1930 book *The Halfway Sun*, anthropologist R. F. Barton told a story about tribal people in the Philippines with whom he lived for many years. The story, which involves a negotiation between two families over some pigs, teaches a sobering lesson about standards and norms.

Barton reported that a man of the Ifugao people (the name of the tribe) once borrowed two pigs from his neighbor. Two years later, the man who loaned the pigs asked for the debt to be repaid. His son was getting married, and he needed pigs to give as presents at the wedding. The two men then fell into a dispute over how many pigs were owed.

Within this tribe, there was a standard "interest rate" for borrowing animals. The standard called for repayment according to the "natural rate of increase" of the animals during the term of the loan. There was general agreement that a two-year loan of two pigs called for a repayment of four—double the original number.

That was the standard. The problem was implementing it. The lender, an ambitious man who wanted to make a lavish wedding display, insisted that the borrower owed him a total of *six* pigs. He argued that slightly more than two years had passed and that one of the pigs had been of a special, larger breed that should draw a higher rate of interest. The borrower angrily replied that everyone knew the right number was four.

Aroused by the lender's greed, the borrower then escalated the dispute. He suddenly recalled that the lender's grandfather had, many years earlier, failed to repay a chicken he had borrowed. The natural rate of increase on that chicken, he said, equaled roughly one pig. So he reduced his offer from four pigs to *three*—to account for the chicken debt. The lender responded that he would accept five pigs, but not one less.

After much haggling and many insults, the two families engaged the services of a respected elder to act as a go-between. Not long after the elder began shuttling back and forth, however, the lender's son sneaked into the borrower's hut and stole the borrower's most valuable possession, an ancestral gong. That brought the whole negotiation process to an abrupt halt.

Now the wives got involved. The gong was believed to house the spirits that protected the borrower's home. The borrower's wife could not imagine spending even one night without the gong in its proper place. The lender's wife was also fed up with the dispute; the family's fields were rotting while her husband fussed over a couple of pigs. Both women told their men to stop arguing and settle the matter.

The elder finally put together a deal. First, the lender promised to restore the gong. Next, the borrower promised to cancel the chicken debt and pay the five pigs demanded by the lender.

But there was a twist: The elder passed along to the lender only *three* of the five pigs paid by the borrower, keeping the other two for himself as his fee. Thus, under this ingenious solution, the borrower paid pigs at the rate last demanded by the lender (five), the lender received pigs at the rate last offered by the borrower (three)—and the elder kept the difference as his tax for restoring the peace.

◄ From Pigs to Price Lists: ► The Role of Standards

What are we to make of this story? Few of us today are busy borrowing and lending pigs. Yet like people in every culture, we are inclined to negotiate on the basis of authoritative standards and norms. And when parties deviate too widely from these norms, they risk irritating others and causing trouble for themselves. They are seen as being unreasonable.

Standards very similar to the Ifugao natural rate of increase for borrowed animals play equally important roles in our more modern world. Global financial markets set interest rates for borrowing money. Used-car buyers consult a buying guide for average car prices—then negotiate final prices based on factors such as the actual condition of the car, the buyer's budget, and the seller's need for cash. Real estate brokers talk about "comparable transactions." And investment bankers argue over the true value of a business based on discounted cash flows and earnings multiples.

Such fancy terms and complex analyses are nothing more or less than techniques that help buyers and sellers form opinions about the right price. These standards, like the one in the two pigs story, bracket the bargaining zone and permit all participants to talk about their preferred end of the range without appearing, at least in their own eyes, to be unreasonable.

Nor are market standards such as interest rates and comparable sales the only examples of normative arguments and formulae that carry weight in negotiations. When children negotiate over who should play with a toy, they argue using norms such as "First come, first served" or "It's my turn." When executives argue over corporate strategy, they discuss their positions using norms such as "profitability," "benchmarking," and "efficiency." And when layoffs loom, people negotiate over who will stay and who will go using standards such as "seniority" and "productivity." Finally, the single most common tactic for closing a negotiation is an allocation formula: splitting the difference.

Finding the standards that apply in a negotiation and doing your homework on how to make your best case using these standards gives you a "speaking role" in the negotiation process. You have something to talk about beyond your self-serving assessment of what you want. This in turn gives you a fair basis on which to be an energetic advocate for your goal. And you had better be ready to respond to arguments the other side will advance. If the accepted standards lend themselves to a variety of interpretations (and most do), the other party will come prepared to argue the interpretation that most favors him or her.

In short, as part of your preparation, you must become an advocate for your goals using the most persuasive standards you can find. Which standards might those be? As my opening quotation from Samuel Coleridge suggests, the arguments the other party accepts as legitimate or has used to his or her own advantage in the past are usually the most effective.

◄ A Psychological Fact: ►
We All Want to Appear Reasonable

Why are standards and norms—particularly standards the other side has adopted—such an important part of bargaining? Because, all else being equal, people like to be seen as consistent and rational in the way they make decisions.

Psychologists have a name for this need-to-appear-reasonable phenomenon. They call it "the consistency principle." Social psychologists have discovered that people have a deep need to avoid the disjointed, erratic, and uncomfortable psychological states that arise when our actions are manifestly inconsistent with previously expressed, long-held, or widely shared standards and beliefs.

Most of us have complex "consistency webs" that are interconnected at many levels of our personality. Because we like to keep these webs intact, we rationalize our actions so they appear (at least in our own eyes) to be consistent with our prior beliefs. We are also more open to persuasion when we see a proposed course of action as being consistent with a course we have already adopted.

Negotiations are fertile ground for observing the consistency principle at work. Whether we are aware of it or not, we sometimes feel a tug to agree with the other party when the standards or norms he or she articulates are consistent with prior statements and positions we ourselves have taken. We also feel uncomfortable (though we may keep this to ourselves) when the other side correctly points out that we have been inconsistent in one of our positions or arguments. In short, standards and norms are—or can be—more than just intellectual pawns in bargaining debates. They can be strong, motivating factors in the way negotiations proceed.

◄ The Consistency Principle and ► "Normative Leverage"

The consistency principle can give you what I call normative leverage in negotiation. Normative leverage is the skillful use of standards, norms, and coherent positioning to gain advantage or protect a position. You maximize your normative leverage when the standards, norms, and themes you assert are ones *the other party views as legitimate and relevant to the resolution of your differences.*

If you set up your own needs, standards, and entitlement as the only rational approaches to a negotiation, you will not inspire agreement. Instead, you will have a fight on your hands pitting your principles against the other party's. The best practice is therefore to anticipate the other side's preferred standards and frame your proposal within them. If you cannot do this, prepare to argue for a special exception to his standard based on the special facts of your case. Attack his standard only as a last resort.

Let's look at a couple of examples.

Suppose you are involved in a budget negotiation in a hospital system. You are a nurse executive pushing for more money for training and nursing services; others are pushing for more money to increase the number of doctors' offices in the surgery department. If the top decision makers in the hospital have previously made policy statements about the importance of "quality patient care" in hospital operations, you have some normative leverage in this debate.

Provided you do your homework, gather data, and make an effective presentation, your budgetary requests will appear more compelling because they will be closely linked to the hospital's announced priorities. The surgery department's request, by contrast, will not enjoy this tight linkage. The administrators will then feel constrained by their prior policy statements to make a decision consistent with their policy. The surgeons are powerful players in a hospital, but a well-prepared case for your budget based on the institution's announced priorities will improve your chances of achieving your goals.

If the hospital has announced a different goal—such as "attract the best physicians"—then you will need to anticipate how the surgeons will use this standard in their plea for funding. Your best move will be to show how a quality nursing staff attracts more and better physicians than do lavish offices.

Here is another, harder case. Suppose you are a corporate division chief faced with a downsizing mandate. Each division must slash 10 percent of its staff. You study the situation and determine that, with a 10 percent cut, there will simply not be enough people to do the work. Your initial instinct may be to go to your boss, show her you cannot do your job with the proposed cuts, and request permission to retain staff.

Will this be persuasive? Probably not. Everyone is going to say the same thing, and she will not make her downsizing target if everyone retains staff. She will counter your "not enough people to do the work" argument with a lecture on efficiency and send you back to find ways of getting more work from fewer people.

How can you gain better normative leverage for your request? By anticipating what standards and norms *the boss* believes to be relevant in this sort of situation and making your arguments based on *her* standards—not yours. If she likes to think about ways to be more efficient, give her arguments based on efficiency. Tell her you have evaluated the assortment of tasks your department is doing and have determined that your group is superbly efficient at tasks 1, 2, and 3 but is ill equipped to perform tasks 4 and 5. Even after a 10 percent cut, you could do considerably more of tasks 1, 2, and 3 if the boss would assign tasks 4 and 5 to other groups better equipped to handle them.

Alternatively, you might try to demonstrate how, by retaining more of your staff and cutting more heavily elsewhere in the organization, you could sharply reduce the time and cost of an entire business process spanning several divisions. That would save the firm money—which is the underlying point of downsizing—while improving an area on which the boss herself is evaluated.

Will such arguments carry the day each time you use them? No. But they have a better chance of advancing your goals than arguments based strictly on your own point of view. In fact, none of the Six Foundations alone guarantees success in bargaining. But attention to each one improves your chances incrementally. Effective negotiators move step by step.

By positioning your needs within the normative framework the other party uses to make decisions, you show him respect and, as a result, gain his attention and sympathy. Because the difference between success and failure in negotiation is often very small, anything that systematically improves your chances of getting agreement to your terms will pay off in the long run.

◄ Beware of "Consistency Traps" ►

Skilled negotiators know about the human need to appear consistent and try to use it as often as they can. Truly manipulative people go beyond identifying their counterparts' standards for positioning purposes and try to trick their opponents by using what I call consistency traps. The goal of a consistency trap is to precommit you to a seemingly innocent standard and then confront you with the logical implications of the standard in a particular case—implications that actually turn out to run against your interests. This is a form of intellectual coercion, and you should be ready to defend against it.

Collection agencies, credit card companies, and high-pressure sales companies routinely use consistency traps as part of the scripts they give telemarketing people to read on the telephone when they call you at dinnertime. You can learn to see a consistency trap coming if you know what to look for. The tip-off is when the trapper tries to get you to agree with some statement before telling you why the statement is important. "Would you like to save some money?" says the long distance company telemarketer. "Sure," you reply. Snap! The trap closes. "Our records of your monthly phone usage indicate you will save more than one hundred dollars by switching to our service. How about starting to save right now?" You are logically committed to saying "yes." You have to invent some new reason or excuse to say "no," and the telemarketing company has a well-rehearsed answer for them all.

At the bargaining table, consistency traps are a favorite of aggressive, competitive negotiators. The pattern is the same as that used by telemarketers. Manipulative negotiators try to get you committed to a relatively innocent-sounding principle or standard ("A fair price for this company should reflect comparable sales of like companies, don't you think?"), then spring their trap by arguing that your bargaining position violates the principle you just endorsed ("Your proposed selling price is 30 percent more than the comparable sales you just agreed should be the benchmark").

How can you defend against consistency traps? By being alert to them. When the person you are negotiating with begins asking leading questions before you know where he is going, slow the pace. Turn the tables on the trapper. Elicit as much information as possible about why these questions are important before committing to anything. If you are nevertheless pressed into agreeing to a standard, qualify it or phrase it in your own words and use the broadest possible terms, leaving ample room for interpretation later. "I believe comparable sales may be relevant to our discussions, although I am not sure just what time frame or industries we should be looking at," you can say to the competitive negotiator. "Why don't you show me all your data?"

Even with these precautions, locking horns with a determined consistency trapper can be uncomfortable and unsettling. You have to be alert to every move he makes. If you are caught in an inconsistency, you have two choices. Either you can adjust your position to conform to the standard that you have admitted applies or you can hold your ground, admitting that you made a mistake when you agreed to the standard. This latter move will cause you to lose some face, but that may be less costly than a bad bargain.

◄ Using Audiences ►

Relying on the other side's standards and norms to frame your proposals is fine, as long as your goals can be positioned within those standards. But suppose they cannot. Suppose the other side's standard directly contradicts your position and there are no exceptions or interpretations that can save you. Should you attack the standard and try to change the other party's mind? You can try, but chances are the other party will cling to his beliefs.

In these difficult cases, you will need to resort to explicit leverage and search for an ally—a third party to whom your bargaining counterpart is answerable and who is sympathetic to your norms. Once you can locate such a person, you need to arrange things so you negotiate in the third party's presence or under the third party's protection. Allies serve as audiences or witnesses to guarantee the application of standards that ought, in fairness, to apply. In essence, you leverage the audience's consistency principles to bypass the party that opposes your goals.

◄ Mahatma Gandhi Rides First-class ►

One way of understanding how audiences can help in asserting standards in negotiations is through example. This one comes from the life of Mahatma Gandhi, the father of modern India. It involves a train ride and comes from Gandhi's autobiography, *The Story of My Experiments with Truth.*

Gandhi's early life as an activist was spent in South Africa, where he worked as a lawyer fighting for the rights of Indians in South African society. Gandhi had earned a law degree in England. He arrived in South Africa ready to use his knowledge of both English law and English social norms to help in the cause of Indian civil rights.

South African law required Indians (or "coolies," as they were called by white South Africans) to travel third-class on trains. The Indians in South Africa were reluctant to challenge this rule, preferring to "pocket the insult" and make their livings in peace. Soon after arriving in South Africa, Gandhi learned firsthand about this rule when he was thrown off a train for trying to ride in a first-class car. It was an insulting episode in Gandhi's life and made a deep impression on him. What is less well known is that Gandhi immediately looked for a second opportunity to challenge the rule on a train ride from Durban to Pretoria. This time he succeeded. He did so by skillfully using an audience to outflank a negotiation opponent.

Gandhi's standard in this negotiation was that "well-dressed and well-behaved people can travel first-class, regardless of race." He anticipated that the railway company's standard would be "Coolies must travel third-class." The law was on the railway company's side. Gandhi's step-by-step approach to achieving his goal is a model of effective preparation and strategy in the most difficult circumstances.

Gandhi's first move was to locate a decision maker and find a way to present his request for a first-class ticket personally in a face-to-face meeting. He obtained the name of the stationmaster in Durban, the city from which he would be departing, and sent him a letter. Gandhi wrote that he was a barrister who was accustomed to traveling first-class. He said he would present himself personally at the stationmaster's office the following day to obtain his ticket. By leaving no time for a reply by mail, Gandhi successfully dodged the possibility of getting an easy "no" by mail. The stationmaster would have to discuss Gandhi's request person to person, and Gandhi knew he would have a better chance if he could plead his case personally.

Gandhi appeared before the stationmaster the next day in what Gandhi describes as "faultless English dress": a frock coat and necktie. He wanted to impress the stationmaster with a basic fact—that the stationmaster and Gandhi were from the same social class, even if they were of different races.

"You sent me the note?" asked the stationmaster when Gandhi presented himself at his desk.

"That is so," said Gandhi. "I shall be much obliged if you will give me a ticket. I must reach Pretoria today."

Now came a bit of good fortune, brought about by Gandhi's insistence on a personal interview. "I am not a Transvaaler [a South African white]," said the stationmaster. "I am a Hollander [a native of the Netherlands]. I appreciate your feelings, and you have my sympathy."

The stationmaster said he would issue the ticket—but only on condition that Gandhi not involve him if the train conductor later challenged the ticket. Gandhi agreed, although this eliminated an authoritative ally who could have proven useful later.

"I wish you a safe journey," the stationmaster concluded. "I can see you are a gentleman."

Now came the hard part. Gandhi had to figure out how to persuade the conductor, who would not be from his own social class and who *would* be a Transvaaler, to let him stay in the first-class car.

Here is where Gandhi made use of the "audience" principle. He needed to find someone who would be sympathetic to his "well-dressed and well-behaved people can travel first-class" standard and to whom the conductor would feel, in some sense, answerable.

Gandhi walked along the corridor in the first-class car until he found just the audience he was looking for: an Englishman sitting in a first-class compartment by himself, without any South African whites present.

Gandhi sat down, holding his first-class ticket and waiting for the conductor to arrive.

When the conductor came, he immediately saw that Gandhi was Indian and angrily demanded that he move to third-class. Gandhi showed him his first-class ticket. "That doesn't matter," said the conductor.

Then Gandhi's "audience," the Englishman, spoke up. "What do you mean by troubling the gentleman?" he asked. "Don't you see he has a first-class ticket? I do not mind in the least his traveling with me." The Englishman then turned to Gandhi. "You should make yourself comfortable where you are," he said.

"If you want to ride with a coolie, what do I care?" said the exasperated conductor. The conductor retreated, and Gandhi completed his trip in first-class.

Gandhi used his Englishman as an audience to (temporarily) overcome the unjust standards of South African law. Later in his life he would use world public opinion as an audience to expose Great Britain's unjust treatment of the Indian people—and help win India's independence.

◄ Standards and Norms in Markets ►

Standards and norms rely on the consistency principle for their power in negotiation. But some standards and norms are more powerful than others, especially in market transactions. The strongest market standards act as anchors or focal points in bargaining. The natural rate of increase standard for borrowing animals in the Philippines had this quality. It provided a single, definitive solution to an otherwise negotiable issue. Most market standards are not so preemptive. Instead, they serve as range finders, bargaining devices that bracket the bargaining zone within which parties can haggle to settle an issue.

Examples of standard terms and formulas that serve as preemptive norms for negotiations can be found everywhere in modern business. For instance, the practice in the residential real estate industry in the United States is for real estate agents to receive a fixed percentage (6 percent) of the selling price of a home. In the literary and entertainment industries, agents receive a standard percentage of royalties and fees (usually 15 percent) earned by their clients. Authors of hardcover books typically collect a 15 percent royalty on U.S. sales based on the book's retail price.

These standards are completely arbitrary from a financial point of view. Real estate brokers, book agents, and publishers could negotiate fees on a case-by-case basis and sometimes do in very special situations. But it would take time and energy to negotiate each and every transaction. The result: Each industry has converged on a payment standard that eliminates the need to negotiate.

Acceptance of institutionalized bargaining standards is a hallmark of social membership in a given industry or group. A feeling arises that it is slightly insulting or presumptuous to negotiate a variance from the standard. This connection between the standard and group membership gives the standard extra bite—because questioning the standard threatens a negotiator's status in the group. And that is just the way the groups that benefit from these powerful standards like it.

When you are new to a market, one of your first moves should be to investigate and abide by the prevailing standards and norms. Otherwise, people will think you are at best clumsy and at worst unreasonable. Similarly, when you are new to a company or institution, you should take time to understand the underlying conventions and norms of that organization if you want to negotiate change effectively.

Eventually, you may have enough leverage or skill to propose a deviation from an institutionalized norm and get away with it. But such a move is a calculated risk best taken by an experienced negotiator, not a novice. An old piece of wisdom from the American South applies here: "Pigs get fat, but hogs get eaten." In the "two pigs" story, the lender ended up with an angry spouse and fewer pigs than he was due because he was greedy and tried to vary a preemptive standard.

Institutionalized standards aside, most norms in market negotiations are contestable. These are the range-finding standards. They provide a basis for arguing in a civilized way about preferred results, but they do not dictate what the final agreement will be. They legitimize offers and demands and narrow the range within which bargaining will take place.

In many buy-sell situations, "fair market value" is the relevant standard and the market provides abundant, useful data as you prepare to advocate your goals. Facts from published and private sources based on prior transactions are usually critical, and it is no surprise that research confirms that such data significantly affect negotiation results. But fair market value is a relative concept in virtually any purchase or sale.

The same principle is even truer for less quantitative standards and norms such as quality patient care in health care institutions or undergraduate educational excellence at colleges and universities. People will interpret such standards differently depending on their goals within their institutions, but data can usually be assembled to support linkages between any given proposal and the applicable institutional norm. The better the data, the stronger your argument.

The biggest mistake you can make with range-finding norms is to come to the table unprepared to argue for your end of the range permitted by the legitimate standards. The better prepared you are and the closer your proposal comes to being viewed as fair within the range described by the standards, the more successful you will be both in obtaining your price and in negotiating additional concessions on important nonprice issues.

◄ Positioning Themes: ►
"Part-time America Won't Work"

A final, powerful way the consistency principle operates in negotiations is through what I call positioning themes. A positioning theme is a crisp, memorable phrase or framework that defines the problem you are attempting to solve in the negotiation. Asserting such a positioning theme early in a negotiation helps the other party see why you are there and what overall interests and norms tie your various bargaining positions together. "We're buying a vehicle to use as a second car at home," you tell the car dealer. "We want reliability, small size, and a low price."

A good positioning theme not only shows the other party why you are there, but it also helps you keep your eye on your own goals. When the going gets tough and the deadline is approaching, a good positioning theme can hold your bargaining position together just as sturdy ropes and bracing hold together a ship being tossed about by a strong wind.

Let me give a simple example of how good positioning works.

Some years ago, the Teamsters Union won a major strike against United Parcel Service of America (UPS), the biggest door-to-door package delivery service in the United States. It was the first major strike won by organized labor in the United States in years.

What made the difference? The union developed and then repeated at every opportunity a carefully constructed positioning theme: "Part-time America won't work." Many of UPS's 180,000 workers and delivery truck drivers were part-time employees. These workers wanted the company to convert their positions to full-time jobs. The theme resonated with these and other workers throughout the United States who were unhappy about being forced to accept part-time jobs. The union made it appear that everything in the negotiation hinged on UPS's increasing use of part-time workers.

UPS tried to counter the union's theme with a "We must stay competitive" theme of its own, but UPS was unable to match the galvanizing power of the union's well-prepared attack. "Part-time America won't work" showed up everywhere: on thousands of placards, in newspaper editorials and stories, on the lips of pundits on television news shows, and on the Internet. The phrase united the 180,000 UPS strikers—no small feat—and appealed to public opinion, a vital audience in a high-visibility strike that would disrupt America's daily commerce and cause average people a lot of inconvenience.

The leverage the Teamsters gained from their persuasive positioning ultimately translated into a win for them at the bargaining table. The company agreed to a wage increase; it dropped its demand for control over the workers' pension fund; and it agreed to promote 10,000 of its part-time workers to full-time jobs over a number of years. As UPS Vice Chairman and strategist John W. Alden ruefully commented after the strike was over, "If I had known that . . . [I] was going to go from negotiating for UPS to negotiating for a part-time America, we would've approached it differently."

People do not usually think of slogans and themes as being an important part of negotiation. But they can be vital, not only in highly visible events such as the UPS strike but also in more ordinary negotiations. Persuasive positioning of our needs and interests helps us organize our thoughts, communicate consistently, and tailor our message so the other party will be most likely to hear it. If other parties become convinced that you are committed to a consistent position, they will respect that and you will gain important normative leverage.

◄ The Power of Authority ►

In addition to the consistency principle, there is a second psychological lever that makes standards and norms persuasive. This is the human tendency to defer to authority. In negotiations, this tendency can affect both the process and the results of an exchange in a number of ways. Standards and norms have power in negotiation in part because they carry an authoritative message about what the market, the experts, or society has determined to be a fair and reasonable price or practice. In addition, most of us occupy a number of social roles in our negotiations, and we may feel a strong need to act in ways that are consistent with our own vision of what these roles require—including being deferential to people and principles that appear to have high status or enjoy broad acceptance.

Psychologists have discovered a firm fact about human nature: We are inclined to defer to authority. Some cultures emphasize obedience to authority more than others, but even Americans, who tend to be highly individualistic, defer to authority in many situations. Deferring to authority is useful most of the time. Society would not work well if we spent all our time questioning the boss's taste in office decor and the various OUT OF ORDER and DO NOT ENTER signs we encounter every day.

But authority becomes a problem in negotiation in two instances. First, others may seek to exploit our natural tendency to defer to authority by presenting us with unfair terms wrapped in authoritative packages. Second, our deference to authority sometimes inappropriately interferes with our ability to assert our own legitimate interests. Let's look briefly at each of these authority problems.

Skilled negotiators use a host of ploys to combine the use of standards with our willingness to defer to authority. They present us with dense, authoritative-looking standard form contracts written in unintelligible legalese and resort to other expert talk in explaining what they call the routine aspects of a transaction. Have you ever heard someone you are negotiating with justify their position using explanations based on company policy, standard procedure, and the like? That is a standards-based argument that gains additional power from being combined with an authority ploy.

Herb Cohen tells a story in his book *You Can Negotiate Anything* that illustrates in an amusing way just how easy we are to manipulate based on our deference to authority. *Candid Camera*, a TV show that uses a hidden camera to observe ordinary Americans reacting to set up situations, once placed a large outdoor advertising sign on the expressway between Philadelphia, Pennsylvania, and the neighboring city of Wilmington, Delaware. The sign read DELAWARE CLOSED. The producers placed a staff member near the sign with a lantern to slow traffic.

The hidden camera then recorded people as they went by in their cars. Some people just drove by, ignoring the sign. But others stopped and inquired. The staff member simply referred people to the sign. One dismayed driver even pleaded, "When do you think it will reopen? I live there, and my family is in there!" Such is the power of the printed word—when you print it in billboard-size letters.

Next time you are signing a lease you don't understand or hearing an argument from a supposed "expert" that makes no sense to you, remember this amusing story. The other party may well be telling you that "Delaware is closed," hoping to trigger unthinking acceptance of his or her unfair or unnecessary demands.

Our deference to authority can also needlessly interfere with our ability to initiate negotiations or express our points of view appropriately within organizations. For example, health care workers such as nurses sometimes mindlessly defer to physicians' judgment in the administration of medicines and carry out orders they know to be nonsense, such as putting eardrops into people's eyes. Virtually anyone who wears a uniform on the job or works in a hierarchical organization must be constantly alert to the possibility that his or her deference to authority could interfere with the proper discharge of his or her duties.

On a more serious note, let me illustrate how our need to maintain consistency with social roles and routines can interfere with our abilities to communicate and, ultimately, negotiate effectively. This tragic example comes from an actual conversation between the captain and copilot of an Air Florida flight departing from Washington, D.C.'s National Airport on a cold, snowy day. The cockpit conversation was recorded by the plane's "black box" and recovered later, after the crash that terminated this conversation.

[The plane is at the gate, awaiting clearance to depart. A heavy snow is falling.]
Copilot: See all those icicles on the back there and everything?
Captain: Yeah.
[Time passes while the plane continues to wait at the gate.]
Copilot: Boy, this is a, this is a losing battle here on trying to de-ice those things. It [gives] you a false feeling of security, that's all that does.
[More time passes. The snow keeps falling.]
Copilot: Let's check these tops [wings] again since we [have] been sitting here awhile.
Captain: I think we get to go here in a minute.
[The plane begins to taxi to the runway.]
Copilot [referring to engine instrument readings]: That doesn't seem right, does it? [Pause.] Ah, that's not right.
Captain: Yes, it is. There's eighty [referring to an instrument].
Copilot: Naw, I don't think that's right. [Seven-second pause.] Ah, maybe it is.

Captain: Hundred and twenty.
Copilot: I don't know.
[The plane takes off, struggles to gain lift, and then begins to fall into the Potomac River.]
Copilot: Larry, we're going down, Larry.
Captain: I know it.
[Sound of impact.]

The copilot in this example failed to overcome his deference to authority in this situation, with tragic results. Sixty-nine of the seventy-four people on this flight, including the captain and copilot, died. The subsequent government investigation of the accident confirmed that the copilot had been correct—the instrument readings were abnormal and the captain should have aborted the takeoff. Partly in response to this and other incidents like it, some airlines now give their flight crews special training on how to communicate regarding safety issues in more direct, effective ways.

If you feel the "deference to authority" tug before initiating a negotiation or before expressing your true views in an ongoing discussion, examine the situation closely before deciding to defer. Make sure your deference or concession is warranted by a basic, interest-based justification, not just your counterpart's title or position.

◄ Summary ►

Arguments about standards, norms, positioning themes, and authority are the bread and butter of negotiation. But virtually all the examples used in this chapter illustrate another important truth about the criteria of fairness and consistency: Unless the issue is relatively trivial or the social roles especially strong, authoritative standards and crisp positioning themes alone seldom carry the day against negotiators with high aspirations.

When stakes are high, people do not make a concession just because they are caught making an inconsistent statement or realize that the other side has a good argument. They make it because they decide after careful consideration that it is within their reach and helps them advance toward their goal. The J. P. Morgan quotation that led this chapter summarizes this point: There are usually two reasons people do things—"a good one and the real one."

Put yet another way: A reasoned argument supporting your position is an admission ticket that establishes your request as legitimate and gets the other side's attention. But argument alone is seldom sufficient to achieve bargaining success. Your request must also be within the zone of the other party's capability and interests, and your manner of communicating the standard you wish to apply must be persuasive. In the end, only two things determine the right price of something: what a buyer is willing to pay and what a seller is willing to accept.

In the two pigs example, a very important part of the negotiation was the theft of the ancestral gong. Because the gong was the home of important family spirits, this move amounted to nothing less than a hostage taking by the lender's son. It added urgency to the borrower's need to settle the dispute. However, the theft also caused the lender to lose face in the eyes of the elder. Both factors contributed to the final settlement under which the borrower paid the full five pigs demanded and the lender ended up getting only three of them.

And Gandhi's argument with the train conductor in South Africa was not the whole story either. The presence of the Englishman gave Gandhi leverage. The conductor faced an uncomfortable choice: He could either throw Gandhi off the train and cause a scene with a dignified-looking and perhaps powerful English citizen or he could leave the situation alone and complain later that someone was illegally selling first-class tickets to coolies. All in all, it was in the conductor's personal interests to accept Gandhi's first-class ticket argument and avoid the trouble of an overt conflict.

◄ GAINING NORMATIVE LEVERAGE: ►
A CHECKLIST

✓ Survey the applicable standards and norms. Identify the ones the other party views as legitimate.
✓ Prepare supporting data and arguments.
✓ Anticipate the arguments the other side will make.
✓ Prepare a positioning theme and anticipate the other side's.
✓ If necessary, consider making your arguments before a sympathetic audience.

4

The Fourth Foundation:
Relationships

If you treat people right, they will treat you right—at least
90 percent of the time.

—FRANKLIN D. ROOSEVELT

Leave a good name in case you return.

—KENYAN FOLK SAYING

Negotiation is about people—their goals, needs, and interests. Your
ability to form and manage personal associations at the bargaining
table is therefore the Fourth Foundation of Effective Negotiation. Personal relationships create a level of trust and confidence between people
that eases anxiety and facilitates communication.

Relationships can help us achieve our goals, and they may also prompt us to modify them. Most of us, for example, would not charge a close friend the same price for a professional service that we might charge a large corporate client. In the introduction to the book, I gave a simple example of a negotiation I had with a neighbor's daughter over citrus fruit she was selling to fund a school trip. Why did I buy any fruit at all? Because of the relationship between our families.

At the core of human relationships is a fragile interpersonal dynamic: trust. With trust, deals get done. Without it, deals are harder to negotiate, more difficult to implement, and vulnerable to changing incentives and circumstances.

What is the secret to creating and sustaining trust in negotiation? A simple but sturdy norm in human behavior: the norm of reciprocity.

◄ The Norm of Reciprocity ►

Dr. Alvin Gouldner has described the general obligation of reciprocity as "duties that people owe one another, not as human beings, or as fellow members of a group, or even as occupants of social statuses within the group, but, rather, because of their prior actions. We owe others certain things because of what they have previously done for us, because of the history of previous interaction we have had with them."

The psychological and anthropological research on the norm of reciprocity has confirmed its power in all sorts of transactions, big and small. People are more likely to send Christmas cards to people who first send cards to them, make charitable donations to organizations that have given them a small gift, and make bargaining concessions to others who have made compromises in their direction.

When it comes to reciprocity, we have long memories. Two-career couples often take turns accommodating each other's jobs over many years. Ethiopians made a substantial donation to a relief fund to aid Mexico City after a terrible earthquake in 1985. Why? To repay Mexico for Mexico's aid to Ethiopia when Ethiopia had been invaded by Italy in 1935.

We also keep short-term reciprocity accounts. In ordinary business negotiations we keep a minute-by-minute tally of each disclosure and accommodation. "I've told you a little about my needs," we might say. "Let's hear a little about yours." Or "I made the last concession," we argue. "Now it's your move."

Old school economists often have trouble understanding the role of norms such as reciprocity in exchange relationships. They assume everyone is always out to get the most he or she can from every transaction. Skilled negotiators and businesspeople know better. They understand that stable relationships and reliable interactions based on reciprocity are enormous sources of both economic well-being and personal satisfaction. An ounce of well-grounded personal trust in a business partner is worth a thousand pounds of formal contracts and surety bonds. And being a trustworthy person gains us more than future business. It also gains us self-respect.

◄ J. P. Morgan Makes a Friend ►

A simple example drawn from American business history helps underscore the role that reciprocity plays in negotiations. The example comes from the lives of two of America's great business tycoons, Andrew Carnegie and J. P. Morgan.

Carnegie, the great steel mogul of the late nineteenth century, tells a story about the banker J. P. Morgan in his autobiography. It is a story about how, relatively early in their careers, Morgan established a "special" business relationship with Carnegie.

During the financial Panic of 1873, Carnegie found himself desperate for cash to meet his obligations. Sensing that a favorable bargain might be struck, Morgan asked if Carnegie might be interested in selling his share in a partnership the Morgan family had previously entered into with Carnegie.

The cash-strapped Carnegie quickly replied that he would "sell anything for money." Morgan asked for his price, and Carnegie said he would gladly sell out for $60,000—$50,000 for a partnership "credit" plus an additional $10,000 of profit. Morgan agreed, and the two men had a deal. Though $60,000 was nowhere near the millions these two sometimes dealt in, it was a substantial amount in 1873—the equivalent of many hundreds of thousands of dollars today.

The next day, Carnegie called on Morgan to collect his money. To his surprise, Morgan handed him two checks—one for $60,000 and an additional one for $10,000.

In response to Carnegie's surprised look, Morgan explained that his own reading of the partnership accounts had revealed that Carnegie was mistaken about the credit he was owed—the credit was for $60,000, not $50,000. Hence, Morgan was paying $60,000 for the credit plus the additional $10,000 profit agreed to the day before. Carnegie was distressed.

"Well, that is something worthy of you," said Carnegie, as he handed the $10,000 check back to Morgan. "Will you please accept these [sic] $10,000 with my best wishes?"

"No, thank you," replied Morgan, "I could not do that." Carnegie kept the $70,000.

The fact that Morgan saved Carnegie from a $10,000 mistake made a great impression on Carnegie. In his autobiography, he goes on to write that he determined then and there that "neither Morgan, father or son, nor their house, should [ever] suffer through me. They had in me henceforth a firm friend."

Morgan had the legal right to buy Carnegie's interest for $60,000, but he declined to exercise it. Why? Because he saw an opportunity to place his relationship with Carnegie on a special footing—something "more" than the contractual, "everyone for himself" model of the marketplace.

Notice the dynamic here: Morgan did nothing to endear himself to Carnegie as a likable person with warm, personal charm. He simply used the occasion to send Carnegie a signal that he was trustworthy, handing Carnegie two separate checks to emphasize what he was doing. Both men lived many years beyond 1873, and their ability to rely on each other in business affairs paid off many times, dwarfing the extra $10,000 they exchanged that day.

◄ The "Ultimatum Game": ►
A Test of Fairness

Boiled down to its essence, the norm of reciprocity in negotiation amounts to a simple, three-step code of conduct. First, you should always be trustworthy and reliable yourself. You have no right to ask of others what you cannot be yourself. Second, you should be fair to those who are fair to you. This simple rule sustains most productive bargaining relationships. Third, you should let others know about it when you think they have treated you unfairly. Unfair treatment, left unnoticed or unrequited, breeds exploitation—followed by resentment and the ultimate collapse of the relationship.

Let me illustrate just how powerful these three rules are as a "code of fair behavior" in bargaining. Negotiation researchers have repeatedly used a simple experiment to prove how sensitive people are to notions of equity and fairness in their bargaining relationships. It is called the "ultimatum game." It works as follows.

Suppose you are sitting next to a stranger at a bar. Someone comes in and hands the stranger $100, telling the pair of you that, if you can agree on a division of the $100 between you, you can both keep whatever you agree to. Here are the rules: The stranger must make a single offer to you for some number between $0 and $100. You must then either accept or reject that offer—no haggling allowed. If you accept, you split the money as agreed. If you reject, neither of you gets any money. After a first round of play, the stranger will get another $100 and you will play again.

Now assume the stranger makes you the following offer: He gets $98 and you get $2. Would you accept or reject? Although $2 is better than nothing, many people in negotiation experiments involving even one round of this game reject this patently unfair division. In fact, some people reject offers going all the way up to 25 or 30 percent of the total amount being divided. Why? Because these divisions are not a "fair" split of the money and by saying "no" people punish the person who has made the unfair offer. True, you lose some money if you turn the $2 offer down—but the other guy loses $98. Many people think it is worth a few dollars to stand up for "fairness."

In a two-round game, our inclination to insist on fairness is bolstered by the fact that our behavior in round 1 affects the way the other party will treat us in round 2. Suppose you accept the stranger's unfair $2 offer in the first round. Now the stranger (not a stranger any longer) gets another $100. What do you think he will offer you in round 2? Probably $2. But what if you had turned down his first offer? What would his second offer be? Something more than $2—and maybe as much as $50. Your insistence on fairness in round 1 would set the stage for establishing a norm of fairness and reciprocity between you in future rounds.

Now imagine that instead of being greedy, the stranger is a fair-minded person who offers you $50. Almost everyone would say "yes" to this. The $50 split is a manifestly fair division and deserves a positive response. You and the stranger could go on playing this game all evening—until the person supplying the money got tired and went home.

Finally, suppose the stranger offers you $55 of the $100? This is, in essence, what J. P. Morgan did for Andrew Carnegie during the Panic of 1873. You might, like Carnegie, try to give your generous new friend $5 back to keep your accounts at the "fair" and equal level. But the game does not permit this, so you would have to accept the $55 offer.

You would also begin thinking about your relationship with the other person somewhat differently. You would "owe" that person something. After J. P. Morgan saved Carnegie from his $10,000 mistake, Carnegie was faced with the problem of finding a way to reciprocate in kind. There was no immediate opportunity, so he determined to look out for Morgan as a firm friend well into the future.

The lesson to take from these examples of how reciprocity works is straightforward: Just because you have power in a given situation does not mean it is smart to use it. In fact, it may be wiser to follow the lead of J. P. Morgan and use the situation as an opportunity to establish the foundation for a future relationship. Generosity begets generosity. Fairness begets fairness. Unfairness ought to beget a firm response. That's the norm of reciprocity in relationships. You can also count on the reciprocity norm to help you through the information exchange and concession-making stages of bargaining. Always take turns. After you make a move, wait until the other party reciprocates before you move again. Reciprocity is a reliable guide of proper conduct at the bargaining table.

◄ The Relationship Factor in ► Negotiation Planning

People are complex and unpredictable. No matter how stable your relationship with the other party may be, you must grapple with the problem of trust each and every time you negotiate. That means you must get into the habit of reviewing the relationship factor as a routine part of effective negotiation planning.

How does one do this? A personal experience may help to show you how it is done. The story involves an American businessman—I'll call him Barry—who attended the Wharton Executive Negotiation Workshop and whom I later advised regarding a complex global business deal. I have changed a few of the facts to ensure confidentiality, but the story is true.

At thirty-five, Barry was the president and chief operating officer of his family's $25 million chemical engineering firm in Ohio. He was energetic, hard-driving, and extremely competitive. Under his leadership, the firm had prospered and grown.

Barry called me because he was talking with a large Swiss firm about a possible joint venture and needed some negotiation advice. The Swiss company wanted to exploit a special chemical formula developed by Barry's firm to create an entirely new product line with enormous global sales potential. If consummated, the deal could dwarf Barry's current operation and quickly lead to more than $100 million in profits.

Barry was anxious for this deal to work, but he was having trouble moving the negotiations along. He was especially keen to decide whether he should be the first one to name a price for his firm's chemical formula or wait for the Swiss company to open with its own valuation.

Barry sent me copies of his correspondence with the Swiss firm and his notes from various face-to-face meetings. We then had several long discussions about the situation. The deal had many interesting business terms, price issues, and possible structures, but as I studied the situation I concluded that the most important strategic variables centered on relationships.

First, Barry and his counterpart—a Swiss executive who was slightly older than he was—had been strangers to each other prior to the Swiss firm's inquiry regarding Barry's technology. As I reviewed the correspondence, I was struck by the collegial tone and "we can work it out" spirit that underlay virtually everything the Swiss executive—I'll call him Karl—said or wrote. Barry's responses, by contrast, had a very competitive, defensive air, focusing on matters such as possible disputes in the future and the risk that the Swiss company might steal Barry's technology. From the workshop, I knew that Barry was a competitive type—and he was running true to form.

In addition, Barry's notes reflected his frustration at not being able to get Karl to talk specifics about the deal at various meetings. Barry suspected that Swiss companies were secretive and that this one might have a hidden agenda.

I did not discount the possibility that something suspicious was going on in Zurich, but competitive people like Barry have trouble taking others at face value. Although it pays to be prudent, people are sometimes exactly what they seem. I questioned Barry closely about Karl's behavior in the casual conversations and social situations they had shared. I then made an informed guess about Karl—that he was a genuine problem solver who could be both fair and creative if Barry would only give him a chance.

I advised Barry to relax and begin approaching Karl as a possible confederate rather than as a potential pickpocket.

I suspected that what Barry was experiencing as delay might well be an unstated need by Karl to form a better personal relationship with him as a foundation for a long-term business opportunity. By focusing exclusively on the current transaction, Barry was missing a lot of signals his would-be Swiss friend was sending him.

This was an important insight, but the most important relational issue in the deal still lay ahead. Something Barry mentioned in one of our talks prompted me to ask him about his relationship with the CEO and majority owner of Barry's own firm: Barry's father. And that opened a floodgate of frustration and anxiety. It turned out that Barry's father, the firm's founder, was getting on in years but was not relinquishing his control over strategic business issues. This deal was a classic example.

Barry's father was avoiding the subject whenever it came up, expressing exaggerated and unrealistic expectations for the formula in question so that funds derived from it would "take care of your mother when I'm gone," and indicating in subtle ways that he did not quite trust Barry to negotiate the best possible terms.

This, of course, raised some complex and important issues about Barry's relationships within his family. It was clear that, even if the Swiss firm made an attractive offer, the deal might fall through because Barry's father would fear losing control of the company. When Barry and I focused on this issue, we agreed that his chances for success with the Swiss firm were low without clarity on the home front.

Interestingly, while Barry's father was avoiding a realistic discussion of the deal, Barry himself had been avoiding a confrontation with his father over the simmering issue of control. Family relationships that involve business can be both the most dependable and the most explosive imaginable. Barry's family had developed a sophisticated avoidance mechanism to keep the risk of an explosion by its strong-willed patriarch as low as possible.

Over the next month or so, the deal began to move forward. Barry made a trip to Europe and spent several days with Karl—this time putting the deal in the background while he let the beginnings of a personal relationship develop. Barry was genuinely surprised when Karl casually dropped a possible price range for Barry's formula into a dinner conversation near the end of this trip. After some discussion, the pair began closing in on a price that was much higher than Barry had thought possible.

Meanwhile, on the home front, Barry had a talk with other family members and a trusted financial adviser about his father's refusal to confront the implications of this deal for the firm. Barry realized that he had been as responsible as his father for deferring the control issue, but he was determined to move the issue forward. Barry gained an important ally when his mother privately agreed that something needed to be done.

In short, Barry's negotiation problems turned out to have important relationship issues both across the table and away from it. Barry began to make real progress only when he started paying as much attention to the "people" issues as he did to the financial terms. The same is true of many important negotiations.

◄ Personal Relationships Versus ► Working Relationships

After the incident during the Panic of 1873, the relationship between J. P. Morgan and Andrew Carnegie was based on a degree of mutual trust. But was this relationship a personal friendship or a working relationship? How about the one between Barry and Karl? There is a subtle distinction between working relationships and personal friendships that can make a major difference in the way negotiations work.

I once interviewed the head of an investment banking firm as part of a negotiation research project. This man had been an entrepreneur before he joined the firm and had done literally thousands of deals in his career. I asked him what aspect of negotiation caused him the most anxiety.

He hesitated for a moment and then replied, "Walking into a negotiation and seeing a friend sitting on the other side of the table."

I was surprised by his answer. "Why would that be a problem?" I asked. "Wouldn't that help you understand each other?"

"In my business," the banker said, "the job is to make as much money for the client as possible. Seeing a friend sitting there makes you worry about something else—the friendship. It's hard to do your job when you're worried about losing a friend."

Research has confirmed this banker's intuition about bargaining with friends. In fact, the closer the personal relationship between two negotiators, the more likely it is that they will seek to minimize conflict and close the deal based on some simple, roughly equal compromise.

Some years ago, three professors conducted a bargaining study to see how dating couples handled bargaining. They gave the same bargaining problem—the purchase for resale of three different appliances—to seventy-four dating couples and thirty-two pairs of men and women who were strangers.

The dating couples were much "softer" in their bargaining styles than the strangers were. They started the negotiation with more modest goals; they made bigger concessions; they argued with each other less; and they told each other the truth about their bargaining positions more often. In short, they were nicer to each other than the strangers were, and reached agreements by straight, simple compromises.

Their "soft" style carried a cost, however. They were much less successful than were the strangers at uncovering hidden, mutually rewarding trade-offs in the scenario they negotiated. Why? Because they focused on simple, equal compromises on all the issues and engaged in less problem solving and probing of priorities than did the more competitively minded strangers. As we shall see in Chapter 9, effective negotiators care about being "fair," but they are also assertive about their goals. They push the other party to help them find the best solutions, not just the simplest compromises.

A second study confirmed that friends are also "soft" on each other when it comes to bargaining. The subjects in this experiment were asked to state the price they would demand or pay for certain items such as used TV sets or concert tickets. In each case, the item being sold had a stated range of fair values (for example, subjects were told that the concert tickets they had or wanted might sell for between $10 and $26). The subjects also told the experimenters how intensely they expected to bargain in an encounter to buy or sell these items. In some cases they were told to set the price for a friend; in others the price was for a stranger.

The results confirmed our intuitions. The relationship factor made a big difference. The opening prices to sell things to friends were toward the lower end of the "fair value" range ($15.50 to sell the concert tickets worth between $10 and $24) and near the midpoint when subjects were offering to buy things from friends ($17.50 to buy the tickets). The subjects also anticipated a relaxed, no-haggle bargaining encounter. The prices for strangers were either very high ($24 to sell the tickets) or low ($14 to buy the tickets). Obviously, the subjects anticipated a lot of bargaining.

So our relationships with others matter when it comes to the allocation norms we apply in bargaining encounters. Close relationships trigger the use of "equality" or "equal sharing" norms. Encounters with strangers cause us to expect and exhibit more competitive, selfish behavior.

But isn't there a middle ground for relationships—something between friends and strangers? There is. Between these two extremes are so-called working relationships. These are the exchange relationships of everyday business life. They are based both on a degree of trust and reciprocity and on the prudent assumption that both parties are looking after their own best interests. Working relationships are somewhat more formal than friendships; they can be sustained through more explicit conflict over relatively higher stakes; and they depend for their existence less on emotional support and feelings of "liking" than on explicit reciprocity in a series of exchanges. My guess is that J. P. Morgan and Andrew Carnegie had a highly reliable working relationship.

◄ Psychological Strategies for ► Building Working Relationships

How does one go about building the trust needed to form working relationships? There are several strategies that can help, but you should remember that sincerity in your conduct is a key to any of these working effectively. People do not respond well when they think others are trying to manipulate them.

THE SIMILARITY PRINCIPLE

At the most superficial level, a simple psychological fact is that we tend to trust people who appear more rather than less familiar to us—people who act like us, share our general interests and experiences, and identify with the same groups.

Remember the story in Chapter 3 about Mahatma Gandhi's controversial first-class train ride in South Africa? The stationmaster gave Gandhi a first-class ticket. "I wish you a safe journey," he said. "I can see you are a gentleman."

Gandhi had no personal relationship with the stationmaster to smooth the way toward getting his ticket, but he did use the basic principle of similarity to help him. The similarity principle applies to aspects of negotiation such as communication style as well as to things like appearance and group membership. When I was coaching Barry in how to relate better to Karl, my main effort was to get him to match Karl's collaborative approach to communication—to emphasize the positive aspects of the deal and make an effort to discuss shared interests. As soon as Barry began suppressing his more overt competitiveness in favor of cooperative communication, the deal began to move ahead. Chapter 8, on the rapport building that goes on during the information exchange stage of negotiations, explores the similarity principle in more detail.

THE ROLE OF GIFTS AND FAVORS

Another time-tested way to encourage the delicate process of establishing trust in working relationships is to give the other side something as a symbol of good faith. Think back to the two examples that led off the book. The first involved the sale of Harcourt Brace Jovanovich to General Cinema. As you will recall, the negotiation started off with a surprise: HBJ's CEO, Peter Jovanovich, presented General Cinema's Dick Smith with a symbolic gift, an engraved HBJ watch. Even more important, he gave Smith some information—an admission that Jovanovich thought General Cinema was the "right" buyer for his company. This latter move involved some risk, which made it all the more meaningful.

In the second case—the settlement of the land dispute between the two Arusha neighbors in Tanzania—the negotiation began with the parties making extreme demands and accusations. In the language of the Arusha people, the neighbors were "talking to the mountain." But the negotiation *ended* with an exchange of gifts: a small goat and some homemade beer.

In both of these negotiations the gifts served an important communication purpose that helped build trust. They were symbols of an underlying relationship between the parties. The HBJ watch helped initiate a relationship between businessmen who were strangers to each other; the goat and the beer helped reestablish order in a long-standing relationship between two neighbors.

The favor J. P. Morgan performed for Andrew Carnegie by saving Carnegie from his $10,000 mistake also served as a kind of gift. And like a gift, Morgan's favor set the norm of reciprocity in motion.

Behavioral economists have argued that gifts—especially gifts between unrelated strangers—often serve as signals regarding intentions to invest in a future relationship. They cite as examples everything from certain animal courtship behavior to gift giving in business mergers such as the HBJ example. Gifts, kindnesses, and a thoughtful regard for other people's feelings are all ways of helping to establish and maintain close personal relationships—and the same acts carry symbolic weight at the bargaining table even though the relationships there may be more professional than personal in character.

TRUST AND RELATIONSHIP NETWORKS

A third way to establish a measure of trust at the bargaining table is through the operation of relationship networks. Such networks often help us gain access to and credibility with those we are seeking to influence. The mere fact that we share a mutual acquaintance with our counterpart may help us appear more familiar and establish a minimal condition for trust. If our counterparts know someone who can specifically vouch for our trustworthiness, this helps them gain even more confidence that we will treat them fairly.

Many cultures around the world have highly refined and explicit ideas about the operation of relationship networks, much more so than we do in the West. The Japanese have a ceremonial ritual of exchanging business cards (called *meishi*) when first meeting a potential business contact. Both parties bow and hold the card a certain way, treating it with great seriousness. This helps the relationship process get started based on reciprocal signs of respect.

While doing research in Japan on negotiation practices, I learned that Japanese firms often send their young executives out for days at a time to collect as many *meishi* as possible. Why? Because once *meishi* are exchanged, both sides are free to make a future call without embarrassment. Asian networking is also accompanied by obligatory giving and receiving of small gifts, underscoring the reciprocal nature of these relationships. There are even gift-giving consultants in Japan to help people decide just what sort of gift is appropriate in each business situation. Once gift giving is established, negotiations become merely an episode in an ongoing association in which the parties no longer have to worry quite so much about the issue of trust.

In China, the ceremonial aspects of networking are somewhat less formal but networks are just as important. The Chinese even have a special name for networks: *guanxi* (pronounced "gwang-chi"). As one prominent Asian business publication put it, "Connections are a fact of life in Asian business. With the right *guanxi,* doors open and deals get done. Without it, the simplest deals can disintegrate."

Guanxi has its strongest connotations with respect to family affiliations. But it expands outward from that core to encompass any and all relationships that have at their source a commitment to reciprocal benefits and obligations.

Just how does *guanxi* work? A U.S. newspaper recently reported a typical story. A young third-generation Chinese-American woman quit her well-paying job in Boston and traveled to Gwangzhou, China, looking for opportunity. After teaching conversational English to "Chuppies" (short for "Chinese young urban professionals") for a few months, she decided to open a café and bar where fellow Americans in Gwangzhou could find a friendly and familiar atmosphere while consuming pepperoni pizza, beer, and homemade cheesecake.

She had the money she needed, but, like many foreigners doing business in China, she had trouble negotiating with local officials to obtain her business permit. As she later described it, "The rules [in China] depend on whoever is behind the counter that day."

Then she called on her *guanxi*—some former "Chuppie" students who worked for the local government in Gwangzhou. She did not have to pay the "Chuppies" bribes or make under-the-table payments. She just approached them and asked for help. They liked their American friend and saw an opportunity to become part of her "network." They spoke to a few officials who were part of their own *guanxi* and bureaucratic wheels began to turn. Her café soon opened as planned.

Guanxi is so important to Asian business that a magazine called *International Business Asia* publishes an annual directory it calls its "*Guanxi* List." This list features the people in Asia with the most influential networks of personal connections. "While [everyone on the list] possesses business acumen in their own right," the magazine notes, "a constant in their success has been access to the best business and political circles."

We Americans tend to be slightly disdainful and even a little suspicious of the idea that people get ahead through their "connections." In our public ceremonies and rhetoric, we honor people based on what they achieve rather than who they know. In the Western news media, the Chinese idea of *guanxi* carries the smell of corruption and unsavory business practices. What Asians and Latin Americans think of as "gifts," we sometimes see as "bribes" or "kickbacks." Where they see public officials exercising discretion, we see violations of the rule of law.

Yet in our own way, we Americans believe in the power of *guanxi*, too. We are just less forthright about it. One of my first jobs out of college was at a fund-raising consulting firm that published what amounted to an American "*Guanxi* List." My firm compiled an annual directory listing the names of every trustee, board member, and executive director of every major foundation and nonprofit funding source in the United States. The directory included every scrap of personal information we could glean from public sources about the people on the list: their spouses, where they had gone to college and graduate school, their clubs and other affiliations, their interests and hobbies.

The programs these foundations funded dealt with high-minded issues such as world hunger, human rights, and curing cancer. But the directory sold out every year because it provided hints about the *guanxi* networks of the elite decision makers who distributed grants. Fundraisers could then find out where their own institutional *guanxi* networks crossed paths with the donors' networks. This was the starting point for strategic planning to approach a funding source. Other examples of American *guanxi* include college alumni networks, relationships gained through community activities, mutual acquaintances made through children and family, and so on.

◄ Relationship Traps for the Unwary ►

Relationships are critical to negotiation success in all the ways I have discussed, but they pose significant risks, too. Fair-minded, reasonable people in particular can fall prey to tricks and traps set by "sharks" at the bargaining table. When the stakes are small, being victimized by such tricks becomes a simple learning experience: Pay for your mistakes and be more careful next time. When the stakes are high, however, you may not be able to afford the lesson. Here are a few common traps to watch out for.

TRUSTING TOO QUICKLY

Cooperative people assume that most people, like them, are fair and honest. Not wanting to appear greedy or suspicious, they take big risks too early in a bargaining encounter. This can happen when negotiators on the other side ask for substantial sums of money or performance commitments up front without sufficient assurances that they will fulfill their side of the bargain.

The solution here is to take your time and build trust step by step. It helps if you can use your relationship network to check the other party out. If this is not possible, take a small risk before you take a big one. See if those on the other side reliably reciprocate in some little matter that requires *their* performance based on trust. If they pass the test, you have a track record on which to base your next move.

RECIPROCITY TRAPS

Sharks can manipulate the norm of reciprocity, triggering a feeling of obligation in well-meaning people when none is appropriate. Many of us have experienced this in everyday encounters with various con artists. How about the people at the airport who give you a flower and then ask for a donation to their charity? You try to give them the flower back, but they insist you keep it. You feel angry, but you also feel obligated. This is nothing less than a well-crafted reciprocity trap designed to trigger donations that far exceed the flowers in value.

At the bargaining table, watch out for people who make small concessions and then ask for much bigger ones in return. Similarly, beware of those who reveal a little information of their own and then ask you to disclose your entire financial position and cost structure.

These are patently unfair exchanges, but the norm of reciprocity is so strongly ingrained in many of us that we respond to the form of the exchange more than the content. Once those on the other side make a cooperative move in our direction, we feel compelled to reciprocate, and we sometimes do not pause to consider whether their suggestion about how to do so is really prudent or appropriate.

If you feel yourself feeling pressured to reciprocate when it does not feel quite right, take a break and consider the overall situation before making your next move. Do you really owe the other party something, or are you falling into a reciprocity trap?

NEGOTIATING WITH FRIENDS WHEN THE STAKES ARE HIGH

As was mentioned earlier, friends and lovers make bad bargaining partners when the stakes are high. People in very close relationships tend to rely on equal-split norms to make divisions. In the $100 "ultimatum game," they split $50-$50 in round after round.

But as many a broken business partnership can testify, very high stakes can bring out the shark in even a close friend or associate. Suppose the ultimatum game involved a final round in which the stakes were raised to $10 million. Your friend now has a choice of what to offer you. Do you think he might be tempted to offer you $1 million or even $500,000, figuring you could not say "no" to that kind of money and deciding that for $9 million he can live without your friendship? It may not say much for human nature, but many people would yield to this enticement.

When the stakes rise, people in close relationships are well advised to seek help in negotiating tough allocation issues. Equity norms (such as "To each according to his inputs" or "To each according to her risk") might become more appropriate division norms than simple fifty-fifty splits.

Even if both parties are operating in good faith, equality norms tend to leave large areas of potential value unexplored. Energetic problem solving can sometimes bring these opportunities for gain to light better than simple compromises. Letting relationship concerns overwhelm the negotiation may eliminate these potential gains.

When the stakes are high, therefore, it is often wise to delegate the bargaining task to professional advisers. If this sounds too confrontational, finding a single adviser trusted by both sides to act as a mediator or go-between might help. Such neutral parties can ensure that the maximum amount of imagination is brought to the transaction without endangering future cooperation between the principals.

◄ Summary ►

The relationship factor is a critical variable in your ability to succeed as a negotiator. Here are some tips that will help you get the most from relationships every time you negotiate.

◄ THE RELATIONSHIP FACTOR: ►
A CHECKLIST

✓ Gain access and credibility through relationship networks.

✓ Build working relationships across the table with small steps such as gifts, favors, disclosures, or concessions.

✓ Avoid reciprocity and relationship traps like trusting too quickly, letting others make you feel guilty, and mixing big business with personal friendships.

✓ Always follow the "Rule of Reciprocity":
  • Be reliable and trustworthy.
  • Be fair to those who are fair to you.
  • When other parties treat you unfairly, let them know about it.

The Fifth Foundation:
The Other Party's Interests

It is not from the benevolence of the butcher, the brewer or the baker that we expect our dinner, but from their regard to their own interests.

—ADAM SMITH (1776)

If there is any one secret of success, it lies in the ability to get the other person's point of view and see things from that person's angle as well as from your own.

—HENRY FORD

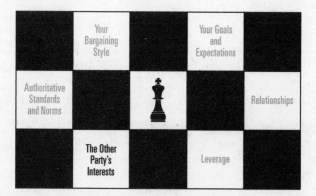

Effective negotiators exhibit a very important trait: the ability to see the world from the other party's point of view. To succeed at negotiation, you must learn to ask how it might be in the other party's interests to help you achieve your goals. Then you should determine why the other party might say "no" so you can remove as many of his or her objections as possible. Understanding what the other party really wants is critical to Information-Based Bargaining, and it is not as easy as it sounds.

I once advised a U.S. hospital that was conducting a clinical trial of a new drug for a foreign pharmaceutical firm. These tests form the basis for new drug applications to the U.S. Food and Drug Administration (FDA). The overseas drug company was refusing to follow an FDA recommendation about how the trial should be conducted. The FDA wanted one sort of informed consent form used with patients taking the experimental drug, and the foreign firm was adamant that it would use its own form. The disagreement was threatening the whole project because the FDA might ultimately reject all the findings in the study if the wrong form was used.

The issue was all the more bizarre because the hospital and the foreign firm shared significant interests. Both wanted to see the project through to a successful conclusion, and millions of dollars as well as the professional reputations of both parties were at risk.

This negotiation had all the earmarks of a disaster until I asked the hospital's research director to identify the specific decision maker at the drug firm who was saying "no." This question forced the executive to focus his attention on a specific person instead of "the client." It turned out that a foreign-trained physician with no U.S. medical experience was calling the shots. Then I asked why this particular physician might be saying "no."

All of a sudden the ideas started popping. First, the foreign physician's experience was with his country's version of the FDA, and that agency would not throw out a study based on this sort of issue. Next, the hospital was being represented in the negotiation by a midlevel project manager who was not a physician and who lacked professional credibility with the foreign doctor. Physicians are professionally oriented toward hierarchies, and the foreign physician's national culture reinforced his tendency. Finally, the research director speculated that the specific form the foreign firm wanted to use might be linked—at least in the physician's mind—to the firm's success in enrolling patients in the study, a critical factor.

From these ideas, none of which had to do with any conflicts between these parties, came a series of recommendations for action. The problem was now framed as one of persuasion. A particular foreign physician working for the client had to be given compelling arguments by a credible source (preferably a physician from his own country who was familiar with U.S. drug approval processes) that the FDA was serious about its recommendation. The hospital had physician contacts abroad. The wheels began to turn. The negotiation gridlock was broken, and a strategy for going forward emerged.

◄ Discover the Other Party's Goals ►

The CEO of one of America's fastest-growing banks once explained the best way to prepare for a negotiation: "You have to get outside your own wants and needs and learn all you can about what's meaningful to the other person. And it's not always another billion dollars." Entrepreneur H. Wayne Huizenga follows a similar approach. As one colleague has described Huizenga's preparation process, "He is good at acquisitions because he knows how to treat people. He studies or thinks about the other side of the table a lot, and he may change his opinion from one day to the next because he's thinking about the other side . . ."

Effective negotiators draw from a wide range of talents. From effective leaders they borrow the habit of committing themselves to specific, ambitious goals. From good advocates they get the skill of developing arguments based on standards and norms. From effective salespeople, they acquire the gift of valuing relationships and seeing the world as the person they are trying to influence sees it. Research suggests that the ability to understand your bargaining opponent's perspective may be the most critical of these skills and one of the hardest to use in practice.

Why is it so hard to get into the other party's shoes? For three reasons. First, most people suffer to greater or lesser degrees from a common human limitation: We see the world through the lens of our own interests. If we favor welfare reform, we tend to notice stories about how people are cheating the welfare system. If we oppose it, we notice the stories about how bad homelessness is and how much worse it will become if welfare policies change.

Negotiation theorists call this having partisan perceptions. This was the main problem with the clinical trials team at the hospital. They assumed they were "right" and the client was "wrong." They needed to step back and take responsibility for failing to understand the client's frame of mind. Whatever the problem in a negotiation, it is usually a safe bet that both sides are contributing to it.

Second, even the most accommodating person brings a somewhat competitive attitude to negotiation. There are, by definition, conflicting needs on the table. This leads us quite naturally to focus on divergent interests in our preparation and to sift what the other side says and does through a competitive filter. The hospital's executives assumed there must be some conflicting interest that was holding up the study on the other side of the table. They were stuck because they could not imagine what it could be. Only when they asked the open-ended question "Why are they saying no?" did they start to identify the personal interests that were causing the delay.

Negotiation scholar Max Bazerman has documented people's tendency to fixate on the competitive aspects of negotiation in a series of research studies. Bazerman and his colleagues have shown that people assume negotiations center on dividing a fixed pie. However, by looking for common ground and nonconflicting interests, there is often a chance to make the pie bigger. The collaborative approach to the chair situation in Chapter 1 is a good example of making a bigger pie. By seeing past the obvious compromise solution of splitting $1,000 to the possibility that both parties could make $1,000 if they moved quickly enough, the problem solver created value for both sides. In Chapters 8 and 9, I explain the bargaining processes that will help you create more value for both parties.

Third, the dynamics of the negotiation process itself often work against finding shared interests once discussions begin. Professor Leigh Thompson and a colleague analyzed thirty-two different negotiation research studies involving more than five thousand participants in an effort to see whether people are good at finding shared priorities and interests in complex negotiations. The results were striking: At least in a laboratory setting, people failed to identify shared goals in negotiations about 50 percent of the time.

Most of this confusion arose because the parties were bluffing each other during the negotiation process, pretending they were compromising when they were really getting exactly what they wanted. Some additional confusion came from people not being explicit about their real interests and motivations. In such cases, it was up to the other side to actively seek the common ground. For example, one could hardly have expected the foreign physician in my example to say, "I am not listening to you because you lack the proper cultural and status credentials to meet my demanding standards." It took an imaginative effort by the Americans to uncover this problem. They needed to note their own frustration, see the discomfort the foreign physician was exhibiting, and move toward some possible hypotheses to explain his behavior. Many people are not willing to take these extra steps.

With all these barriers, it is not surprising that people have trouble focusing on the other party's interests in their negotiations. Is it worth the substantial effort it sometimes takes to locate the common ground? The research evidence suggests very strongly that the effort pays big dividends, as long as you do not forget your own goals in your enthusiasm to accommodate the other person.

◄ The Planning Behavior of ► Skilled Negotiators

The Rackham and Carlisle study of English negotiation professionals discussed in Chapter 1 supports this point: The more skilled the negotiator, the more likely he or she was to focus during planning on possible areas of common ground between the parties, including feasible options for settlement. This study was unusual in that researchers actually listened in on real planning sessions involving real deals conducted by fifty-one different negotiators over fifty-six planning sessions. The subjects had previously been identified as having a high degree of experience and bargaining skill. The sessions involving the skilled group were then compared with planning sessions led by negotiators who were rated by peers as average.

Note well: Both the average and the skilled groups spent more time focusing on their own goals and the areas of potential conflict with the other party than they did looking for the bigger pie. But the skilled negotiators focused nearly four times more of their time during the planning sessions, 40 percent in all, on possible areas of shared or complementary interests—the common or at least nonconflicting ground between them. The group of less skilled negotiators focused on the common ground only about 10 percent of the time and spent the remaining 90 percent figuring out how to make or defend against demands arising from conflicting positions on issues such as price, power, or control.

The skilled negotiators' focus on areas of common ground led to another significant difference between the groups. The skilled negotiators developed about twice the number of possible settlement options in their planning as did the less skilled group and appeared to try harder to anticipate options the other side would suggest. One area the groups did not differ on was their formal education—neither group had many people with advanced degrees from business or law schools. In short, being a skilled negotiator did not require education. Instead, it required experience, judgment, and imagination. Laboratory studies have confirmed that people who are able to judge their opponents' interests more accurately achieve consistently better outcomes than those who focus solely on their own goals.

Given the importance of focusing on the other side's interests to create opportunities for favorable trades, how should one go about doing so? The following steps will help you focus your attention on what the other party wants and how these interests can be used to advance your own goals.

1. Identify the decision maker.
2. Look for common ground: How might it serve the other party's interests to help you achieve your goals?
3. Identify interests that might interfere with agreement: Why might the other side say "no"?
4. Search for low-cost options that solve the other party's problems while advancing your goals.

◄ Identify the Decision Maker ►

To understand what the other party needs, you must first identify who the person on the other side of the table—the decision maker—is. Companies and institutions have policies, goals, and relationships, but as my hospital's dispute with its clinical trials client shows, *only people negotiate.* The decision makers' needs, including their status, self-esteem, and self-fulfillment interests, will drive the negotiation. I am amazed at how often people forget to identify these pivotal people before they begin negotiating.

At business school, each entering MBA class starts on a two-year quest with a single goal: to get a good job upon graduation. The students' second year is often spent interviewing, flying around the country to "callbacks," and, usually, nailing down the terms of a concrete offer sometime in the spring semester.

Every year I am approached by numerous students who are nervously engaged in the final stage of the job-hunting process. They want advice on how to resolve such negotiating issues as salary, the amount of a signing bonus, relocation expenses, and the like.

My first question is "With whom are you negotiating?" More often than not, they are speaking with someone in a general corporate role, such as a director of human resources or a division recruitment coordinator. These are people who usually implement hiring decisions made by others. I then ask, "Is there a person who has higher decision-making authority who knows you and wants *you*, not just any recruit, at the firm?" Their eyes light up. They see that they need to take initiative in the negotiation process and select a person to negotiate with who can make or influence decisions and who has a specific need for their services.

One MBA student I counseled several years ago managed to persuade his new employer, a South American firm that had never hired anyone with an MBA before, to pay off his entire business school tuition debt as part of the package of benefits he would receive. He negotiated this extraordinary deal by arranging to meet directly with the entrepreneur who owned the firm in an airport lounge, appealing to the entrepreneur's own experience as a debt-burdened student, and describing what this payment would mean in terms of the student's commitment to the company. His appeal was persuasive because he took the trouble to make it in person to the ultimate decision maker and to couch it in terms of the other party's experience and interests.

➤ Look for Common Ground: ➤
How Might It Serve the Other Party's Interests to Help You Achieve Your Goals?

After you have a clear idea about who is on the other side, think carefully about what his or her needs and interests might be. Do you have any interests in common? Why might a proposal achieving your goal be a good option for this person?

An excellent way to explore the other side's interests is through a technique called "role reversal." Let's say you are in a negotiation with your boss over a promotion. In a role reversal, you pretend for a moment that *you* are the boss. Then you ask a spouse, colleague, or friend to play you. After briefing your friend on the issues, you stage a pretend meeting in which to discuss the promotion problem. As you sit in the "boss's" chair, ask yourself, "How might it serve my interests to help this employee achieve his (or her) goals?" When the role play reaches a natural conclusion, write down the reasons why it might make sense from the boss's point of view to promote you. Talk to your colleague about your conclusions. See if you can discover what the boss might really be thinking.

Usually, there is a solid foundation of shared interests on which you can build a persuasive proposal. In fact, even the most contentious situations harbor a surprising core of common or nonconflicting interests.

An executive I know was recently involved in a tough negotiation among several hospital systems in New England over a possible merger. At the opening meeting, one side brought a large ax and put it on the bargaining table. "That's what we will be able to use on our competition if we can do this deal," they said. It is a testament to the brutal competition characterizing the U.S. health care market that an ax was seen as a shared interest, but this gesture got the negotiations off to a focused start.

Take consumer situations. Most of us assume that firms selling us goods and services have interests that conflict with ours over the issue of price. We want to pay less, and the sellers want us to pay more. This is true, but it is not the whole story. Surprisingly, many consumer companies have an additional interest that sometimes trumps their interest in a higher price: They have an interest in maintaining you as a satisfied customer. That is an interest you share with the firms, and it gives you an opening to request all sorts of accommodations.

One of my negotiation students recently undertook an interesting experiment. After listening to my lecture on shared interests, he called the toll-free numbers of all the magazines he subscribed to and asked for a discount. Note carefully: He did not threaten to drop his subscription; he just asked for the best discount the magazine was giving other customers. On several occasions he needed to take his request to a supervisor, but all eventually fell into line and gave discounts. They wanted to keep him as a satisfied customer.

When he reported his success to the class, another student mentioned that he had tried the same experiment, only he had done it at Macy's department store. He was in a hurry to buy a tie and located one at Macy's, where he was a regular customer. Mindful of a course requirement I impose to "haggle" for something, he asked for 10 percent off, pointing out that the tie was wrinkled. The attending clerk looked a little concerned and said it was not store policy to grant discounts, but my student persevered very tactfully and quickly received 10 percent off the price. A third classmate then volunteered that his wife had once been employed as a clerk at Bloomingdale's. Floor clerks, she reported, were authorized to give 5 to 15 percent off many high-end items if the discount was needed to maintain customer satisfaction.

By the end of the semester, the class had something of a contest going to see who could report the best story about receiving a discount for customer satisfaction. One woman in the class took the prize with a $350 discount off her wedding dress in a small upscale wedding boutique.

In the world of business-to-business relationships between sellers and customers, the same principle of customer satisfaction applies with even bigger payoffs. *BusinessWeek* magazine recently reported that business buyers are becoming increasingly savvy negotiators, asking for and getting such things as long-term agreements with "no price hike" promises, improved quality at no extra charge, free aftermarket service and upgrades, and favorable financing. The shared interest in keeping customers happy in a competitive marketplace is a huge source of value, prompting the magazine to headline its article "Ask and It Shall Be Discounted."

What are the lessons to be learned from these stories? First, there seem to be two prices for many things in the United States (and everywhere else in the global economy). There is the full price for easy-to-satisfy customers who dislike negotiation, and there is a discount price for customers who are willing to ask for it. Which are you?

Second, you may be entitled to more customer satisfaction of many kinds than you are currently getting simply because you do not realize that for many firms your satisfaction is a shared interest, not a conflicting one. In fact, the best firms with the best products are typically the ones most interested in your satisfaction. Note that you need not be pushy or aggressive to make your own satisfaction an issue. Just note politely, "I would be a really satisfied customer if you could _____."

If magazine publishers, department stores, and other service providers have vital interests they share in common with their customers, how much more is this the case for the people and firms with which you work? Do you want to start your new job later rather than sooner? Perhaps your new employer is waiting for an office to open or wants to keep its payroll down for the next quarter and would prefer you to start later. Why not ask? Do you want your new customer to pay that big bill sooner rather than later? Perhaps the division that made the purchase is trying to spend its budget allocation before a new budget cycle starts. It might be happy to pay. You will never know if you do not raise the issue.

Shared interests are the "elixir of negotiation," the salve that can smooth over the issues which you and the other party genuinely disagree about. The shared interests that are hidden in all negotiation situations are the foundations on which to build your proposals.

◄ Identify Interests That Might ► Interfere with Agreement: Why Might the Other Party Say "No"?

To be fully prepared to meet the other side's objections, you must identify likely areas of conflicting or ancillary interest that might cause the other party to resist or reject your proposal. In negotiations, you want to *lead* with your shared interests, but you need to anticipate objections and problems so you will be able to respond constructively.

During the role reversal part of your preparation, you should spend time asking why the other side might say "no" to your proposal. The answers you get to this question often provide the breakthrough insights that clinch a deal.

Of course, most parties will say "no" because you are not offering them enough on issues where your interests directly conflict: Your price is too high or your bid too low. These are predictable objections, and your response will need to be based on such things as leverage (Chapter 6), prevailing standards (Chapter 3), or relationships (Chapter 4).

However, a surprising number of cases will hinge on some completely separate reason that you had not anticipated and might not even care much about. Often these reasons have more to do with self-esteem, status, and other nonfinancial needs of the individuals involved in the negotiation than they do with the more obvious institutional and dollar issues on the table. Once you bring these reasons out into the open, you can set about to address them.

For example, some years ago First Union Corporation acquired CoreStates Financial Corporation for more than $16 billion, one of the biggest bank mergers up to that time in U.S. history. Near the end of the negotiations, it became clear that CoreStates' CEO, Terry Larsen, was hesitating to recommend the deal even though First Union's Ed Crutchfield had come most of the distance to meet Larsen's financial demands. The problem, as it turned out, had nothing to do with price. Larsen was deeply concerned that First Union, a North Carolina institution, would abandon the many charitable commitments both he and CoreStates had made in Pennsylvania, New Jersey, and Delaware, CoreStates' area of operation.

This would hurt the local community and subject Larsen to the charge that he had sold out the region where he made his home.

The two firms had different charitable giving policies, but they shared an interest in providing corporate support to worthy causes. Once Crutchfield uncovered this issue, he offered to set up a $100 million independent community foundation to be organized by Larsen. The foundation would make grants in the CoreStates area after the merger. This $100 million "extra" totaled only about .5 percent of the $16 billion purchase price, relatively small change for the key that unlocked the deal. With the foundation in hand, Larsen became an advocate for the merger and recommended approval to the CoreStates board. The deal eventually went through.

◄ Search for Low-Cost Options That Solve ► the Other Party's Problems While Advancing Your Goals

Once you have determined some of the less obvious reasons why the other side may object to an agreement, think of low-cost options that may address the other side's concerns while advancing your own goals. Once again, our tendency is to assume the other side is saying "no" because it wants the same thing we do—money, power, reduced risk, and the like. The best negotiators strive to overcome that assumption and search for additional, secondary interests that can be used to advance the deal.

My favorite example of an "outside the box," low-cost option that broke open a deal for an enterprising negotiator involves the city of Oceanside, California, and its garbage. A young woman named Kelly Sarber, representing an Arizona-based garbage company, was trying to win the contract to be the garbage hauler for the city of Oceanside. Faced with stiff competition from other haulers and the possibility of a bidding war, she managed to get Oceanside to accept her $43-per-ton bid to haul the city's garbage even though her bid was $5 *higher* than her competitors'. How did she do it?

An avid surfer in her spare time, Sarber was keenly aware that the beaches in Oceanside, a major source of tourist money and real estate values, were slowly but surely eroding. Her company's waste dump sites were in the Arizona desert, and if there is one thing a desert has in abundance, it's *sand*. Sarber won the Oceanside contract at a premium price by promising that her trucks would not only take the garbage out of town but also return with a load of clean, fresh Arizona sand to dump onto the town's disappearing beach. Oceanside officials thought they wanted cheap garbage-hauling services, but Sarber was able to win the contract with a premium price by showing the city she understood its beach and tourist problems.

Ms. Sarber's story is instructive for another reason. If you are able to identify the other side's interests, you are not far from understanding specifically what it needs that you may have to offer. And as we shall see in the next chapter, the greater the other party's need for what you have and the more it will feel the loss if you choose to walk away from a deal, the more leverage you have to insist that the other party agree to your terms.

◄ Summary ►

Finding out what the other party is worried about sounds simple, but our basic attitudes about negotiation make this surprisingly difficult to do. Most people tend to assume that other people's needs conflict with their own. They also restrict their field of vision to the issues that they themselves are troubled by, forgetting that the other side often has its own problems based on its own worldview.

The best negotiators overcome these assumptions with a relentless curiosity about what is really motivating the other side. Indeed, research suggests that they spend up to four times more time thinking in a strategic way about what the world looks like to the other party than average negotiators.

The lesson here is simple: Find the shared interests that will motivate negotiators on the other side to agree with your proposal and explore why they might say "no." These inquiries will give you a checklist of questions to ask in the negotiation. Lead with the areas you have in common, then probe for and try to meet the other side's objections one by one with the lowest cost concessions you can make. As you move into the areas in which you have genuine and significant conflicts, you will have gained the momentum you need to keep talks going. You will also be well positioned to exploit the next subject we will cover: your leverage.

◄ **EXPLORING THE OTHER PARTY'S** ►
INTERESTS: A CHECKLIST

✓ Locate the decision maker.
✓ How might it serve the other party's interests to help you achieve your goals?
✓ Why might the other party say "no"?
✓ What low-cost options might remove the other party's objections?

The Sixth Foundation:
Leverage

Every reason that the other side wants or needs an agreement is my leverage—provided that I know those reasons.

—BOB WOOLF

You can get much further with a kind word and a gun than you can with a kind word alone.

—ATTRIBUTED TO AMERICAN GANGSTER AL CAPONE

By now you should be feeling new confidence in your understanding of negotiation. You have knowledge about personal bargaining styles, goals, relationships, and interests. But the most important factor for high-stakes bargaining is still ahead of us. It is the Sixth Foundation of

Effective Negotiation: leverage. Leverage is your power not just to reach agreement, but to obtain an agreement *on your own terms*. Research has shown that, with leverage, even an average negotiator will do pretty well while without leverage only highly skilled bargainers achieve their goals. The party with leverage is confident; the party without it is usually nervous and uncertain. Let's start with several simple negotiation stories to illustrate what leverage means.

EXAMPLE 1: SHIFT THE BALANCE OF NEEDS

A major U.S. airline once faced a big problem. Its fleet of aircraft was aging, and it needed to purchase some of the latest jumbo jets. The trouble? It had recently taken on a large amount of new debt to pay for an acquisition and had no money left to buy new planes. At the time, two U.S. airplane manufacturers, Boeing and McDonnell Douglas, had a virtual monopoly on plane sales in the Unites States, and they were not interested in doing business with a customer that was broke.

But within a few months of confronting this issue, the airline's CEO proudly announced that his company would be acquiring fifty of the latest jumbo jets in a deal valued at close to $1 billion. How was he able to achieve this remarkable result?

Answer: The world's *third* major airplane manufacturer, Europe's Airbus consortium, had a new jumbo jet ready for sale. But Airbus had gone for an entire year without selling a single airplane. More important, Airbus leaders viewed the American market as critical to its future because airlines from other countries took their cues from sophisticated American buyers.

When the CEO showed interest in Airbus, it pulled out all the stops to arrange an innovative leasing deal that involved borrowed funds from one American and two French banks, General Electric (the firm that made Airbus engines), and Airbus itself. The French government even threw in millions of dollars' worth of export credits to subsidize the deal. In short, Airbus supplied not only the airplanes the CEO needed, but also *all the money to purchase them.* The CEO (Frank Borman of Eastern Airlines) got his jets by looking past the obvious sources of supply to find a seller that needed a buyer even more than he needed planes. He improved his leverage by shifting the "balance of needs" in his favor in the transaction.

EXAMPLE 2: LEVERAGE OF THE OTHER PARTY'S EGO

The entertainment business is rife with examples of how the personal ego needs of the participants in a deal can be sources of leverage just as often as corporate business needs. One of the most famous (or infamous) movie executives Hollywood spawned in recent times is hairdresser-turned-producer Peter Guber. Guber made one of his better deals early in his career when he obtained 20 percent of the stock of a booming record company owned by Neil Bogart called Casablanca Records in exchange for a modest 5 percent interest in his next movie, a second-rate sequel to *Jaws* called *The Deep*. How did Guber arrange this favorable trade?

Like many on the periphery of Hollywood, Bogart craved the legitimacy of being a "movie mogul." As one associate put it, "What Neil wanted more than anything was to get into the movie business and he was willing to pay anything to get it." Guber became aware of Bogart's movie mogul fantasy and offered to give him a role in producing *The Deep* for a big chunk of Bogart's record company. Bogart's self-esteem needs provided all the momentum needed to close the deal. The arrangement turned out doubly well for Guber because, as a fruit of the partnership, one of Casablanca's top artists, Donna Summer, sang the title track for *The Deep*. The film's soundtrack, released by Casablanca, sold two million copies.

EXAMPLE 3: GENERATE COMPETITIVE PRESSURE

A public utility in Houston, Texas—Houston Power & Lighting Company—was paying $195 million a year to the Burlington Northern Santa Fe railroad ("Burlington Northern") to carry coal to its giant generating station. Janie Mitcham, the head of purchasing for the utility, was fed up with the outrageous rates and poor service she was receiving, but what could she do? Burlington Northern had a monopoly on rail access to her plant. And rail was the only way to supply the enormous quantities of coal needed to run a generating facility. She tried to negotiate lower rates based on fairness arguments and appeals to the firms' relationship, but all she got from Burlington Northern was a shrug.

Then she got an idea: She would build a railroad of her own connecting her plant to tracks owned by the rival Union Pacific railroad, ten miles away. She mentioned the idea to Burlington Northern in a last-ditch effort to get it to reduce its rates, but Burlington Northern was not impressed. It was a lame threat, Burlington Northern executives figured, because the cost of such a project would be prohibitive, more than $24 million. Even Mitcham's staff was skeptical, calling her idea "The Rail of Dreams."

But Mitcham persisted. She got approval from her bosses to go ahead, had plans drawn up, and started building her own ten-mile-long railroad, now nicknamed "Janie Rail." It was no picnic. Burlington Northern sued her and went to rail regulators to complain; she had to move 300,000 cubic feet of soil, design around graveyards and historic sites, and put up with complaining neighbors. But in the end she got the job done. "Janie Rail" is now a reality—and Union Pacific bid for her business at a 25 percent discount off the rates Burlington Northern was charging. She is saving $10 million per year and stands to save about $50 million a year in the near future.

Mitcham is enjoying her newfound position of power. In fact, when Union Pacific recently was late with some deliveries, she switched some shipments *back to Burlington Northern,* prompting a personal visit and apologies from Union Pacific officials, who promised to do better. In short, Janie Mitcham improved her leverage by thinking outside of the box to create a new alternative for solving her supply problem. "Janie Rail" gave her leverage over *both* her old and new railroad service providers by creating competition for her business.

◄ Leverage: The Balance of Needs and Fears ►

As Chapter 5 revealed, skilled negotiators pay close attention to the other party's needs and interests. But let's be clear: They do so for a purpose. They are not negotiating in order to solve other people's problems. They are negotiating to achieve their own goals. And the most reliable way to achieve your goals at the bargaining table is to acquire and use something everyone wants but only negotiation "naturals" fully understand: leverage. Leverage derives from the balance of needs and fears at the bargaining table.

For all its importance, many people are confused about exactly what leverage is and how to use it. They also have trouble coping with the fact that leverage is a *dynamic* rather than a static factor in bargaining. It can change moment by moment.

The best way to test your own understanding of leverage—let's call it your "leverage IQ"—is to work your way through an example of a tough, high-stakes bargaining situation, asking yourself each step of the way, "Who has the leverage?" and "Given the leverage situation, what should the parties do next?" If you can understand how leverage works in a concrete situation such as this, you are ready to begin analyzing leverage in your everyday business and professional negotiations.

The example I have chosen to introduce the dynamics of leverage involves the kind of crisis that makes even expert negotiators break out in a cold sweat: a hostage taking. Many people feel that negotiating with hostage takers sets a bad precedent, but it is safe to say these critics have not had the bad luck to become hostages themselves. Moreover, as unique as a hostage situation may appear, the leverage lessons learned here apply broadly to any business or personal situation in which one side seems to have complete control and is dictating your moves. As you read the following story, watch carefully as the police authorities gradually take a situation that is totally out of their control and carefully turn it around by developing leverage from three sources: information on what the other party wants (both explicitly and implicitly), the power to make the other side worse off, and norms or values the other side respects.

◄ The Hanafi Hostage Situation ►

In March 1977, 12 heavily armed members of a little-known religious sect calling themselves the Hanafi Muslims seized three buildings in Washington, D.C., killing 1 radio reporter, wounding many other people, and taking 134 hostages. The three buildings included the District of Columbia's city hall, the national headquarters of the Jewish organization B'nai B'rith, and the Islamic Mosque and Cultural Center on Massachusetts Avenue.

The leader of the Hanafi Muslims, Hamaas Abdul Khaalis, had recently been the target of a brutal crime himself. Hit men from the largest and most powerful black Muslim group of the day, Elijah Muhammad's Nation of Islam, had broken into Khaalis's Washington home and murdered five of his children and several women living there. Seven members of the Nation of Islam had been tried for these murders; five had been convicted. But Khaalis was not satisfied. As his group stormed the B'nai B'rith building, Khaalis exclaimed, "They killed my babies and shot my women. Now they will listen to me—or heads will roll!"

With the Washington police blockading the three buildings, the Federal Bureau of Investigation called to full alert, and the media streaming in, Khaalis made his demands known to the press.

He wanted three things: the immediate removal from all U.S. theaters of a movie starring Anthony Quinn called *Mohammed, Messenger of God;* the return of a $750 fine imposed against Khaalis for misconduct during the hit men's trial; and the surrender to Khaalis of the five men convicted of murdering his children. Barricaded in their respective buildings, the Hanafi Muslims continued to terrorize their hostages and announced that they were prepared to die in defense of their beliefs.

Let's stop this newsreel here—at a time when the action also stopped for the participants. Assume you are an adviser to the FBI and the Washington police chief. You must decide what to do next. What will it be? Storm the buildings and free the hostages, who are clearly in grave danger? Send for the five Nation of Islam murderers and trade their lives for the 134 hostages? Call the distributor of *Mohammed, Messenger of God* and tell him to stop the show? Your answer, regardless of what it is, will depend on your understanding of the relative leverage the parties had at this point in their confrontation. Let's assess the situation.

◄ Who Controls the Status Quo? ►

First, it always helps to know who, if anyone, controls the status quo and who is seeking to change it. Leverage often flows to the party that exerts the greatest control over and appears most comfortable with the present situation. Prior to the assaults, the status quo was working against the Hanafi Muslims. They were a marginal group at the fringes of the black Muslim movement and drew, at most, casual monitoring from people in power.

The hostage taking changed all that. Now the Hanafi Muslims controlled the status quo. In fact, the strategic nature of the Hanafi Muslim action is an important part of the leverage equation. These events were not random acts of violence or botched robbery attempts. Khaalis took the hostages precisely to gain leverage—both to get the attention he craved and to acquire something he could offer in trade. Khaalis was willing to kill others and die himself, but his purpose in taking hostages was neither murder nor suicide; he sought hostages as leverage to achieve specific goals.

So the Hanafi Muslims gained at least a temporary advantage by seizing control of the status quo. Now what? Both sides were heavily armed; both could harm each other by using their weapons. The power to make the other side worse off by taking away things they have—in this case life itself—is an important source of leverage.

◄ Threats: They Must Be Credible ►

Threats, sometimes explicit but often implied, are a factor in many negotiations. In fact, the other party will ordinarily sense a threat anytime you suggest an option that endangers its status quo (however they conceive of that important reference point). And using threats in most negotiations is like playing with fire—dangerous for everyone concerned. Tell a union during an employment negotiation that you will not give workers an increase in health benefits, and you may get a spirited objection. Take away an existing benefit of any kind, however, and you risk a full-fledged labor strike.

A second point about threats: They are effective only if they are credible. That means the opposing negotiators must share your assumption that implementing the threat will make them worse off, and they must believe there is a good chance you will carry the threat out. If you yourself would be hurt as much or more than they by carrying out a threat, your threat may lack credibility.

Which side in the Hanafi Muslim situation could make credible threats? The Hanafi Muslims demonstrated right away that their threats were credible. They killed one person and wounded many others.

But the police had a credibility problem. They could not use their weapons without placing hostages at risk, a step they were unwilling to take given the hostages' large number and diverse locations. This significantly reduced the police threat leverage.

Moreover, the Hanafi Muslims improved their position further by announcing that they were ready to die. At least some of them probably were. Why did this matter? The police weapons did not count if they could not make the Hanafi Muslims worse off. The Hanafi Muslims' weapons, however, continued to count as the means of both killing the hostages and injuring the police.

As if all this were not enough, the police were further hamstrung by a variety of laws related to duress and the use of force that constrain civil authorities in hostage situations and govern both parties in ordinary commercial disputes. The police could not go to Khaalis's house and take hostages of their own, for example. Nor, for obvious reasons, would a threat about the legal consequences of taking hostages and murdering them be useful. It was too late for that. Finally, moves to make life unpleasant in the buildings by cutting off water and electricity would affect the hostages as much as or more than the Hanafi Muslims. In short, the police's ability to make Khaalis worse off was sharply limited.

The Hanafi Muslims controlled the status quo and had a definite edge in threat leverage. If your first instinct was to storm the buildings and free the hostages with a SWAT team, think again: The leverage in this situation at this time did not favor the use of force.

The police weapons in the Hanafi Muslim situation were helpful in one respect, however. By completely surrounding the buildings the Hanafi Muslims had seized, the police regained a degree of control over the situation. Khaalis gradually became aware that he, too, was a hostage. At one point during the thirty-eight-hour ordeal, Khaalis even requested that the police check his home and make sure his wife and remaining family were alive and well.

Overall, given the leverage situation that exists early on in most hostage crises, the best move is a counterintuitive one: You should acknowledge the hostage taker's power, indicate that you have relinquished control of the immediate situation to him, and, as odd as it may sound, look for opportunities to build a working relationship.

➤ For Whom Is Time a Factor? ➤

What else can we puzzle out about the leverage dynamics in this situation? Another good question concerns time. Which group had time on its side? Although you might think that time favored the Hanafi Muslims, it did not. Khaalis needed time to deliver his message and figure out where he stood vis-à-vis his goals, but he knew that he could not sustain his control over the status quo forever.

Psychologists have discovered a fascinating fact about time in hostage situations: The passage of even a small amount of time makes a huge difference in terms of the life expectancy of hostages. Experienced hostage negotiators report that if hostages live through the first fifteen minutes of an ordeal, their chances of surviving are quite good.

Why might this be so? First, time takes a toll on the hostage taker's "do-or-die" commitment. As one commentator has explained it, "The thought of one's own death grows tasteless when one has chewed on it for [many] hours."

Second, even if the hostage takers maintain their discipline, they sometimes develop relationships with their captives that make killing them in cold blood harder. It appears that such relationships were formed during a more recent, four-month hostage crisis at the Japanese Embassy in Lima, Peru, which ended in a hail of bullets as 140 police officers stormed the 14 rebels holding 72 hostages in the embassy. During the last moments of the government attack on the compound, the Peruvian agricultural minister reported that his guard pointed a rifle at him, then simply lowered his weapon, turned, and walked away to meet his death.

So time favors the police in a hostage situation. But how does one buy time from a nervous religious fanatic such as Khaalis? By establishing a communication link.

Khaalis himself took care of the communication link. He had his son-in-law contact an African-American television reporter to announce the Hanafi Muslims' demands. This reporter continued to serve as the messenger throughout the crisis, and the police tape-recorded all their conversations, carefully analyzing them to plot their next moves.

◄ Create Momentum: ►
Give Them Little Things

With a communication link in place, the police set to work building their leverage position by finding things Khaalis wanted that they could deliver. Note the qualifier "that they could deliver." One of the trickiest aspects of hostage situations is the unrealistic demands that hostage takers usually make. For example, Khaalis wanted to have the five Nation of Islam hit men who murdered his children delivered to him for execution. The authorities could never comply with this request, so they simply deferred the topic, talking instead about other things they might be able to do. The goal was to make Khaalis feel like a player in the situation—to keep him talking.

Khaalis's agenda, like that of many negotiators, was a mix of explicit demands and implicit needs. His actions and silences spoke as loudly as his words. Beginning with the first few telephone calls, the authorities began to assemble a list of concessions Khaalis might value.

To start the ball rolling, the police made a strategic decision to meet two of Khaalis's demands. First, they arranged for movie theaters around the country to stop showing *Mohammed, Messenger of God*. Second, an official from the city government delivered a certified check for $750 to Khaalis's house, a gesture Khaalis's wife confirmed via telephone. The police used these concessions to buy time and to establish their credibility. Then they probed to see what they should do next.

One curiosity was why Khaalis, himself a Muslim, had seized the Islamic Mosque and Cultural Center. As police monitored Khaalis's telephone conversations, they discovered that Khaalis fancied himself a spokesperson for black Muslims, a role that nobody in the Muslim community acknowledged for him. When Khaalis requested that he be put in touch with the ambassador from Pakistan, an Islamic country, to discuss religious issues, the authorities saw an opening.

Joined by the ambassadors from Egypt and Iran, the Pakistani diplomat spoke to Khaalis by phone during the first night and second day about Muslim theology and various religious teachings. The diplomats were impressed with Khaalis's knowledge. He knew his Koran. More important, the authorities confirmed that Khaalis liked playing the role of Muslim religious leader in front of a distinguished audience. They began to see that Khaalis had revealed an important need when, upon storming the B'nai B'rith building, he had shouted: *"Now they will listen to me."*

◄ Create a Vision That the Other Side Has ► Something to Lose from No Deal

In a tough negotiation, it is not enough to show the other party that you can deliver things he wants. He will almost always discount this sort of demonstration and raise his demands. To gain real leverage, you must eventually persuade the other party that he or she has something concrete to lose in the transaction if the deal falls through. As the Hanafi Muslim situation developed, the focus of negotiations gradually shifted from the hostages to Khaalis's interest in Islamic theology as well as his self-image and self-esteem. The authorities wanted Khaalis to realize that his best hope of becoming a black Muslim leader resided in his bringing the crisis to a successful rather than a disastrous close.

During the second day of the crisis, Khaalis requested a face-to-face meeting with the Pakistani ambassador on the main floor of the B'nai

B'rith building. This caused a stir in the police camp. How to respond? Sending one person alone into the Hanafi Muslim stronghold simply risked adding a high-level diplomatic hostage to the ones already being held. The Pakistani ambassador felt he had established a rapport with Khaalis, however, and he was ready to go. Eventually, the police proposed and Khaalis agreed to a meeting with all three diplomatic ambassadors accompanied by two unarmed police officials. This face-to-face encounter was to become a turning point in the negotiation, with the personal integrity and credibility of everyone present placed squarely on the line.

The officials sat with Khaalis at a folding table in a first floor corridor. For three hours, the ambassadors and Khaalis discussed Islamic theology, with an emphasis on the role of compassion and mercy in Islamic thought. Then, a little after midnight on the third day of the crisis, the ambassador of Pakistan asked Khaalis to make a gesture of good faith and release thirty hostages.

"Why not release them all?" Khaalis asked. That was the breakthrough.

As tension eased, discussion turned to the terms of the hostage release. To save face with his movement, Khaalis requested that, after being criminally charged later that night, he be released without bail to await trial at his home. Meet that condition, said Khaalis, and the crisis would be over.

This last-minute, unexpected request illustrates nicely how leverage can dictate the last moves in the closing moments of a negotiation. Although Khaalis was clearly at a disadvantage at this point, having signaled his willingness to bring the crisis to an end, his men still had what the authorities wanted—the hostages. With this last move, he offered to give his opponents everything they wanted in return for a relatively small concession. His power to deliver the goods favored him in this trade. Would he give up the hostages if they said "no"? He was not saying. It is a testament to the power of face-to-face human communication that this closing condition sealed the deal. The authorities believed Khaalis would keep his word, and he believed they would keep theirs.

Telephone calls to the U.S. attorney general and a local judge secured, after some heated debate, agreement to Khaalis's condition. The Hanafi Muslims peacefully laid down their arms, and at 2:18 A.M. the hostages walked free. To the surprise and dismay of some, the authorities kept their promise and let Khaalis return to his home that morning to await trial under house arrest. He caused no further trouble, however, and several months later a jury convicted him and his men of murder, kidnapping, and related offenses. Khaalis will be eligible for release from prison when and if he reaches the age of ninety-six.

What changes in the leverage equation caused Khaalis to relent? First, in spite of his terrorist bravado, he gradually came to see he had more to lose by pressing ahead to a violent death than by resolving the crisis peacefully. Most hostage takers, particularly criminals who take hostages in a panic when their escape route becomes blocked, come to the same realization.

Second, the authorities deftly used the negotiation process to make Khaalis feel his needs were important. He stopped the showing of the offensive movie, at least for several days. Authorities returned the insulting $750 fine. Perhaps most important, the Muslim ambassadors made him feel like a national spokesperson for black Muslims. He began to imagine a future in which he played a meaningful role in the world, even from prison. Meanwhile, the violence of the assault may have sated his rage and need for vengeance. By the time he met with the Muslim ambassadors in the B'nai B'rith building, he had dropped all mention of having his children's murderers delivered to him.

Many people have taken issue with the way the Hanafi Muslim hostage situation concluded. Public officials at the time were particularly critical of the decision to let Khaalis return to his home instead of going to jail the morning after the event, despite the promise made in the B'nai B'rith building. After all, a promise made under such duress can hardly be said to be binding. And failing to put Khaalis in jail set a dangerous precedent.

But who can say what incentives reliably prompt would-be hostage takers to refrain from acting, or once they have taken captives, from killing their victims? Events like these may not be subject to the usual rules of precedent. Meanwhile, we know for sure that in this case all but one of the hostages walked out of their buildings thirty-eight hours after the assaults. And the perpetrators went to prison for long terms. The officials charged with making decisions in this confusing and life-threatening situation demonstrated a profound understanding both of the leverage positions they faced and of the negotiation process.

◄ The Three Types of Leverage: ►
Positive, Negative, and Normative

Let's step back from the Hanafi Muslim story and look again at the overall question of what leverage is. There are many ways of thinking about leverage. One common approach is to think in terms of alternatives. Roger Fisher, William Ury, and Bruce Patton speak in *Getting to Yes* of parties' having a "Best Alternative to a Negotiated Agreement" (BATNA). As these authors put it, "The better your BATNA, the greater your power."

They use a simple example of an employment negotiation. If you are negotiating with a prospective employer over the terms of a job offer, you have more power if you have two other job offers than if you have none. If the employer refuses to meet your demands, your BATNA in the former case is to take one of your other offers; in the latter case, your BATNA is unemployment.

There is wisdom in the BATNA conception of leverage because good alternatives away from the table can increase your confidence when you are negotiating. But alternatives do not capture the essence of what leverage really is. Khaalis did not improve his alternatives by taking hostages. Instead, he got people's attention by making the authorities' alternatives worse. And the authorities' alternative to agreement—an assault on the Hanafi Muslims—was very poor and never changed even though their leverage improved as the negotiation progressed.

A better way to understand leverage is to think about which side, at any given moment, has the most to lose from a failure to agree. In the employment example used by Fisher, Ury, and Patton, the employee's multiple offers will not improve his leverage if he really wants to work for one particular employer, the employer knows it, and that company has a firm policy of never negotiating job offers. The employee has too much to lose from "no deal" to insist on his own terms regardless of whether he has two other offers. So a more basic test for leverage is to ask which side needs the deal more to achieve its goals.

What goes into a good leverage analysis? The Hanafi Muslim example displays three different types of leverage: leverage based on the relative abilities of each party to supply things the other wants, leverage based on the parties' relative power to take away things each currently has, and leverage based on application of the consistency principle discussed in Chapter 3. I call these three types of leverage, respectively, positive, negative, and normative leverage. Let's review each type briefly, keeping in mind the overall idea that we are always trying to assess, at each changing moment, which side has the most to lose from no deal.

POSITIVE LEVERAGE

The first and most common type of leverage in commercial situations is needs-based, positive leverage. Every time the other party says "I want" in a negotiation, you should hear the pleasant sound of a weight dropping on your side of the leverage scales. Your job as a negotiator is to uncover everything the other side wants and to investigate as thoroughly as possible just how urgent are his or her various needs. Donald Trump summed this up nicely once when he said, "Leverage is having something the other guy wants. Or better yet needs. Or best of all, simply cannot do without."

Janie Mitcham's story of her crusade to build her own railroad exemplifies how leverage relates to needs. Before Ms. Mitcham built her own rail line, her firm was totally dependent on one railroad company to supply its coal. She needed this railroad, they knew it, and they charged her a premium price as a result. By building her rail connection to a rival line, she reduced her firm's dependency and simultaneously increased her suppliers' need for her business as a customer. Mitcham's case shows how a better BATNA can *sometimes* increase your power—by adjusting the needs of the parties for things they can offer one another.

In the Hanafi Muslim situation, each time Khaalis asked for something that the authorities could deliver during the standoff, the authorities gained both time and leverage. As the authorities came to understand Khaalis's underlying psychological drives better, their leverage improved even more. In the end, they were able to deliver what Khaalis craved more than anything: self-esteem as a Muslim leader. With that need met, Khaalis suddenly found he urgently wanted something else the authorities had to offer—a way out of the crisis with his life intact. By that point, the authorities had turned the leverage tables on Khaalis completely.

NEGATIVE LEVERAGE

The second type of leverage is negative, or threat-based, leverage. Khaalis got everyone's attention by showing he had the power to make his opponents worse off. The Hanafi Muslim situation was an extreme, illegal example of threats, but the same principle applies in commercial settings provided people act within the law.

Because threats often engender ill will, resistance, and resentment, skilled negotiators use them with great care. Unlike Khaalis, they display their power to make the other side worse off with hints rather than shouts.

Let me offer a story about real estate and casino entrepreneur Donald Trump to illustrate how experienced businesspeople make "civilized" threats that preserve their working relationships. When Trump was planning his signature building in New York City, the Trump Tower on Fifth Avenue, he needed the air rights over a small, classic building owned and occupied by Tiffany & Company, the famous jeweler. Trump was willing to pay $5 million, but he was afraid that Tiffany would turn him down in order to maintain the architectural integrity of its section of Fifth Avenue.

An old-style, impeccable New Yorker named Walter Hoving ran Tiffany, and Trump set up a meeting with Hoving to negotiate the air rights. To prepare for this meeting, Trump had his architect construct not one, but two different models of the proposed Trump Tower.

At the meeting with Hoving, Trump presented both models. The first was an elegant, fifty-story building that Trump argued would be a classy neighbor for an upscale jewelry store. That was the building Trump proposed to build if he could acquire the Tiffany air rights. The second was an awful, ugly building—one that Trump said the New York City zoning authorities would force him to build if Tiffany would not cooperate. This building featured tiny lot-line windows covered with wire mesh on the entire wall facing Tiffany. The two fifty-story models sat side-by-side in Hoving's office. It was Hoving's choice. He got the message and agreed to Trump's terms.

Threat leverage gets people's attention because, as astute negotiators have known for centuries and psychologists have repeatedly proven, *potential losses loom larger in the human mind than do equivalent gains*. But a word of warning is in order: *Making even subtle threats is like dealing with explosives.* You must handle threats with care, or you can hurt yourself. You cannot raise a child without a measure of discipline, but a parent-child relationship based on threats is a failure. The police contained the Hanafi Muslim situation by surrounding the hostage takers with overwhelming force, but their success came in never using it. Moreover, if others use threats against you, you should respond in kind if necessary. Highly competitive people, in particular, sometimes need to hear that you can match their threat power "tit for tat" before they will settle down and negotiate based on the merits of a deal.

NORMATIVE LEVERAGE

The third and final type of leverage is normative leverage, which de-rives from the consistency principle discussed in Chapter 3. This source of leverage played a role in the Hanafi situation in several ways. First, as the Pakistani ambassador drew out Khaalis's knowledge of and commit-ment to the Koran, the ambassador laid the groundwork for Khaalis to make a compassionate gesture by releasing hostages. Most religious texts—including the Koran—favor compassion over revenge and love over hate. By the time Khaalis arrived at his fateful moment of decision on the third day of the crisis, the Pakistani ambassador had used passages from the Koran to remind Khaalis that a truly visionary Muslim leader would be a living model of Islamic virtues, not a cold-blooded killer of in-nocent people.

Second, the authorities found themselves in a consistency trap of their own creation by Khaalis's surprise request to remain at home under house arrest pending trial. The agreement allowing him to do so was the explicit quid pro quo for releasing all the hostages and, even more im-portant, was made after three hours of discussion about the Koran and the meaning of virtue. To have reneged on this promise would have meant, among other things, loss of face for three distinguished Islamic ambassadors who had pledged their word and risked their lives to resolve the crisis. The authorities felt bound in a moral sense to keep their prom-ise even if they had no legal obligation to do so.

Leverage is a complex mixture of ideas. It includes opportunities that will be lost if the parties fail to reach a deal, threats to each party's status quo, and possible losses to each side's self-esteem should their actions ap-pear inconsistent (in their own eyes) with a prior or professed standard of conduct or dealing.

But there is a way to assess leverage in a single, easy-to-remember test: *Ask yourself, as of the moment when you make the assessment, which party has the most to lose from no deal. The party with the most to lose has the* least *leverage; the party with the least to lose has the* most *leverage; and both parties have roughly equal leverage when they both stand to lose equivalent amounts should the deal fall through.*

This way of thinking about leverage also points to more sophisticated ways of enhancing your leverage that go beyond just improving your BATNA. Your goal is to alter the situation (or at least the other party's perception of the situation) so you have less to lose, the other side has more to lose, or both. You can achieve these goals by gaining more information about what the other side really needs, acquiring credible power to make the other side worse off, framing your needs under principles and norms that are hard for the other side to walk away from, binding yourself to a course of action that forces the other side to concede, and, finally, improving your BATNA, that is, seeking alternative solutions to your underlying problem that do not require the other party's cooperation.

◄ The Power of Coalitions ►

One of the most important ways to gain all three types of leverage is by using relationships and shared interests to help you create effective coalitions to support a bargaining position. When you can make common cause with others who share your bargaining priorities, you gain advantage in three important and distinct respects.

First, in multiparty situations, group dynamics often favor those who are first to achieve a dominant position in terms of numbers. Research on American juries suggests that the first verdict to gain a majority vote during jury deliberations ends up being the verdict the jury unanimously endorses.

The same is true at many business meetings. One person makes a suggestion, another picks it up, and pretty soon it is the consensus even though there may be good reasons for doing something else. You can greatly improve your chances of getting your point of view across to a group if you take the time to assemble a coalition before the meeting starts. That way, your position can gain momentum as the members of your coalition take turns expressing support for their shared goal.

Second, coalitions gain power from a psychological phenomenon social scientists call social proof. In ambiguous situations, people take their cues from what other people do. If you are going down a crowded street and you notice some people looking up in the sky, you will probably look up, too. Then the person behind you will look up, and so on. Negotiations can work the same way if the issues being discussed are complex and others tend to look to experts to lead the way. Your coalition can provide the cues that prompt others to follow.

Finally, coalitions often improve your leverage by either giving you better alternatives, making the other party's alternatives worse, or both. For example, American cattle ranchers in the mid-1990s were desperate because beef prices were so low that 85 percent of the ranchers in some areas of the Midwest could have qualified for federal food stamp assistance if they had not been too proud to apply. Their problem? A few giant agribusiness firms controlled the meatpacking and slaughtering industry, and the ranchers had no choice but to sell their cattle to these companies. The ranchers were losing $30 for each calf they sold while the meatpackers made $30 in profit on each calf they slaughtered.

The ranchers in North Dakota began digging their way out of this situation when they formed a coalition and started their own meatpacking operation, a cooperative called Northern Plains Premium Beef. When the ranchers competed with one another to sell their cattle to the giant slaughterhouses, they lacked leverage. But by combining with other ranchers and slaughtering their own animals, they gained a way to attract consumer dollars directly to their high-quality, distinctively branded beef. In short, they created an alternative distribution system and, in the process, improved their leverage vis-à-vis both the giant slaughterhouses and the restaurant chains. Cooperatives have been successful in getting contracts from some of the biggest steak house chains in the United States. The big firms are taking notice.

◄ Common Misconceptions about Leverage ►

Leverage is a difficult subject for people who negotiate infrequently because we all have certain routine ways of viewing the world that we assume apply to bargaining. For example, we assume that people with a lot of economic, social, and political power always have the advantage. Big companies, high-ranking officials, and the rich usually get their way. So we think that such parties always have leverage when they negotiate.

We also tend to accept situations as we find them, assuming that power relationships are fixed. Why waste a lot of energy getting ready to bargain when we are selling a widely available commodity and there are only a few buyers in the market? The buyers will simply tell us what they want to pay, and we will say, "OK." It is all fixed and cannot be changed.

Finally, we usually believe that our power to influence our surroundings depends on the facts affecting us. We are unemployed; therefore we are in a weak position in a job negotiation. We are the sole source of an important computer component; therefore we are in a strong position and can name our price.

All three of these beliefs and assumptions about leverage are dangerously wrong. They are dangerous because a skilled counterpart can take advantage of you if you make them. These mistaken assumptions can also lead to self-defeating strategies. In the next few pages, I will explain why these convenient assumptions about the world at large don't apply in negotiations and what assumptions you should use instead to protect your interests.

MISCONCEPTION 1: LEVERAGE AND POWER ARE THE SAME THING

Not true. Leverage is about situational advantage, not objective power. Parties with very little conventional power can have a lot of leverage under the right circumstances. Let's look at a couple of examples.

The first concerns negotiating with small children. Assume you are the father or mother in a household with a five-year-old daughter. The menu this evening features one of nature's healthiest foods, broccoli. Your daughter does not want to eat it.

"Eat your broccoli, dear," you say sweetly. Your daughter looks you in the eye and says, with emphasis, "No! I hate broccoli!"

Who has the leverage?

You may be big, rich, powerful, and strong, but your daughter has a lot of leverage in this situation. Why? *Because she and only she can eat the broccoli.* She controls what you want and, at the moment, has nothing to lose by saying "no." And that isn't all. She probably senses that the issue is important to you. That improves her position. You may be willing to offer something for her cooperation.

This critical leverage insight can apply just as readily to negotiations with stubborn politicians, cranky customs officials, and tightfisted budget officers as it does to children. Regardless of how important you are, you had better treat such people with care when they control the decision you want made.

But back to the dinner table. What can you do about the broccoli? You could try reasoned persuasion, but your daughter is not likely to care much about nutritional standards. So whatever normative leverage you may have will not be worth much.

Another option is to offer your daughter bribes to encourage her cooperation. Concrete offers of things she likes such as desserts or treats may create attractive visions in her mind. She would lose these delights if negotiations were to break down. The promise of treats might gain you some leverage.

However, parents everywhere know that using this form of leverage with children carries risks. Bribing your child to do things she should be doing anyway eventually spoils her, making your life difficult, not easy.

How about resorting to explicit threats, such as spanking her, sending her to her room, or eliminating dessert from the menu? Your size and vocal power make it easy to use threats, but it is risky to do so over an issue like broccoli. If she complies based on your threat, you will pay a price. She will eat her broccoli as slowly as she can, with periodic grim looks in your direction. A participant in the Wharton Executive Negotiation Workshop once told me his child took four hours to eat his dinner one night after he tried the threat strategy. Dinner turned into a contest of wills. Worse still, suppose she calls your bluff and forces you to carry out your threat? You send her to her room, but she still has not eaten the broccoli. You must then either escalate the dispute even further or concede defeat.

Conclusion? Your child may look small and weak in terms of conventional power, but she has leverage in this situation. Your solution should therefore acknowledge your child's preferences in some way—either by giving her a choice of another healthy vegetable, compromising on the amount of broccoli, adding a sauce, or serving the broccoli in some heavily disguised form. You will do better as a parent if you recognize your child's leverage in this situation and frame your strategy to address her interests in some way, particularly her interest in feeling like she controls decisions that affect her. You will also do better as a professional if you take the same approach with the stubborn politicians, customs officials, and budget directors who control implementation of things you want done at work.

My second example of how little people can gain leverage concerns the casino business in Atlantic City, New Jersey. Like the Tiffany air rights story, this one involves Donald Trump—but this time he does not do as well.

An elderly widow named Vera Coking owned a small boardinghouse in a prime location in Atlantic City, New Jersey. She was a woman of modest means who had lived in the house practically her whole life. When the casino business came to Atlantic City, several would-be developers expressed interest in buying Ms. Coking's property to put up a casino.

First came *Penthouse* magazine publisher Bob Guccione. He reputedly bid as high as $1 million for her land in the 1980s, but she turned him down. Guccione eventually failed to get a gaming license and abandoned his plans to build a casino. Next came Donald Trump, who was not interested in paying $1 million and simply tried to negotiate with her on the basis of the home's fair market value. He, too, struck out. Trump eventually developed the Trump Plaza Hotel and Casino nearby and, during a major expansion, tried to negotiate with her again. She asked for $1 million. He declined.

After more than a decade of fruitless jockeying, lawsuits, and media attention, Trump gave up and expanded the Trump Plaza so it surrounded Coking's boardinghouse on three sides. The Atlantic City casino authority then intervened at Trump's request to condemn and clear her property so it would not be an eyesore. Coking was not disturbed. She hired a lawyer to defend her land and went on enjoying her reputation as "Trump's ulcer." Her case eventually attracted support from a legal foundation interested in constitutional protections for private property rights. Meanwhile, Trump became the butt of jokes nationwide as cartoonist Garry Trudeau featured Trump's Atlantic City property disputes in a series of newspaper comic strips.

Vera Coking was elderly and alone, but she had leverage. Why? She had legal title to her home, Trump needed her land, she knew it, and she was obviously in no hurry to sell. She controled what Trump needed, and, at least as she saw it, she had nothing to lose by saying "no." In fact, a psychologist might say she used the situation to get something priceless she had probably wanted all her life: attention.

So leverage is not the same thing as conventional social or economic power. Examine the specific situation you face and ask: What do I control that the other side wants, what do they control that I want, and who stands to lose the most if no deal gets done? Don't make assumptions about leverage based on wealth or position.

MISCONCEPTION 2: LEVERAGE IS A CONSTANT THAT DOESN'T CHANGE

Wrong. Leverage is dynamic, not static. Leverage changes as negotiations proceed. Some moments are therefore better than others for making your needs known and insisting that they be met.

The Hanafi Muslim example illustrates this point well. Khaalis needed to take hostages before anyone would listen to him. The police needed the Muslim ambassadors to develop a relationship with Khaalis before they could introduce the idea of freeing some hostages as a gesture of good faith. Khaalis was smart enough to ask for temporary house arrest instead of jail while he still had enough leverage to get this concession.

All this may seem obvious, but many very smart people fail to understand the relationship between time and leverage. For example, there is a "golden moment" when job hunters should negotiate for extra benefits such as relocation expenses, bonuses, and company cars. That moment comes *after* they get an offer from a firm but *before* they accept the offer.

During this peak leverage interval, the employer has explicitly committed itself, but the prospect is still free to say "no." This puts the employer at a potentially greater risk of loss than the prospect, improving the prospect's position considerably. As compared with the period before the offer is made or the period after the prospect has said "yes," this golden moment is the time when an employer will give maximum attention to a prospect's special needs.

Of course, there are no guarantees the employer will agree to sweeten a deal, even at the golden moment. The employer still controls its job, and, in any given case, the prospect may have more to lose if the offer falls through. But timing matters in every leverage analysis. You improve your chances of success if you ask for things when your leverage is at its height.

MISCONCEPTION 3: LEVERAGE DEPENDS ON THE FACTS

Incorrect. Leverage is based on the other party's *perception* of the situation, not the facts. When Joshua won the Battle of Jericho in the Bible, he did it with a few cymbals and some torches, not a mighty army. The leaders of Jericho surrendered based on their perception that they had a lot to lose. In the Hanafi Muslim example, Khaalis surrendered when he was treated like a Muslim leader even though he wasn't one in fact. And the police made a prominent display of their weapons around the hostage buildings even though they could not use them. In short, you have the leverage the other side thinks you have. If the other party thinks you are in a strong position, you are—at least for the moment.

But the perceptual nature of leverage can also work against you. You may mistakenly assume the other party is stronger than they really are. You may also be in a good position, but the other side may not believe you. In such cases, you must find ways of proving your worth, importance, or power. Some things, such as your ability as an employee or your product's true value to a customer, are hard to prove. If so, you may need to give away some of your time as a low-paid intern or volunteer to prove your worth or offer some free samples of your product to prompt a later sale. On the negative side, you may need to make a subtle demonstration of your ability to affect the other side's status quo. It is up to you to see that the other side understands the true leverage situation before it acts unwisely based on a miscalculation.

◀ Leverage Within Families, ▶
Firms, and Organizations

Leverage works differently inside a family, firm, or organization than it does in competitive markets. The parties' interdependence based on their shared web of affiliations makes bargaining and persuasion more subtle. You still gain leverage from controlling things that other people need and the advantage still goes to the party with the least to lose, but some important leverage rules are reversed because of the need to preserve and enhance relationships.

For example, having good walk-away alternatives usually helps you in market transactions. As we discussed, having a good alternative may mean you need the other side less and have less to lose if no deal happens. But inside families and firms—at least healthy ones—people do not rely on or talk about walking away. Such moves look too much like threats and make the speaker appear shrill and unreasonable. Instead of walking away, people rely more on normative leverage, the values and norms the members of the group share. They try to position their proposals in a positive light with reference to these standards, often with objective data and information. I discussed this subject in Chapter 3.

Similarly, displays of urgency ordinarily weaken your leverage in a market-based transaction. You tip off the other negotiator that you need his agreement very badly indeed and stand to lose a lot if he says "no." But a show of passionate commitment and persistence can *help* you get what you want inside a family or an organization. With important relationships on the line, people listen when you come out strongly for your point of view—particularly if you do not make a habit of doing so on every occasion.

Let me give one brief but notable example of this point. In May 1940, just before the United States entered World War II, the U.S. Army chief of staff, General George C. Marshall, attended a meeting in the White House with senior cabinet officials and President Franklin Roosevelt. On the agenda was the possible mobilization of men and equipment in anticipation of United States participation in the European war. Public sentiment in the country at the time was distinctly isolationist. Roosevelt did not want the United States to go to war in Europe, and he did not want to talk about getting ready for one. No one was even thinking about a war with Japan.

Marshall was a reserved, very controlled person. He never got emotional about anything. But that day something snapped. After sitting quietly and noticing that the president was not paying attention, Marshall requested permission to speak for three minutes. It was granted.

Marshall then stood and proceeded to put on one of the most effective, passionate displays anyone ever saw from him. Marshall's words literally "spilled out" as he catalogued the short supplies, unbuilt weapons systems, and outnumbered troops that would, if hostilities broke out, face Hitler's well-oiled war machine. Marshall went on and on—well past his three-minute allotment. As one of the meeting's attendees, Secretary of the Treasury Henry Morgenthau, recorded in his diary, "[Marshall] stood right up to the President." After this presentation, Roosevelt changed his approach completely. The United States began preparing for war in earnest and, after war broke out, Roosevelt put Marshall in charge of the entire war effort.

This example may be dramatic, but it is surprisingly typical of life within many organizations. Intensity, particularly if it is coupled with expertise, gets people's attention. A show of passion backed by solid facts brings abstract argument down to the level of personal concern. It can be very persuasive.

There is no research I am aware of on why displays of urgency and passion are effective inside an organization, but I have a theory. I think people who work or live together in groups subtly monitor the level of intensity shown by other group members to see what sort of priority an issue has. A display of urgency—particularly by someone who is usually reserved—is a strong signal that "I must win this one." Interpersonal conflict disrupts an otherwise cooperative group, so people tend to defer to others when this signal goes out.

Overall, this "intensity" form of leverage probably works best for people within an organization who are by nature reasonable and soft-spoken. If you do not speak with passion often, people will usually pay special attention to you when you do. The "squeaky wheels" who are always complaining and pushing their agendas, by contrast, gain no extra leverage from being noisy and intense. To the contrary, most of us learn to tune them out.

◄ Summary ►

Leverage is a critical variable in negotiation. The party with the least to lose from no deal generally is the party that can afford to insist that critical deal terms break its way. You can improve your leverage using many different moves, including finding good alternatives to achieve your goals away from the table, gaining control over assets the other side needs, forming coalitions, arranging the situation so the other party will lose face if there is no deal, showing the other negotiator you have the power to make him worse off materially, and so on.

Watch out for the common misconceptions about leverage. Even less powerful people can have leverage in any given situation. And leverage is a dynamic factor based as much on perception as fact. Finally, you can gain power within an organization by showing passionate commitment rather than cool indifference. That is just the opposite of the way leverage works in most market transactions.

◄ A LEVERAGE CHECKLIST ►

✓ Which side has the most to lose from no deal?
✓ For whom is time a factor?
✓ Can I improve my alternatives or make the other party's worse?
✓ Can I gain control over something the other party needs?
✓ Can I commit the other party to norms that favor my result?
✓ Can I form a coalition to improve my position?

PART II

---->

THE NEGOTIATION PROCESS

<----

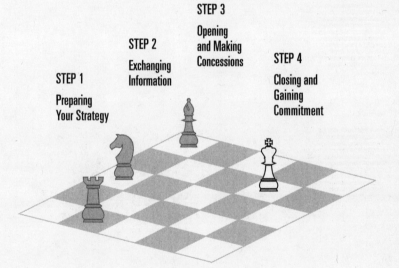

STEP 1

Preparing
Your Strategy

STEP 2

Exchanging
Information

STEP 3

Opening
and Making
Concessions

STEP 4

Closing and
Gaining
Commitment

7

Step 1:
Preparing Your Strategy

In all negotiations of difficulty, a man may not look to sow
or reap at once, but must prepare [the] business and so
ripen it by degrees.

—SIR FRANCIS BACON (1597)

For tough meat, sharp teeth.

—TURKISH FOLK SAYING

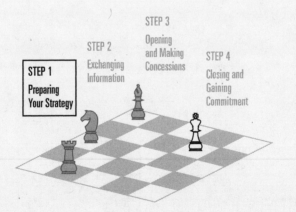

STEP 1
Preparing
Your Strategy

STEP 2
Exchanging
Information

STEP 3
Opening
and Making
Concessions

STEP 4
Closing and
Gaining
Commitment

We have come a long way toward understanding what makes bar-gaining work. Part I presented the Six Foundations of Effective Ne-gotiation. We discussed:

- Different bargaining styles
- The importance of specific goals and expectations
- How authoritative standards and norms bracket the bargaining zone
- The ways that relationships influence negotiations
- How the other party's interests can unlock deals
- What leverage is and how to use it

These six key factors will reliably prepare you for success in negotiation. Moreover, each of these six elements rests on deep, psychological foundations that are often invisible to the untrained eye. These motivational influences, summarized on the following chart (see Figure 7.1), are what give negotiations their emotional rhythm.

FIGURE 7.1
The Psychological Foundations of Negotiations

Foundation	Psychological Basis
1. Your bargaining styles	Attitudes derived from family, gender, culture, and experience
2. Your goals and expectations	Beliefs about what is possible and what you deserve
3. Authoritative standards and norms	The consistency principle and deference to authority
4. Relationships	The norm of reciprocity
5. The other party's interests	Self-esteem and self-interest
6. Leverage	Aversion to loss

◄ The Four Stages of Negotiation ►

In Part II of the book, I will show you how the Six Foundations and their associated psychological bases can help you achieve your goals as you move step by step through the negotiation process. Part II's organization will reveal a simple but important truth: Negotiation is a dance that moves through four stages or steps. This and the following chapters will cover these four steps, each in turn. Let's look at a simple example from real life to see how the four-step sequence works in practice.

Imagine you are approaching a traffic intersection in your car. You notice that another car is nearing the intersection at the same time. What do you do?

Most experienced drivers start by slowing down to assess the situation. Next, they glance toward the other driver to make eye contact, hoping to establish communication with the other person. With eye contact established, one driver waves his or her hand toward the intersection in the universally recognized "after you" signal. Perhaps both drivers wave. After a little hesitation, one driver moves ahead and the other follows.

Note the four-step process: preparation (slowing down), information exchange (making eye contact), proposing and concession making (waving your hand), and commitment (driving through). This may seem like a unique case, but anthropologists and other social scientists have observed a similar four-stage process at work in situations as diverse as rural African land disputes (the Arusha example in Chapter 1), British labor negotiations, and American business mergers. The four stages form an unstated and often unseen pattern just below the surface of negotiations.

Of course, in complex bargaining encounters, people vary the sequence and pacing of these steps. They may reach an impasse in the concession-making stage, so they go back to exchanging information. And some aspects of a deal may move faster than others—commitments may come on issues "A" and "B" while information exchange and concession making continue on issue "C."

People in different cultures also tend to go through the stages at different speeds. Task-oriented negotiators from Western industrialized countries often move hastily past information exchange, eager to "put something on the table" and get down to the business of opening and making concessions. They then spend an extended time exchanging, testing, and arguing over proposals.

Relationship-oriented negotiators from Asia, Africa, South America, and the Middle East prefer a more leisurely process of information exchange to establish a degree of mutual trust before they bargain. With a relationship established, the explicit concession-making stage often goes very quickly. A consultant I know once closed a multimillion-dollar deal in Saudi Arabia over coffee, after spending ten days attending what an outsider might consider a boring series of formal dinners and social events. Beneath the surface, however, a carefully planned minuet of relationship development was unfolding. When this stage was completed, the actual deal took only a few minutes to conclude.

Regardless of culture, skilled negotiators everywhere are a bit like good dancers. They are alert to their counterpart's pace, striving to stay "in step" as the process moves along.

With that introduction to what lies ahead, let's get started. This chapter will deal with the first step in the negotiation process—preparing your strategy.

◄ Preparation Step 1: ►
Assess the Situation

The goal of good preparation, even for a relatively simple negotiation, is to construct a specific plan of action for the situation you face. There are basically four different types of bargaining situations, depending on (1) the perceived importance of the ongoing relationship, if any, between the parties (how much might the parties need each other's help and cooperation in the future to achieve their respective goals?) and (2) the per-

FIGURE 7.2

The Situational Matrix

Perceived Conflict over Stakes

		High	*Low*
Perceived Importance of Future Relationship Between Parties	*High*	I: Balanced Concerns (Business partnership, joint venture, or merger)	II: Relationships (Marriage, friendship, or work team)
	Low	III: Transactions (Divorce, house sale, or market transaction)	IV: Tacit Coordination (Highway intersection or airplane seating)

ceived conflict over the stakes involved (to what degree do both sides want the same limited resource such as money, power, or space in this particular transaction?). Every negotiation—no matter how friendly or apparently confrontational—combines some measure of conflict over substantive issues with a degree of sensitivity to the way people should treat each other.

Relationship concerns can be relatively high or low compared with the stakes and vice versa. The Situational Matrix (see Figure 7.2) combines these two factors relative to one another and describes the four situation types: Tacit Coordination, Transactions, Relationships, and Balanced Concerns.

Let's examine each type of situation beginning with the simplest (Quadrant IV) and working up to the most complex (Quadrant I).

QUADRANT IV: TACIT COORDINATION

The most rudimentary of all negotiation situations is the one found in the lower-right-hand box: Quadrant IV, "Tacit Coordination." Quadrant IV is characterized by both low conflict over stakes and a limited future relationship. My example of two drivers meeting at a traffic intersection given above is a Quadrant IV event. There is no need for a collision at the intersection (managed correctly, there is little need for conflict over the space), and the parties are unlikely to see each other again (the future relationship is not a factor). Tacit Coordination situations do not call for negotiation so much as tactful avoidance of conflict.

QUADRANT III: TRANSACTIONS

Now move left to Quadrant III, "Transactions." These are the situations in which the stakes matter substantially more than any future relationship. House, car, and land sales between strangers, business acquisitions in which the incumbent management will be thrown out after the purchase, and many other market-mediated deals are typical Transactions.

It is tempting to think of Transactions as simple "haggling" or "winner-take-all" events in which the relationship between the parties is irrelevant. Transactions can be this simple, but often they are not. The bargaining situation itself usually creates the need for a form of working relationship between the negotiators if they are to close the deal. In the West, this relationship is often limited to mere civility unless the negotiators are professional agents who deal with each other on a repeated basis. In other cultures, a personal relationship (or at least the appearance of one) remains a necessity, even in a Transaction. How do sophisticated negotiators treat each other in a high-stakes Transaction? Let me illustrate with a story.

◄ "Mr. Morgan, There Must ► Be Some Mistake"

My example of a Transaction situation comes from the "gilded age" of American business and involves three of its most memorable historical figures: Wall Street tycoon J. P. Morgan (whom we met in Chapter 4 handing two checks to Andrew Carnegie); Standard Oil's founder, John D. Rockefeller, Sr., and Rockefeller's young heir, John D. Rockefeller, Jr.

In 1901, J. P. Morgan was intensely interested in buying an area of land rich in iron deposits known as the Mesabi ore fields. Morgan was putting together his steel trust, which eventually became U.S. Steel Corporation, and these iron fields were a vital source of supply for the minerals needed to make steel.

The elder John D. Rockefeller owned this valuable property. Rockefeller was in retirement at this point of his career and had made it clear he had no particular interest in buying or selling major assets such as the Mesabi ore fields. He repeatedly refused to discuss the matter with Morgan, a man whom he personally disliked.

But Morgan wanted the Mesabi ore fields. He pestered Rockefeller into finally granting him an audience at Rockefeller's New York City mansion. At this meeting, Morgan asked Rockefeller to name his price for the ore fields. Rockefeller demurred, instructing Morgan to take up the matter with one of his newest advisers, his twenty-seven-year-old son, John D. Rockefeller, Jr.

Sensing an opportunity for advantage, Morgan invited the younger Rockefeller—a stranger to him—to come to his Wall Street office for a discussion. A few weeks later, the younger Rockefeller presented himself at Morgan's Wall Street address.

As a Morgan aide ushered Rockefeller Jr. into Morgan's office, Rockefeller took in the scene. This was not just an ordinary office; it was the hub of the most important financial empire of its day. And Morgan took pains to make sure Rockefeller knew it.

Bent over paperwork and speaking intently with an adviser, Morgan at first gave no indication that he knew Rockefeller had come in. Rockefeller, for his part, stood patiently while Morgan continued to ignore him. At length, Morgan looked up and glared at the younger man.

"Well," Morgan growled, "what's your price?"

Rockefeller Jr. looked back intently at the great man.

"Mr. Morgan," he replied quietly, "I think there must be some mistake. I did not come here to sell. I understood you wished to buy."

The two men held each other's glance. Morgan, impressed by the young Rockefeller's firm demeanor, was the first to blink. He adopted a friendlier tone. As the two men discussed the possible sale in general terms, it became clear that neither was willing to state an opening price. Morgan had been privately advised by his friend Judge Elbert H. Gary that an "outside figure" of $75 million was the top price he should pay for the ore fields. But Morgan was too smart a negotiator to mention that or any other specific figure.

Sensing Morgan's uneasiness, Rockefeller finally suggested that Morgan engage someone to serve as a go-between to help him establish a fair value for the ore fields. They agreed that Henry Clay Frick—someone trusted by both Morgan and the elder Rockefeller—could serve in this role.

Once appointed, Frick quickly discovered that Morgan did not intend to pay more than $75 million. Frick brought this number to the elder Rockefeller and discovered that Rockefeller did not like the idea of saying "yes" to anything Morgan suggested.

"I frankly object to a prospective purchaser arbitrarily fixing an outside figure," Rockefeller said to Frick, "and I cannot deal on that basis. That seems too much like an ultimatum."

Frick and Rockefeller discussed the ore fields and finally agreed that $80 million was a fair value Frick could endorse. Frick took this number back to Morgan and Judge Gary. Judge Gary urged Morgan to reject it as too far beyond the outside figure.

But Morgan knew what he was up against. Even at $80 million he could not walk away from the ore fields, and he knew Rockefeller did not need to sell. To cap it off, the neutral Frick had endorsed Rockefeller's offer.

"Write out an acceptance," he told Gary.

And the deal was done.

It turned out to be a good bargain for Morgan. The fields went on to yield hundreds of millions of dollars' worth of ore.

So a Transaction is a situation in which the stakes are substantially more important than the relationship. The parties may need to cooperate to arrange meetings, explore the issues, and communicate effectively. But as the case between the Rockefellers and J. P. Morgan shows, no accommodations need to be made for the purpose of securing cooperation in future periods. Leverage counts.

QUADRANT II: RELATIONSHIPS

Our next situation is the exact opposite of Quadrant III. In Quadrant II—the upper-right-hand square—the relationship matters a great deal, and the particular item being negotiated is secondary. This is the Relationships box. Negotiations between couples in healthy marriages, employees working on well-functioning executive teams, and certain kinds of recruitment tasks fall into this category.

When relationships are the most important factor, we should strive to treat the other party well, observing careful rules and limits to our bargaining conduct. To illustrate this important idea, let's look at another example from history. This one involves probably the greatest scientist of the twentieth century, Albert Einstein. It arose when Einstein was in the market for a job.

► "Unless You Think I Can Live on Less" ►

In the early 1930s, a new research organization, the Institute for Advanced Study in Princeton, New Jersey, was looking for world-class scholars and researchers to create one of the world's first "think tanks." The faculty of this institution would not teach. Instead, they would do basic research, share meals and seminars together, and publish papers.

The institute's new director, Abraham Flexner, approached Albert Einstein to join his new organization. Einstein, who was then living in Europe and looking for a new situation, said he was interested. As their discussions advanced, Flexner eventually asked Einstein what his salary requirements might be.

Einstein replied that $3,000 per year would suffice him, unless, as he put it, Flexner thought he would be able to "live on less." The director's response? He more than tripled Einstein's request, offering him $10,000 per year. After further discussion about relocation and pension needs, Einstein ultimately received a final package that some sources say was worth close to $15,000—a superstar sum in the Depression-scarred 1930s.

Einstein's story shows how negotiations look when they focus mainly on the relationship. Flexner's problem was how to make a "crown jewel" professor feel honored and appreciated so he would make the institute his professional home. The amount of Einstein's salary was distinctly secondary. And Flexner's generous treatment of Einstein worked. Einstein went on to become an icon at the Institute for Advanced Study, attracting many other distinguished scholars and firmly establishing the institute's world-class reputation.

QUADRANT I: BALANCED CONCERNS

The upper-left-hand quadrant is the most interesting and complex of the four situation types. This is the Balanced Concerns situation. Here, the future relationship and the immediate stakes are in balanced tension with each other. Quadrant I is where many employment disputes, family business matters, partnerships, mergers (in which incumbent management will remain to manage the firm), long-term supplier relationships, strategic alliances, and institutional relationships between different divisions of the same firm are located.

You want to do well in these situations but not at the expense of the future relationship. You want the future relationship to be sound, but not at too high a price. My example of a Balanced Concerns situation involves Benjamin Franklin, an American founding father.

◄ Benjamin Franklin's Meal Deal ►

Among his many talents, Franklin was an astute negotiator. Perhaps for this reason he played an important role both as a diplomat—representing America's interests in France at a critical time in U.S. history—and as a skilled facilitator who helped the disputing members of the Constitutional Convention of 1787 bridge their differences and draft the Constitution of the United States.

Franklin displayed his talent for finding ingenious solutions to potentially contentious problems at an early age. One example can be found in a negotiation he had in 1722 about vegetables—a deal that ended up putting money into the pockets of everyone involved.

When Ben was a boy of twelve, he moved in with his older half-brother James in Boston and became apprenticed to James to learn the printing trade. James was not married, so he and his apprentices took their meals at a boardinghouse. James paid a monthly fee, and the boardinghouse cook prepared their meals.

Four years into this arrangement, Ben—now an active and inquiring teenager of sixteen—read a book on vegetarianism and was attracted to both its health benefits and its philosophy. He began refusing to eat meat at his meals.

This was fine for Ben, but the boardinghouse cook complained loudly to James about having to prepare special meals. And the other apprentices began to grumble and gossip about what Ben later called his dietary "singularity." James was irritated, and the situation rapidly threatened to escalate into a conflict both within the Franklin household and among the apprentices.

To resolve the situation, Ben proposed a deal. He said he would stop taking his meals with the rest of the apprentices and relieve James of the burden of paying his boarding fee—if James would give Ben 50 percent of what James was paying the cook for Ben's meals. Ben would then use the money to buy his own vegetables and cook his own meals.

Ben Franklin reports in his *Autobiography* that this arrangement worked out especially well for, of all people, Ben himself:

> I presently found that I could save half of what [James] paid me. This was an additional fund for buying of books; but I had another advantage from it. My brother and the rest [of the apprentices] going from the printing-house to their meals, I remained there alone, and dispatching presently my light repast . . . had the rest of the time till their return for study.

In short, by insisting on his vegetarian principles, Franklin found a way for *everyone* to be better off. James saved 50 percent of Ben's boarding fee, and Ben got to keep his vegetarian diet, pocket 25 percent of the fee for himself, and gain some peace and quiet for reading.

This story does not have the same stakes as the negotiation between Rockefeller and Morgan over the $80 million ore fields. Nor does it carry the same momentous relationship implications as did the Institute for Advanced Study's successful recruitment of Albert Einstein. But the boarding fee was important to both James and Ben Franklin, and Ben's insistence on his vegetarian diet threatened to provoke a nasty family feud, spoiling delicate relationships within James's small printing shop.

Ben Franklin's "meal deal" neatly kept the peace, provided a fair, face-saving way out of the dispute for everyone, and created a fund for James and Ben to divide. It was an inspired piece of negotiating.

◄ Preparation Step 2: ►
Matching Situation, Strategy, and Style

As these cases illustrate, different situations call for different strategies and reward different negotiation skills. Chances are, you will be better negotiating in some situations than others. Figure 7.3 will help you see which strategies are best suited for handling each situation.

FIGURE 7.3

The Situational Matrix: A Strategy Guide

Perceived Conflict over Stakes

	High	Low
High Perceived Importance of Future Relationship Between Parties	I: Balanced Concerns (Business partnership, joint venture, or merger) *Best strategies:* Problem solving or compromise	II: Relationships (Marriage, friendship, or work team) *Best strategies:* Accommodation, problem solving, or compromise
Low	III: Transactions (Divorce, house sale, or market transaction) *Best strategies:* Competition, problem solving, or compromise	IV: Tacit Coordination (Highway intersection or airplane seating) *Best strategies:* Avoidance, accommodation, or compromise

If you are personally comfortable using these strategies, you will be able to handle the situations indicated on the chart. If the strategies indicated are awkward or unpleasant for you, it may be wise to find someone to help you as part of your preparation.

Overall, cooperative people are well equipped to negotiate in Relationship and Tacit Coordination situations emphasizing relationships without significant conflicts of interest. Competitive people are good at Transaction negotiations that focus on the stakes and deemphasize relationships. Balanced Concerns situations call for a mixture of both cooperative and competitive traits, leavened with a collaborative dash of imagination. Franklin's suggestion that he and James split the cook's money was a classic imaginative response to a Balanced Concerns situation. It was, at one and the same time, assertive, fair, sensible, and thoughtful.

What personality traits are helpful in executing the problem-solving strategy that works so well in Balanced Concerns situations? First, it helps to be insistent without being too aggressive. Franklin did not compromise his vegetarian principles in his meal deal. He maintained them. Cooperative people sometimes fall short in this regard by discounting their own goals and deferring too quickly to others' needs. Competitive people, meanwhile, sometimes bargain too hard over positions without attention to people's underlying interests and feelings.

Second, good problem solving takes imagination and patience. This means that simple compromises can be the enemy of good problem solving. If you split the difference before you have explored all the options, you miss opportunities to meet both sides' needs more fully.

In fact, if you study Figure 7.3 closely you will notice that although compromise is a useful strategy in every situation, it is usually the second or third best choice. Compromise is therefore better used as a tool to help you when time is short or as a supplement to another strategy than as a one-size-fits-all way to handle all bargaining situations.

◄ Preparation Step 3: ►
Examining the Situation from the
Other Party's Point of View

I have labeled the factors in Figures 7.2 and 7.3 as *perceived* conflict over stakes and *perceived* importance of relationship. That is because negotiation situations are products of people's perceptions, not objective realities. And people often perceive situations differently. In your preparation, you need to consider not only your own view of the situation but also the other side's.

For example, one party may think the relationship is more important than anything else while the other may think the stakes matter most. Each side may behave differently as a result of their different perceptions.

An important function of the information exchange stage of negotiation (see Chapter 8) is to explore what the other party thinks about the situation. If necessary, you will need to persuade the other side to see the situation as you do.

If you are trying to return an appliance to a department store and the clerk is playing hardball, treating the event as a pure transaction, your first move might be to point out that you have a long-standing relationship with the store (see Chapter 4) that the clerk is placing in jeopardy. If you persuade the clerk (or the clerk's supervisor) that the relationship matters, he or she may soften his or her stance. If there is no past relationship to point to, the vision of a potential future relationship can sometimes be just as effective.

If, as in my department store example, the other party is represented by a bargaining agent, this introduces another layer of perception with which to cope. There may be a genuine split between the agent's perception of the situation and his or her client's. In labor-management negotiations, for example, professional union negotiators often have more of a Balanced Concerns view of the situation than do their rank-and-file members. The professional labor negotiators deal repeatedly with their management counterparts and have a stake in maintaining serviceable, working relationships across the table.

Individual union members, by contrast, have little personal contact with management bosses and do not sit at the bargaining table. From the more distant perspective of a factory floor, workers may take a cynical view of the relationship between the union and the company and see wage negotiations as a Quadrant III Transaction. To bridge this perception gap, union negotiators sometimes need to engage in hardball bargaining theatrics to satisfy their members that they have pushed the company to its limit. Wise company negotiators understand the need for these displays and do not take them personally.

◄ Preparation Step 4: ►
Deciding How to Communicate

The fourth step in your preparation is deciding how best to communicate with the other party. There are two important dimensions to this question. First, should you communicate directly with the other side or get an agent involved? If you are a highly cooperative negotiator and find yourself facing off against a bargaining bully, you might do well to hire a hard-nosed agent or lawyer to do your talking for you. Second, if you are going to negotiate yourself, should you communicate face-to-face, by telephone, or by using an electronic medium such as e-mail? If you want to eliminate sales pressure as a factor in buying a new car, decide what car you want and then do your negotiating over the Internet. Because most complex deals these days will inevitably involve some combination of all communication methods, the wise negotiator has a strategy on how best to communicate at each stage of the process.

I faced both of these questions not too long ago when my wife and I sold our townhouse in Philadelphia to move to a nearby suburb. We had lived on our family-friendly block near the University of Pennsylvania for more than fifteen years and felt warmly toward our neighbors, many of whom were colleagues where we both work. In selling our home, we wanted, if at all possible, to replace ourselves with a family that would fit in well on our tight-knit street. We also wanted to get a good price and, if possible, save the customary 6 percent real estate agent's fee. So we studied the recent sales and home listings in our part of the city, paid a real estate agent a small fee for a professional appraisal, and asked our neighbors if they knew anyone who might be interested in buying our home.

Within days, we had the name of a neighbor's college friend—a young professor who was moving into the area with his wife and child to join the university faculty. A week later they visited from New England, inspected (with the help of savvy in-laws) the plumbing, roof, and heating systems, and decided to make a bid. For our part, we immediately felt that this family would match well with the neighborhood. That posed an interesting problem: with our multiple and mutual relationships in the background (and with the other couple somewhat wary that they were up against a negotiation "expert"), what was the best way to negotiate?

We had had a successful person-to-person encounter, so I suggested that we use e-mail. E-mail negotiations can, as I will discuss below, be perilous. But it has some virtues that I thought would reassure the other side in this situation: It would permit them to take as much time as they wanted to consider each proposal, create a clear record of the offers and counteroffers, and eliminate the chance that our side would get away with some clever bargaining move in the context of a face-to-face meeting or telephone conversation.

So that is what we did, and the process worked well. As the seller, we forwarded an offer with our first e-mail message and attached a list of what we thought were comparable listings and recent sales. They came back to us with a counteroffer that was equally well-researched and justified. We then closed in on a bargaining range over the course of a couple of weeks. In the end, I made a phone call to close the last $5,000 gap with a proposal to split the difference between us—and they accepted. The only bumps in the road for this transaction came a few weeks later, when the couple hired a lawyer to help them with the purchase and sale documents. This irritable woman, who was being paid by the hour, tried her best to inject trouble where peace and harmony ruled. Occasional telephone calls directly to our buyers kept things on track, however. The sale went through and we now happily return to our old street for the annual block party with all our relationships intact.

COMMUNICATION ISSUE #1: SHOULD YOU USE AN AGENT?

As you can see from my house-sale example, I am not a fan of using agents unless they contribute more value than they cost. Nevertheless, as I noted above, imbalances in bargaining styles or expertise sometimes make hiring an agent a wise move. In addition, the world is full of real estate agents, financial advisers, lawyers, and brokers of all kinds who act as intermediaries for other parties. So you will often need to deal with them whether you like it or not.

The best reason for using an agent is economic: they can sometimes get you a better deal than you could get yourself. Had my wife and I faced a shortage of buyers in selling our home, an agent might easily have paid his or her way by providing marketing and advertising muscle, showing the house for us when we were at work, and protecting us from annoying contact with rude, unpleasant, and aggressive buyers. The same goes for using a good lawyer to help you negotiate deals. Not only may a lawyer bring negotiation experience and useful relationships to the table, but he or she can often steer the parties past hidden (and genuinely catastrophic) legal and business risks. In fact, the best business lawyers in centers such as New York or California's Silicon Valley are also some of the most sophisticated business strategists in the world. They don't just negotiate choice-of-law clauses, they structure deals for maximum value under complex global conditions. Finally, some agents act as "gatekeepers" to entire industries. For example, top publishers will not look at your book proposal unless it comes from a reputable literary agent. And agents play similar, central roles in the entertainment and sports industries. In all of these cases, using agents makes a lot of sense.

But before adding an agent to your team, you should carefully add up the costs that agents bring to the table. These include:

- *The fee the agent charges.* Negotiate this if possible.
- *The agent's own agenda.* Make sure you know how your agent is compensated and whom he or she is working for. In real estate deals, the listing agent is paid on commission and works for the seller. This has two important implications. First, agents paid on commission usually do better closing a high number of transactions rather than maximizing each and every one. Indeed, research shows that when agents sell their own homes, they leave them on the market longer than when they are selling yours. In addition, be careful how much you reveal to your agent about your true bottom line. Agents working on commission may be tempted to negotiate to your bottom-line level more quickly than you would to get the deal closed. The opposite is often true of an agent paid by the hour. Like the lawyer who represented the buyers in our Philadelphia home sale, an agent punching a time clock may drag out the engagement to increase the fee.
- *Bad feelings.* Sometimes agents get into pointless fights, spoiling the relationship between the principals. Lawyers can be "deal breakers" instead of "deal makers" by battling over clauses neither party cares about, creating bad feelings, tensions, and mistrust. If your agent misbehaves in this way, show him or her the door and get the process back on track yourself.
- *Miscommunication.* Whenever you add layers to a communication process, you increase the risk of honest misunderstanding. And when both sides are using agents, the distortion risk escalates. If you want to get an important message to another party and must work through his or her agent, either ask for a direct meeting with the agent present or put your message in writing.
- *Self-serving bias.* Real estate agents are confident they can sell your house, and lawyers are sure they will win your case. Research shows that agents often suffer from overconfidence in their own abilities, leaving you with the problems when they are proven wrong. Do your own research and get second opinions whenever possible.
- *Time.* An old saying goes: "If God had had an agent, He would still be creating the earth." Using agents creates delays that can prove costly, especially if time is of the essence.

COMMUNICATION ISSUE #2: PERSON-TO-PERSON, TELEPHONE, OR E-MAIL?

The traditional negotiation involves a face-to-face encounter, but our networked world often demands that we use many other means to communicate. In general, face-to-face meetings give everyone the maximum "bandwidth" for communication, allowing people to read between the lines of what is said, ask follow-up questions, get feedback, and develop genuine relationships that can ease the negotiation over many hurdles. We convey more than one-half of the meaning of our messages nonverbally, so you lose a lot of communication channels when you limit yourself to written messages or voice only. The next widest channel for communication is video conferencing, a method that is increasing as geopolitical risks such as terrorism rise and communication technology improves. Next in line is the telephone, which at least permits you to both use and interpret vocal tone and pacing. Last on the list are electronic communications methods such as e-mail and instant messaging.

This list is reversed in terms of convenience—meetings are often the hardest to arrange while an e-mail message is a "click" away. So we are inevitably tempted to use the narrowest communication pipeline (e-mail) the most.

I have already detailed some of the benefits of using e-mail in discussing why I decided it was the best way to negotiate our home sale. These include:

- *Convenience* when parties are at a distance
- *Time to consider* one's next move
- *A clear record* of the proposals
- *Ease in conveying large amounts of data* to back up proposals
- *Leveling of the playing field* between negotiators with different levels of seniority and experience
- *The power to quickly mobilize large coalitions* of like-minded people using group e-mail lists

One additional benefit relates to personality. People strongly inclined to avoid negotiations will prefer using a method such as e-mail because it reduces the risk of a face-to-face disagreement or confrontation.

Because electronic communication is so temptingly convenient, it is especially important to be aware of its pitfalls. Researchers have confirmed these problems repeatedly in experiments. These include:

- *Increased risk of impasse.* Lacking voice tone, facial expression, and conversational pauses, electronic messaging comes across as more aggressive and "in your face" than spoken words. This can trigger reactions in the receiver, who then fires off an angry response. The problem escalates from there. Several detailed studies of e-mail negotiations have confirmed this problem. One pitted MBA students at Stanford and Northwestern University against each other. Half the students were given only their counterpart's name and e-mail address before starting the negotiation. The other half were given a photograph of their opponent and explicitly instructed to exchange social information on hobbies, families, job plans, and hometowns prior to beginning the negotiation. Ninety-four percent of the "schmoozing" groups had no trouble reaching a deal, while only 70 percent of the "strictly business" groups managed to complete the negotiation.
- *Careless clicking.* The informality and privacy of sitting in front of a computer screen tends to put us off our guard, and we forget that our message can easily be copied and sent to unintended audiences. A former student of mine once made the mistake of negotiating his salary using e-mail. His message arguing for a raise came across as arrogant, and he appeared to be taking too much credit for projects others had contributed to. The e-mail circulated widely throughout the leadership group in his company, and he ended up being fired.
- *Delay.* Research on electronic communications shows that the same problem can take much longer to solve using e-mail than using face-to-face or voice communication. The narrower the pipeline of communication, the longer it takes to get information through it. Delay and associated misunderstandings are special problems when it comes to using e-mail to resolve disputes, as opposed to constructing deals.
- *Polarized decisions in groups.* When groups negotiate electronically, they tend to reach decisions that are more extreme in one direction or another than when they meet face-to-face. The lack of social awareness and non-verbal channels for communication seems to reduce our tendencies to compromise.

If you find you must negotiate electronically, even when you prefer using another means, three simple steps will keep you out of trouble. First, *think before you click.* Never send a message when you are in the grip of a strong negative emotion—and assume that once you send the message it will be read by many people other than the person you are sending it to.

Second, go out of your way in all your messages to *engage in a little small talk* and make sure to explain your reasoning when you make requests or demands. This may feel phony, but it works to soften the in-your-face feeling your message will otherwise convey. Even starting a message with a cheerful "Hi, John" instead of just "John" can soften the impression you make.

Third, in prolonged negotiations, *make periodic telephone calls and, if possible, have a few meetings* with your counterparts. These contacts can help convey relationship messages that e-mail excludes. Companies have found that cross-functional project teams working on complicated problems can take longer to complete tasks if they rely exclusively on electronic communication. The solution is to mix electronic communications with conference calls and an occasional meeting.

Instant messaging is an interesting variant of e-mail that is becoming common in corporate communications and real-time trading, especially when several parties are involved. As executive ranks fill with people accustomed to chatting with multiple parties using IM, this form of electronic communication will doubtless become favored in more formal business negotiations.

Unlike e-mail, IM permits parties to carry on several real-time conversations at once, including private "side" communications that others are blocked from seeing. In addition, like e-mail, IM has the capability of creating a precise record of all communications. Even conference calls do not have this combination of features. At the same time, IM suffers from the same in-your-face message presentation problems as e-mail and, in some ways, requires even more caution. Your words can become historical records instantly—there is no "pause" before you click during which you can edit out a hasty phrase or emotional outburst.

Finally, research on IM versus e-mail negotiations suggests that competitive negotiators prepared with intricate arguments to justify their positions have an advantage when using IM. Their opponents, finding themselves at a loss for words in the rapid-fire IM environment, tend to concede points. E-mail, by contrast, gives the slower party a chance to think of and articulate more skillful responses between messages.

In short, IM negotiations call for extra care, preparation, and prudence.

━ Putting It All Together: ━
Your Bargaining Plan

Now that you understand the basics of situational analysis and can anticipate the various strategies that others may use, you need to combine this knowledge with information on the Six Foundations to create a specific bargaining plan. I have given you a simple form (see Appendix B) to organize the information you have gathered. You should refer to this plan and update it as the negotiation process unfolds.

The insight you gain from preparation is a key to Information-Based Bargaining. But good planning is only a start. One of the best uses of preparation is to make a list of specific questions you intend to ask early in the negotiation. Your plan, after all, is based on a number of assumptions about what the other side wants and is thinking. As the next chapter will show, the opening stage of negotiation gives you a chance to test those assumptions against information provided directly by the other party itself.

━ Summary ━

This chapter has introduced you to the basics of good preparation. First, using the Situational Matrix, you should determine the basic situation you face. What strategies are best suited to deal with the situation?

Next, you need to combine your situational analysis with the knowledge you have about your own stylistic preferences to determine how well suited you are to negotiate the problem. If you are basically non-confrontational, you will have a hard time doing well in a Transaction unless you are negotiating against someone just like yourself. If you are aggressively competitive, you will lack some of the tact needed to handle a Relationship situation that calls for delicate diplomacy.

Third, try to imagine how the other party views the situation. Do they see the relationship as important? Do the stakes matter as much to them as they do to you? The situational analysis prepares you to anticipate the range of strategies the other side can be expected to use.

Fourth, decide how best to communicate with the other side. Does it make sense to use an agent? If you negotiate directly, should you meet face to face or rely on telephone or e-mail?

Finally, combine the information you have gathered on the situation with your insights into the Six Foundations to develop a specific bargaining plan. Use this plan to formulate a list of questions to ask the other side early in the discussion phase to test your assumptions.

If all this sounds like too much work for the time you have available, remember that even a few minutes spent reviewing the Six Foundations and the Situational Matrix before you start will yield significant benefits. In fact, research indicates that the single most important step in becoming an effective negotiator is acquiring a habit of preparation. John Wooden, the legendary UCLA basketball coach, once summed up the truth about preparation with a phrase that has stuck with me: Failing to prepare is preparing to fail.

It is now time to move into the interactive stages of negotiation. Bring your bargaining plan along with you as we move to Step 2: Exchanging Information.

8

Step 2:
Exchanging Information

It is better to sound a person with whom one deals . . .
than to fall upon the point at first.
—Sir Francis Bacon (1597)

Who is without knowledge? He who asks no questions.
—Fulfulde folk saying

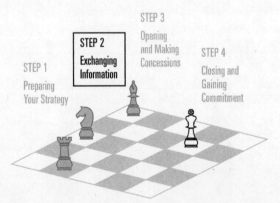

STEP 1
Preparing
Your Strategy

STEP 2
Exchanging
Information

STEP 3
Opening
and Making
Concessions

STEP 4
Closing and
Gaining
Commitment

Think back to the negotiating examples that opened the book in Chapter 1. Do you recall the phrase "talking to the mountain"? The Arusha people of Tanzania use that expression to describe the opening phase of negotiations in which the parties exchange their initial demands and counterdemands. No one takes these opening demands seriously. Rather, they are the means by which Arusha negotiators fix the agenda, test expectations, and establish the legitimacy of their positions. The parties conveniently forget their excessive initial demands through "tolerant amnesia" when they get down to the serious business of bargaining.

And remember the opening stage of the negotiation between Peter Jovanovich and General Cinema's Dick Smith over the future of Harcourt Brace Jovanovich? The opening encounter was a carefully orchestrated minuet, but Jovanovich departed from his script to give Smith an expensive engraved watch and tell Smith he thought General Cinema was HBJ's best hope for survival. HBJ was on the brink of bankruptcy and ruin. Peter Jovanovich's gift and candid admission were important steps in establishing rapport and letting Smith know that Jovanovich would be realistic in light of Smith's superior leverage. This move helped create an atmosphere of mutual cooperation that propelled the parties into a working relationship and, ultimately, a successful deal.

Neither "talking to the mountain" nor preliminary moves such as gift giving are bargaining, at least in the ordinary sense of that word. There is no give-and-take and no explicit testing of concrete, realistic proposals. Rather, these initial steps are part of the ritual of negotiation that always precedes and sometimes loops back upon bargaining: information exchange. A good information exchange process accomplishes several important purposes, each of which I will discuss in this chapter. They are: the development of *rapport* between the individual negotiators, the surfacing of underlying *interests, issues, and perceptions* that concern the parties and the initial *testing of expectations* based on the parties' relative leverage.

It is during the information exchange stage—not during the later phase of explicit bargaining—that we have our first opportunity to explore the Six Foundations in action. We display our style traits—personality, gender, and culture (Chapter 1), express our goals (Chapter 2), probe to discover the other side's interests (Chapter 5), and test our assumptions about such things as applicable standards (Chapter 3), relationships (Chapter 4), and leverage (Chapter 6).

As we share information, we test our counterpart's commitment to the norm of reciprocity discussed in Chapter 4. If this norm can be established in the exchange of information, both parties gain the confidence that will help them get through the hard work of bargaining and commitment. If it does not take hold, the parties will have a very difficult time making a successful deal.

Many of the messages we exchange in negotiation take only seconds to convey. Remember the example of the two cars at the intersection in Chapter 7? A momentary exchange of glances is all it takes to assess the intentions and personality of the other driver and make a decision on how to proceed into the intersection. The same is true of more formal negotiations. Enormous amounts of information can be conveyed by a satisfied look, a frown, or a nervous pause in response to a pointed question.

Cultural differences are also particularly important variables in the information exchange stage of negotiations. As I noted earlier, research on cultural styles reveals that Americans in particular and Westerners in general are relatively "task-oriented" in negotiation. This means that we Americans like to get down to business, cutting the information exchange stage short with remarks such as "So, are you prepared to make an offer?"

By contrast, in many "relationship-oriented" cultures in Asia, Africa, and Latin America, the information exchange stage assumes much more importance. Not only do the parties expect to find out what the negotiation is about, but they also seek to establish a personal or professional relationship that goes deeper than the single transaction at issue. If this relationship fails to materialize during the preliminary discussion stage, negotiations are likely to be very difficult, and the parties may never get to meaningful bargaining.

Let's look more carefully at some examples illustrating each of the three main functions of the information exchange stage of negotiation: (1) establishing rapport, (2) determining interests, issues, and perceptions, and (3) signaling expectations and leverage. As we do, remember that this preliminary phase of negotiation is often the most overlooked part of the process. Awareness of it therefore yields significant competitive advantages.

◄ Purpose 1: ►
Establishing Rapport

The first thing to take care of in the information exchange stage is the mood or atmosphere at the table—the rapport between the negotiators. Information exchange depends on effective interpersonal communication, and rapport facilitates this.

Some people may think rapport is a trivial point, a mere social nicety, but professional negotiators know better. They may, like J. P. Morgan in his negotiation with John D. Rockefeller, Jr., described in Chapter 7, bypass rapport and growl, "What's your price?" But when they do so, it is for a purpose. Either they are deliberately seeking to intimidate the other party or they are responding to an attempt at intimidation against themselves. Meanwhile, in Quadrant II Relationship situations, rapport building is the most important aspect of the negotiation process.

Professional negotiators are full of stories about the carefully planned rapport-building moves they have made to initiate important negotiations. These stories are interesting in their own right, but they also reflect the extraordinary importance that experts place on establishing the right tone early in a negotiation.

When Armand Hammer, the aggressive CEO of Occidental Petroleum, made his first bid to buy the valuable Libyan oil concession from Libya in the mid-1960s, he distinguished his bid by presenting it in an Arab rather than a Western manner. He went to the trouble and expense of having the bid written out on sheepskin parchment, rolled up, and tied with ribbons bearing the Libyan national colors, green and black. He was showing the Libyans that he had studied and had respect for Arab culture. He also won the contract.

A time-honored method of establishing rapport in negotiation is to find some common interest, passion, or background experience—unrelated to the negotiation—that you share with the other negotiator. When the legendary founder of Warner Communications (later to become Time Warner), Steve Ross, was just starting out, he was in the funeral home business. One of the first steps that led him out of that line of work and into big business involved helping a small car rental company negotiate a deal with Caesar Kimmel, the owner of some sixty parking lots in and around New York City. Ross wanted Kimmel to let the car company use Kimmel's parking lots to rent cars and give rental customers free parking. In return, Ross was prepared to give Kimmel a percentage of the car rental business.

Before going into the negotiation, Ross researched Kimmel thoroughly and found out, among other things, that Kimmel was an avid horse racing fan who owned and raced his own horses. Ross knew something about the track because his in-laws owned and raced horses, too.

When he entered Kimmel's office to start the negotiation, he made what was to become a classic Steve Ross bargaining move. Right away, he scanned the room and spotted a framed picture of one of Kimmel's horses in the winner's circle of a big race. He went over and studied it for a moment. Then he said enthusiastically, "Morty Rosenthal [Ross's relative] owned the number-two horse in that race!" Kimmel beamed. The two men hit it off—and went on to launch a very successful venture that eventually became Ross's first public company.

◄ The Similarity Principle ►

Social psychologists have confirmed Steve Ross's (and many other expert negotiators') instincts about the right way to start a negotiation. Psychologist Robert Cialdini calls this the "liking rule." As he puts it, "We most prefer to say yes to the requests of someone we know and like."

Underneath the liking rule is something even more basic: We trust others a little more when we see them as familiar or similar to us. Studies ranging over the past thirty-five years have consistently shown that people like other people more when they display appearances, attitudes, beliefs, and moods that are similar to their own, provided that these similarities reflect well on them. As Armand Hammer's bid on parchment shows, these similarities do not have to go deep to smooth the way to better communication. Indeed, as I discussed in Chapter 4, common affiliation or membership in a given group such as a club, religion, college alumni body, or even nationality (when in a foreign country), is sometimes enough to induce a momentary feeling of relatedness and similarity. And that momentary opening may be all that is needed to establish rapport.

Nor does it matter much that both sides know the other is presenting similarity information solely for the purpose of establishing rapport. The e-mail experiments reported in Chapter 7 suggest that even forced pre-negotiation "schmoozing" reduces the risk of impasse. I am a specialist in negotiation, and I still succumb to the influence of similarity information when someone tactfully opens a discussion with me by telling me about some shared experience, affiliation, or common acquaintance. The similarity principle is a compelling force in human psychology, much like gravity in physics.

◄ Rapport Pitfalls: ►
Over- or Underdoing It

To repeat: Establishing rapport will not and should not gain one side a significant bargaining advantage over the other. If you sense that your counterpart is trying to extract concessions from you on the basis of his or her initial success in establishing rapport, alarm bells should go off. You are being conned, not negotiated with. Armand Hammer did not pay less for his oil concession because he put his bid on sheepskin parchment, and Steve Ross did not get free parking from Kimmel because he expressed interest in Kimmel's race horses.

Rather, both men used their knowledge about rapport to open a distinctively personal channel for communication so they could get their "deal message" across. The goal was to get the other party to think of them as unique people, not just faces coming to ask for something. As both stories illustrate, one good way to get other people to think of you as a unique individual is to show them that you think of *them* that way.

We walk a fine line in the rapport stage of information exchange. Most of us know when we negotiate that other people want things from us. We therefore guard against and discount techniques such as flattery and social niceties designed to gain influence. Overt, manipulative, and ingratiating behavior does not usually work and can be very costly in terms of credibility.

At the other extreme are blunders at the beginning of a negotiation that needlessly upset or offend the other party. These are especially common in cross-cultural situations, although any thoughtless act can interfere with bargaining. One of my favorite examples of a clumsy opening move involves Intel Corporation, the maker of computer chips. This story is also a reminder that everyone in a large organization is on its bargaining team, not just the people who happen to be at the bargaining table.

In the early 1980s, Intel was about to begin some very sensitive negotiations with a company in Japan. The Intel bargaining team had done its homework and was in Tokyo prepared to go through all the social rituals needed to establish a business relationship with a Japanese partner.

Back at its U.S. headquarters, Intel's general counsel, Roger Borovoy, picked up the phone to answer a call from a newspaper reporter and was asked, in a conversational way, whether negotiating with Japanese firms was easy or hard. "Negotiating with the Japanese is like negotiating with the Devil," Borovoy said. The quote soon appeared in the reporter's story.

Shortly after the story was published, Intel's negotiations got under way in Japan. Borovoy's quote quickly found its way to Intel's Japanese counterparts and cast a distinct chill over the proceedings. Intel's would-be Japanese partners were not amused.

Andy Grove, chairman of Intel, was so chagrined by this event that he invented a new in-house Intel award to honor it. The award is called "The Muzzle." It consists of a leather dog muzzle mounted on a wooden plaque. Borovoy was its first recipient, and it stayed in his office until another Intel executive won the honor of hanging "The Muzzle" behind his desk for an ill-timed remark to the press.

To summarize: Establishing rapport at the outset of negotiations is a distinct, separate part of the information exchange process. Everyone, no matter how simple or sophisticated, likes to be acknowledged on a personal level. The more genuine this personal acknowledgment is, the more effective it will be.

◄ Purpose 2: ►
Obtaining Information on Interests,
Issues, and Perceptions

The second major task in the information stage is obtaining basic information regarding the other party's interests, issues, and perceptions. Who are they? Why are they here? What is important to them? What are they prepared to negotiate? What is their view of the situation? Do they have authority to close? This aspect of information exchange is important in all negotiating situations, but the higher the stakes, the more care you should take to acquire answers to these questions.

Determining interests and issues builds on the preparation work you did using the Six Foundations and analyzing the Situational Matrix. In effect, the information exchange stage allows you to test the hypotheses you developed earlier about the other party's needs and arguments and communicate your own basic interests—*without giving up anything.*

To frame our discussion of sharing information on interests, issues, and perceptions, I would like to tell a story about a cross-cultural negotiation that utterly failed on this score. It is another story involving Akio Morita, the chairman of Sony, whom we met in Chapter 2 selling transistor radios in New York. The story shows some very skilled negotiators making some very costly mistakes.

This time the year is 1976—twenty-one years after Morita had vowed to make Sony a household name in quality electronics. The story involves the litigation by which the American movie industry tried to stop the spread of an emerging technology—the videocassette recorder or VCR.

AKIO MORITA GETS A VISIT

In September 1976, Sidney Sheinberg, president of both Universal Pictures and its parent company, MCA, had a problem. Sony was launching a new electronic device called Betamax, the forerunner of what we now call the VCR. The Betamax permitted television viewers to copy and replay TV programs.

As Sheinberg saw it, the Betamax was a threat to his basic business strategy. It would enable consumers to tape Universal's movies and TV shows free of charge and replay them as often as they liked. If the audience already had an original show on tape, what station would pay for a rerun?

"It's [the Betamax] a copyright violation. It's got to be," said Sheinberg when he heard about the Sony machine. "I'd be crazy to let them [market it]."

To complicate matters, MCA and Sony were engaged in a number of joint projects. In particular, MCA was hoping that Sony would become a key manufacturer of playback machines to run the "videodisk"—a new technology MCA had developed to play prerecorded films. The two firms had also cooperated on several deals.

So, from Sony's point of view, the two firms were in a collaborative relationship. But from Sheinberg's point of view, the stakes had just risen sharply. It was a ticklish situation.

As it happened, Sheinberg and MCA's chairman, Lew Wasserman, had a dinner meeting with Morita scheduled in New York to discuss Sony's participation in the videodisk project. Sheinberg hoped the informal setting of a dinner conversation following a cooperative, brainstorming session about the videodisk project would be an effective way to raise the Betamax issue without threatening the overall Sony-MCA relationship.

In preparation for the meeting, Sheinberg had his law firm research and prepare a legal memorandum regarding the legality of the Betamax. Reading the memo, Sheinberg became even more convinced that he could and should stop the advance of this technology. His positioning theme was straightforward: Under U.S. law, the Betamax was an illegal machine. He intended to sue if Morita did not drop it.

FRIENDS DON'T SUE

On the appointed day, Sheinberg and Wasserman met with Morita and Sony's top U.S. executive, Harvey Schein, at Sony's U.S. corporate headquarters. The four men engaged in a lengthy, animated discussion of the videodisk project.

They then moved to a catered dinner in Sony's main boardroom. As the dinner came to a close, Sheinberg reached into his coat pocket and pulled out the legal memorandum. To his astonished audience, Shein-berg explained that Universal would be forced to sue unless Sony either dropped the product or made some other type of accommodation.

Morita reacted with surprise and confusion. Hadn't the parties just fin-ished discussing a major cooperative deal? What was all this about lawsuits?

As a business matter, Morita rejected MCA's analysis regarding the conflict between the Betamax and the videodisk. "I totally disagree with that argument," he said, "because in the future the videodisk and the video recorder will coexist, just as the record and tape recorder coexist in the audio field."

Morita then went on to express his confusion about what the dispute would mean for the MCA-Sony business partnership. It was hard, Morita said, to see how two business partners such as Universal and Sony could be talking about a joint project such as the videodisk one minute and about suing each other the next.

He tried to make his point with an image that any Japanese would understand. "When we shake hands [with one hand]," he told Shein-berg, "we will not hit you with the other hand." That was a basic princi-ple of Japanese business.

After Sheinberg and Wasserman had departed, Morita assured Harvey Schein that MCA could not be serious about a lawsuit. "We've done a number of things over the years, and we're talking about the videodisk," Morita said. "Friends don't sue." Case closed.

Within a month and without telling Sony, Universal had formed a coalition with Walt Disney and other entertainment producers and be-gun drafting its lawsuit. Private investigators were gathering evidence to prove that the Betamax was being used to copy legally protected tele-vision shows. Finally, on November 11, 1976, Universal and Disney filed their lawsuit against Sony.

Morita was getting ready to play golf in Japan when he heard the news. As a colleague later recalled it, "He let out a kind of death cry" when he was told about the lawsuit.

But once he was sued, he accepted the challenge. And Sony eventually won the case. Eleven years and millions of dollars in legal fees later, the U.S. Supreme Court put an end to the dispute by upholding Sony's right to make and sell the videocassette recorder.

By the time the lawsuit was over, everyone involved in the case—from Disney and Universal to Sony—was making millions of dollars selling a new product, videotapes, through an entirely new type of convenience outlet, the video store. Contrary to Sheinberg's fears, TV stations were still paying top dollar for reruns. And everyone was still going to theaters to watch movies—even to see films they could rent and watch on videotape. Morita, meanwhile, had written and given a talk at Harvard University entitled "The Role of Lawyers in Handicapping Entrepreneurial Efforts in the United States."

DON'T BE A "BLABBERMOUTH" NEGOTIATOR: ASK QUESTIONS

Sheinberg made three classic mistakes in his Betamax negotiation: He thought he could gain advantage by surprising an unprepared opponent, he focused on delivering information instead of asking questions and listening, and he ignored a potential cross-cultural difference. For his part, Morita failed to get beyond his own Japanese frame of reference and into his opponent's shoes. He did not listen to what the other side was telling him.

First, what did Sheinberg gain by surprising Morita with the Betamax issue? People who approach negotiation as if it is a game or sport often think they can gain an advantage by tricking or surprising the other side. They think they can score a bargaining point by faking one way and moving in another. But this is usually a mistake in important negotiations. You actually do better when the other side is prepared to deal with the real issues.

A professional labor mediator and I were once called in by management to help facilitate a union-management labor negotiation. The company viewed the union as stubborn and disrespectful. The union leaders, disorganized and new to their jobs, assumed the company was out to take advantage of the workers. Relations at the plant were terrible. What did we do? We spent the first three months of the engagement helping the union become better organized. Why? Because it had not had a real meeting in over a year and the leaders were both inexperienced and out of touch with the real issues. To make progress, management needed an organized and informed opponent at the bargaining table.

Sheinberg's next mistake came from his lack of curiosity about Morita's interests, issues, and perceptions. By framing the problem as a matter of legal rights on which there could be no debate, he shut down communication regarding business interests.

Finally, Sheinberg failed to consider Morita's Japanese approach to business relationships. As I made clear in Chapter 1, cultural differences must be considered for the signaling part of information exchange to work. Americans file literally millions of court cases each year. In America, litigation is not a last resort; it is a normal part of being in business. In Japan, very few disputes go to court. To the Japanese, a lawsuit is a burial service for a productive business relationship, as it was in this case.

◄ Probe First, Disclose Later ►

The research on negotiation effectiveness repeatedly underscores a simple fact about skilled negotiators: They focus more than average negotiators do *on receiving,* as opposed to delivering, information. As I suggested in Chapter 1 when I identified listening as a key effectiveness factor for the skilled negotiator, the best practice in this stage of negotiation is to probe first, disclose later. The average "blabbermouth" negotiator does it the other way around: He carelessly discloses information first and asks questions later.

Look at Table 8.1, reporting the results of a study by Neil Rackham and John Carlisle that monitored the behavior of English labor and contract negotiators engaged in actual transactions. What do skilled negotiators do that average negotiators do not?

First, they ask twice the number of questions that average negotiators ask. These questions have a purpose: They are designed to elicit real information ("When can you make delivery?" or "How did you calculate your offer?"). Next, they test their understanding of what the other side

TABLE 8.1
Information-Gathering Behavior
as a Percentage of All Behavior Observed

	Skilled Negotiators	*Average Negotiators*
Asking questions	21.3%	9.6%
Testing for understanding	9.7%	4.1%
Summarizing	7.5%	4.2%
Total	**38.5%**	**17.9%**

has said ("When you say 'ten days,' do you mean ten calendar days or ten business days?"). Third, they summarize where they think the parties are in the process ("As I understand it, we have agreed to pay you net ninety days of delivery and you have promised to deliver within seven business days of the date you receive our specifications—is that correct?"). Finally, they listen to all of the other party's answers.

The Rackham and Carlisle study shows that skilled negotiators spend 38.5 percent of their time acquiring and clarifying information—as compared with just under 18 percent for these activities by average negotiators. In addition, by testing their understanding, effective negotiators nail down what they have heard and what everyone has agreed to do. This means there are fewer problems in the commitment and implementation stages, when miscommunication is both common and costly.

These findings have been confirmed by other researchers studying a variety of professions. One study of American lawyers found that the most effective negotiators were "skillful at reading cues," "perceptive," and able to "probe an opponent's position." Another study, this time of American bankers, found that "listening skill" ranked as one of the top three traits of the best negotiators in that industry. The other top-rated skills? Willingness to prepare (rated number one), knowledge of subject matter being negotiated and ability to think clearly under pressure (tied for number two), and ability to express one's thoughts (tied with "listening skill" for number three). Yet a third study of working professionals in several different fields found "listening skill" to be the number two rated communication skill after "verbal clarity."

Asking questions and getting clarification regarding others' answers have obvious benefits in terms of information flow. But these techniques also give the people using them additional time to plot their next moves. Most people are so grateful to have an attentive audience that they take little notice of your tactful probing until they suddenly feel the urge to get a few answers themselves. By then the effective negotiator has the information he or she needs to frame just the right responses.

THE STRATEGIC NATURE OF INFORMATION EXCHANGE

It all sounds so easy. All you need to do is ask negotiators on the other side what is important to them and they tell you, right? Not quite. In negotiation, information—especially information about what people want—is power. If the other negotiator is awake (and you must assume he will be), he will want you to disclose your interests and needs before disclosing his own. Why? Because, as U.S. sports agent Bob Woolf said in Chapter 6, "Every reason that the other side wants or needs an agreement is my leverage—provided that I know those reasons." Negotiators on the other side will want to find out what you want so they can see if your needs provide them with leverage.

The leverage effect of information disclosure often gives the opening stage in negotiations a somewhat comic "you first—no, you first" rhythm. I once ran a negotiation seminar for high-level managers at a South Korean firm. I devised a fairly complex, international negotiation scenario in which there were many issues. Some of the issues were more important to one side than the other, and some issues were equally important to both. To give the workshop a realistic flavor, we invited a group of American executives to negotiate against the Korean managers.

One American in attendance was a backslapping, talkative entrepreneur who was obviously used to controlling most situations in which he found himself. He and his team of Americans sat down with their Korean counterparts to begin the negotiation. Before anyone could say anything, this man made a speech.

"Look," he said, "I am sure there are some things here that are more important to you and some things that are more important to us. Why don't you guys just tell us what your 'hot-button' issues are? Then we'll figure out what the best deal is for both of us."

I am sure this speech must work for him in many settings, because he gave it with great confidence. After he finished, the Korean team put their heads together and spoke rapidly in their own language for a few moments. At length, the Korean team leader—who spoke perfect English—gave the team's response.

"Thank you very much for your idea," he said. "We too are looking for a good deal for both sides. However, you must forgive us because we are not sure what you mean by 'hot-button issues.' All of these issues are important to us. Perhaps you could give us *your* 'hot-button' issues first. Then we will see what you mean by this, and perhaps we can give you ours. Would that be acceptable?"

The entrepreneur sputtered and fumed. Finally, one of his teammates suggested that the two sides begin a general discussion of the issues, one at a time, without bothering about "hot buttons." Eventually, both sides arrived at a working understanding of each other's priorities, but they did so by listening to the signals hidden in the give-and-take of discussions and through careful questioning about why one issue mattered or another option was not possible. The entrepreneur's opening gambit and the Korean's clever response were forgotten.

Research confirms that information exchange on interests and issues is a tricky business. As I mentioned in Chapter 5, one recent survey analyzed thirty-two different negotiation research studies involving more than five thousand participants. The survey found that negotiators failed to correctly identify *shared* priorities about 50 percent of the time.

Most of this confusion arose because the parties were bluffing each other during the negotiation process, trying to gain tactical advantage by pretending some issues were more important than they really were. Bluffing distorts the information flow in negotiation in ways that can be costly. In one study, for example, 20 percent of the subjects, including some experienced professionals, ended up agreeing to options that neither side wanted due to bluffs that backfired.

The best way to manage the flow of information about interests is to realize that it is a strategic process and take it slowly. It almost never hurts to talk less.

Open your ears before you open your mouth. *Probe first, disclose later.*

◄ Purpose 3: ►
Signaling Expectations and Leverage

Sidney Sheinberg did a poor job of probing Akio Morita's interests and issues regarding the Betamax controversy, but perhaps that is an unfair criticism. After all, Sheinberg had made up his mind that MCA and Sony had strictly conflicting interests. He was not there to ask questions. He was there to deliver a message: Drop the Betamax or pay us royalties under copyright law. Otherwise, we sue.

If you must deliver an ultimatum (or any other "deal breaker") to the other party in a negotiation, how should you do so? Most experts agree that the best way to deliver bad news is to do it early, clearly, and credibly. That way you condition the other negotiator's expectations and avoid disappointing him later, after he has made plans based on an assumption that you might be flexible. A realistic sense of what is possible saves everyone a lot of time and confusion.

That brings us to the third basic function of the information exchange process: signaling regarding your expectations and leverage. Recall from

FIGURE 8.1
Signaling Leverage

Your Actual Leverage Situation (As You See It)

		Strong	*Weak*
How You Want to Act	*Firm*	Make confident demands and credible threats. Display your alternatives and leave the decision up to the other party.	Emphasize the uncertain future. Bluff (act strong when you are not).
	Flexible	Show the other party you are investing in the relationship. Be generous.	Acknowledge the other party's power and stress the potential gains from future cooperation. Appeal to the other party's sympathy. What would they do in your position?

my discussion in Chapter 6 that your leverage in negotiation is a matter of perception as much as reality. You have only as much or as little leverage as the other side gives you credit for. If you have attractive alternatives or good sources of normative leverage or can easily live without the other party's cooperation, the information exchange stage is the time to signal this to the other party. If you have none of the above, you had better have a plan for dealing with that fact.

I will break down the discussion of signaling into two basic situations: when you think you are relatively weak and when you think you are relatively strong. Figure 8.1 summarizes the signals that you might send in these two situations, depending on how flexible you are willing to be.

SITUATION 1: YOU HAVE A WEAK HAND

If your leverage is weak, I recommend you emphasize the uncertainty that always attends the future. If you are selling something and have no other offers, you can discuss what you will be pursuing by way of additional marketing efforts if no deal happens, or talk about your comfort with the status quo. In short, even if you are in a weak position and have few options, you can still appeal to the other party's desire to minimize future risk by closing a deal now—and the other side can also save himself the expense of continuing his search for a partner. These are not strong signals, but they can keep the process moving without getting you deeply involved in lies or misrepresentations about your own situation.

Some people try to bluff their way through a weak bargaining position by acting in ways that strongly signal strength regarding a deal. A successful bluff can make a great negotiation story, but it is a high-risk strategy. You may, after all, end up with no deal. In fact, experienced negotiators can usually see through ploys of this sort—especially tricks such as the "keep-them-waiting" move. As Leslie H. Wexner, chairman of The Limited, once put it, "The longer they keep you waiting, the more they want the deal." Unless you are an experienced gamesman, leave the bluffing to others and emphasize the inherent uncertainty of the stronger party's future if it passes up your offer.

If your weakness is obvious and you know that they know, it may help your credibility to personalize the situation as much as possible, arrange for a face-to-face meeting, candidly acknowledge the other side's power, and proceed on that basis. Jovanovich's admission to Dick Smith in Chapter 1 that General Cinema was HBJ's best hope was such a move. It helped create a cooperative atmosphere that facilitated a deal.

Finally, when all else fails, you can appeal to the other party's sympathy. Ask the other negotiator what he or she would do in your position. Give the other party a "blank check" question like "What would it take for you to say 'yes'?" If the other side responds, you may discover you have more leverage than you thought.

SITUATION 2: YOU HAVE A STRONG HAND

Suppose you think you have a strong hand—your leverage looks good. What signals should you send to the other side in the information exchange stage? You can either send a firm signal that you have the power to demand a favorable deal and intend to insist on one, or you can show your power, then indicate you intend to be flexible in order to build goodwill for the future.

Suppose you want to send a strong, firm signal. How should you do so without being either arrogant or overly aggressive? Sheinberg's negotiation with Morita is a good example of how *not* to do it. Sheinberg failed to gain any useful leverage from his meeting with Morita because, in the end, he did not convince Morita he would carry out his legal threat. The result was misunderstanding, a ruined business relationship, lost opportunities, and an eleven-year legal battle.

Instead, Sheinberg should have asked Morita to bring his lawyers to a special meeting about the Betamax. "This is what lies ahead," Sheinberg could have said after the lawyers had made their legal arguments. "Do we want to settle this in court, or is there a businesslike way to handle it?" In essence, Sheinberg could have taught Morita how Americans handle business relationships that include litigation.

If you have a lot of leverage, but for one reason or another you are willing to be flexible, how should you go about sending that signal?

A good example is the way J. P. Morgan handled his negotiation with Andrew Carnegie over the partnership interest, a story told in Chapter 4. Carnegie made a mistake and charged Morgan $10,000 less than he meant to for a partnership interest. When Carnegie showed up to get his check, Morgan gave him *two* checks, one for the agreed amount and another for the amount of Carnegie's error. Carnegie tried to give the second check back, but Morgan would not hear of it. Carnegie got his money, and Morgan got credit toward their future relationship.

It is the same in any negotiation when you have leverage but choose not to use it. Let the other side know what options you have before you show you are not going to exercise those options. You don't have to be arrogant about it, just matter-of-fact. You view the transaction as part of a relationship, and people in good relationships do not squeeze every nickel they can out of a situation. They treat each other fairly. Someday it will be the other side's turn.

◂ Summary ▸

The information exchange process is the crucial first stage of the interactive phase of negotiations. In general, it accomplishes three purposes. First, the parties establish open communication by setting, if the situation favors this, a friendly and personal tone. Second, they determine the interest and issues to be negotiated and share information about their perceptions on these matters. Finally, they send signals regarding their respective leverage positions.

Information exchange should be handled differently in different situations. The more the stakes matter relative to the relationship, the more strategic the parties are likely to be. Hard-nosed opening statements and bluffing regarding the issues can be expected in a Transaction situation, whereas the rapport-building effort may be the most important aspect of a Relationship situation. In many cultures of the world, extensive rapport building is a precondition to any negotiation regardless of context.

The preliminary information exchange stage has ended and the bargaining stage has begun when one side or the other makes a concrete, plausible opening offer that requires a reciprocal response. That is our next step in the negotiation process.

◄ INFORMATION EXCHANGE: ►
A CHECKLIST

✓ Establish rapport.
✓ Obtain information on interests, issues, and perceptions. *Probe first, then disclose.*
✓ Signal regarding your leverage.

9

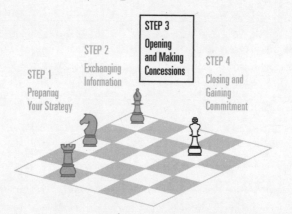

Step 3:
Opening and Making
Concessions

Life cannot subsist in society but by reciprocal concessions.

—SAMUEL JOHNSON

STEP 1
Preparing
Your Strategy

STEP 2
Exchanging
Information

STEP 3
Opening
and Making
Concessions

STEP 4
Closing and
Gaining
Commitment

You have established a degree of rapport, identified the issues you are negotiating, and exchanged signals on your relative leverage position. Now it is time to bargain. This is it: the anxiety-provoking moment that makes accommodating people nervous and starts competitive juices running.

Should you be the first to make a specific proposal? If so, should you open at a fair and reasonable level or more aggressively? What sort of concessions, if any, should you plan to offer? Should you bargain hard to start with and then become more flexible, or should you start with a soft, amiable approach and then plan to harden your position?

Scholars have spent more time researching the dickering and trading procedure at the core of negotiation than any other aspect of the process. This chapter will summarize the highlights of what we know about bargaining and, even more important, show how you can put that knowledge to use.

━ Tactical Bargaining Questions ━

The bargaining stage is dominated by tactics, so let's look at some. As you might expect, good tactics depend on the situation. The right tactic for one situation may not be right for another. And, of course, the other person's style can trump any situational analysis. If you are up against a competitive negotiator, you may need to become temporarily competitive yourself even when the situation seems to call for a softer approach.

Bargaining formally begins when negotiators on one side open with a concrete and, at least in their own mind, plausible offer. It then usually proceeds through a series of reciprocal offers, suggestions, and counteroffers as the parties use various techniques to explore alternatives. Eventually, the process comes down to a distinct "closing and commitment" stage—the subject of the next chapter.

━ Question 1: ━
Should I Be the First to Open?

Let's start with the issue of whether you should open or try to make the other party go first. Many complex negotiations will have lots of issues to discuss, and you may be able to discuss some of them without opening in the sense I am using the word. But there will inevitably come a time when you will have to decide who is going to make the first concrete offer on allocation issues such as price, power, or control. What will you say when someone looks at you the way J. P. Morgan looked at John D. Rockefeller, Jr., in the Mesabi ore field story (see Chapter 7) and growls, "Well, what's your price?"

Many experts say you should never open. The famous film director

Billy Wilder once wanted to hire novelist Raymond Chandler (author of many detective books) to help write the screenplay for a 1940s movie called *Double Indemnity*. Chandler was new to Hollywood but he came ready to negotiate.

In his first meeting with Wilder and the movie's producer, Joe Sistrom, Chandler made the first offer on salary. He demanded that he receive $150 per week—and he warned Wilder that it might take him two or three weeks to finish the project.

Wilder and Sistrom were amused. They had been prepared to pay Chandler $750 per week and knew that movie scripts usually took months to write, not weeks. Had this been a Transaction situation, Chandler would have lost a lot of money.

But the situation was more like the "Einstein versus the Institute" example discussed in Chapter 7, not the "Rockefeller versus Morgan" case. The two Hollywood moguls valued their future relationship with the talented Chandler, so they took pity on him. They called an agent to represent Chandler in the negotiations and started over. Chandler's poorly informed opening was forgotten.

Beatles manager Brian Epstein once made a similar mistake that cost the Beatles considerably more money. He was negotiating for the Beatles' financial share of their first movie, *A Hard Day's Night*. Like Chandler, Epstein knew little about the movie business and opened with what he thought was an aggressive demand: 7.5 percent of the movie's profits. The producers quickly said "yes." They had been prepared to give the Beatles up to 25 percent and were delighted with Epstein's 7.5 percent figure. *A Hard Day's Night* turned out to be a hit, and the Beatles made money—but not as much as they could have.

The Chandler and Beatles stories illustrate the risks you take when you are the first to open. Just keep your mouth shut, the experts counsel, and let the other negotiator name his price. You can always correct him if he is outside the "fair and reasonable" range. And you may be pleasantly surprised to find out that the other side is willing to pay thousands more (or take thousands less) than you expected.

The "never open" rule is easy to remember—but, like most simplistic approaches to negotiation, it is not always good advice. How can you do better? The answer lies in how much information you have. Let's look again at the stories we just discussed.

What was the most important fact common to both Chandler's and Epstein's situations? Neither had experience in the movie business. They did not know enough about the standards and valuation systems used in the business to open with confidence. Being newcomers, they should have sat tight and let the other side do the talking. The same is true anytime you don't know the market value of what you are buying or selling.

If you are well informed about the bargaining range, then you gain an important advantage from opening. When I first started teaching negotiation, I recommended the "never open" rule to my classes. Then one of my better students introduced me to an entrepreneur who had successfully bought and sold literally hundreds of small and medium-sized companies. This man made it his practice to name the first price in every acquisition he did. Being the first to open let him fix the range, he explained to me.

I subsequently learned that there is a substantial and persuasive body of research that supports this entrepreneur's practice. First, by naming the first number, you have a chance to set the zone of realistic expectations for the deal. Your opening often forces the other side to rethink its goals.

Second, social scientists have discovered a psychological quirk they call the "anchor and adjustment" effect. The term refers to a human tendency to be affected by "first impression" numbers thrown into our field of vision. We tend to make adjustments from these often arbitrary reference points.

Researchers have found, for example, that most people seeing the string of numbers $8 \times 7 \times 6 \times 5 \times 4 \times 3 \times 2 \times 1$ for a few seconds estimate that it yields a very high product. Other people, shown the same string in reverse order—$1 \times 2 \times 3 \times 4 \times 5 \times 6 \times 7 \times 8$—think the product is much lower. The two products are identical, so why the different estimates? Because we focus on the first three or four numbers and extrapolate; that is, we anchor and adjust.

In negotiation, research suggests that people who hear high or low numbers as initial starting points are often affected by these numbers and unconsciously adjust their expectations in the direction of the opening number. Of course, a totally outlandish number may trigger a strong negative reaction that could offset this effect. But there is some power in or draw toward these initial numbers nonetheless.

My entrepreneur friend was taking advantage of the opportunity to both lower his opponent's expectations and use the anchor effect. But note well: He did enormous amounts of research before he made a bid to set the range.

Conclusion? Feel free to open if you think your information about market value is as good as or better than your counterpart's. Otherwise, guard against the anchor effect, then ask the other party to open. Finally, remember that the best protection against making a mistake at the opening is negotiating with someone who cares about his or her relationship with you.

◄ Question 2: ►
Should I Open Optimistically or Reasonably?

Okay, either you have decided to open—or the other side opened and it is your move. Should you open aggressively with an optimistic request or make a manifestly fair and reasonable proposal? If you are in a Relationship situation, the answer is obvious: A fair or even accommodating opening is the right move.

How about a Transaction? Assuming that you have some leverage, the research suggests you should open optimistically. Indeed, a recent summary of more than thirty-four bargaining experiments performed between 1960 and 1980 concluded that a hard-line bargaining strategy (open high and concede slowly) is the best approach to transactional bargaining, especially if direct communication between the parties is limited (as may be the case in a home sale or any other transaction mediated by a broker).

That sounds persuasive, you may say, but what exactly is an optimistic opening? I define an optimistic first offer as *the highest (or lowest) number for which there is a supporting standard or argument enabling you to make a presentable case.* Your opening need not be supported by your best argument, just a presentable one.

The difference between an optimistic opening and an outrageous one is this: The outrageous opening has no justification whatever to support it. The optimistic opening, by contrast, is a highly favorable interpretation of some standard or reference point. American lawyers are duty-bound when they argue a legal appeal to make every argument on behalf of their client that they can make "with a straight face." Optimistic openings are like that: You should reach for but not beyond the "straight face" argument.

And remember that in some cultures such as South America, the Middle East, and Africa, anything other than an optimistic opening is a serious social mistake as well as bargaining blunder. For North Americans and some Europeans, part of acclimating to these cultures is getting used to making optimistic (and in some cultures outrageous) opening offers in carpet stores, jewelry shops, and bazaars. Bargaining is a form of recreation in these places.

◄ Why Do Optimistic Openings ►
Work in Transactional Bargaining?

Optimistic openings take advantage of two well-documented psychological tendencies: the contrast principle and the norm of reciprocity. First, let's examine the contrast principle. If I want you to pay me $50 for something and I open with a demand of $75 (supported by a presentable argument about prices that "others have paid"), my $50 final offer looks reasonable by comparison with my opening. If I had opened at $55 instead of $75, and moved down only five dollars before I stopped, you would be less likely to think you had gotten a bargain. An optimistic (but not outrageous) opening sets the other party up to feel both relief and satisfaction (and thus be more willing to say "yes") when the realistic settlement range comes into view.

If you think the contrast principle does not apply to you, think again. It is used successfully against millions of people every day. Why do car dealerships have a special sales force to sell you things *after* you buy a new car? Because they know that you are more likely to spend a couple of hundred dollars on extended warranties and service plans just after you have spent $20,000 on a new vehicle than you would be if you shopped for these things by themselves. The same is true of furniture dealers who sell $75 fabric treatments for your new $1,000 sofa and travel agents who push $150 trip insurance policies just after you book a $3,000 vacation. These add-on sales look inexpensive in comparison to the big money you just paid for the thing you really wanted. But they are usually expensive when compared with the alternatives you could find if you shopped for them separately. That is why the dealers don't want you to leave the store without giving you these strong after-sell pitches.

Second, the optimistic opening permits the person making it to trigger the norm of reciprocity, discussed in Chapter 4. It works like this: Person A makes an optimistic opening; person B rejects it. Person A then moderates his demand by making a significant concession. Person B then feels pressure imposed by the norm of reciprocity to make a reasonable response, or even to say "yes."

Psychologists have found that this "high opening, rejection, then moderation" procedure works for all kinds of requests, not just bargaining demands. In controlled field experiments, scientists have induced people to agree to all manner of things—including volunteering to take underprivileged children on a trip to the zoo, signing petitions, or giving up smoking for short periods of time—simply by asking them for a big favor first, getting a rejection, then presenting the smaller, apparently more reasonable request. The norm of reciprocity induces people to say "yes" much more frequently after they have rejected your first demand than when you open with your modest request.

◄ A Word of Warning on Optimistic Openings ►

Does an optimistic opening *always* work in a Transaction situation? No—but you can anticipate the occasions when it will not.

WHEN YOU LACK LEVERAGE

The first exception concerns leverage: Don't open optimistically if you lack leverage and the other side knows it.

If you are a new college graduate applying for an entry-level position in cities such as San Francisco or Boston, which have a lot of colleges and universities, don't ask for the moon when an employer inquires about your salary expectations. An overly optimistic opening will make you look unreasonable and scare the employer away.

WHEN THE OTHER SIDE WON'T BARGAIN

The second exception concerns special markets in which there is, for one reason or another, no expectation of bargaining. A friend in the management consulting business pointed this out to me.

When someone calls and asks him to do an engagement, he quotes a price and, nine times out of ten, either gets the job or does not. Haggling is not part of the normal engagement process. His asking price conveys a message to his customers about his reputation and sophistication. His prospective customer, meanwhile, is shopping for the right level of sophistication by assembling price quotes. My friend has learned to name a price that is high enough to carry a "premium services" message, but not so high that prospective clients think he is out of their league.

WHEN IT'S MORE THAN JUST A TRANSACTION

As you move from Transactions toward Balanced Concerns situations, in which relationships take on more importance, highly optimistic openings do not work well.

For example, when Wayne Huizenga, the deal maker who built Waste Management, Blockbuster Video, and Republic Industries, makes business acquisitions, his strategy is not to start with lowball offers and move up into a reasonable range after a lot of haggling. Instead, he starts within 5 to 10 percent of the final price he is willing to pay—and negotiates mainly on nonprice issues. Huizenga has firm, fair, high expectations for all his deals—he is an excellent negotiator—but he is not a "haggler."

Why? Because he does his homework. He knows as much or more about the value of the firms he buys as the sellers do. He is also mindful that he is buying from people who have invested their lives in building their businesses. A lowball offer insults their pride. He wants the owners to stay and run their companies as part of his megaenterprises. Relationships matter. "No matter what he does, he's fair about it," says one associate. "He leaves you with the feeling that . . . 'I got, I guess, what I really deserved.'"

In other words, an aggressive highball or lowball opening is usually a bad idea in a Balanced Concerns situation, but an opening offer that reflects legitimately high expectations (see Chapter 2) is still appropriate. Try to find a favorable proposal supported by good, solid arguments (not just "presentable" ones) that still leaves you some room to negotiate.

◄ Question 3: ►
What Sort of Concession Strategy Works Best?

Even if you are inclined to be reasonable in your opening, it pays to leave yourself bargaining room to make concessions during the course of negotiations. When I was a lawyer negotiating lawsuit settlements, I used to think that the haggling aspect of negotiation was a silly, pointless ritual. Both sides knew they were going to end up somewhere between the plaintiff's and defendant's initial numbers. Why not just name an objectively fair figure, stick to it, and settle the case?

The answer to this question can be found in a story and some research. The story involves the automobile dealers of America. In the early 1990s, sensing that Americans did not like to haggle about price at car dealerships, roughly two thousand dealers across the United States instituted "no haggle," one-low-price selling policies for new cars. It was a big deal. Corporate America was finally listening to consumers who wanted a fair price for cars just as they wanted a fair price for soap. The dealers were going to transform car buying from an anxiety-provoking, pressured ritual into a simple event like going to the shopping mall.

Within a few years, about half of these dealerships—more than one thousand of them—had dropped the policy, and more were dropping it every day. Why? For one thing, the group of people who genuinely hated haggling turned out to be much smaller than anticipated (only about 15 percent of Americans). In addition, many people, armed with abundant information on car pricing from Internet Web sites, wanted to use this newfound bargaining power. Finally, people wanted the satisfaction of telling their friends about the "great deal" they had negotiated. One consumer expert who studied the decline of the "no haggle" policy explained it this way: "Automotive consumers need to feel that they get a good deal when they purchase a vehicle, and, for most, the only way they feel that they get a good deal is through negotiation."

Research confirms that people receiving concessions often feel better about the bargaining process than people who get a single firm, "fair" price. In fact, they feel better even when they end up paying *more than they otherwise might*. One experiment compared three different concession strategies: (1) start high, then refuse to move, (2) start moderately, then refuse to move, and (3) start high, then gradually concede to the moderate point. The last of these strategies was the most successful by far. More agreements were concluded using this strategy. The parties employing the third strategy made more money per transaction than did those using the first two. And the people who faced negotiators using the third strategy reported much higher levels of satisfaction with their agreements than did people who faced those who refused to move.

Concessions are the language of cooperation. They tell the other negotiator in concrete, believable terms that you accept the legitimacy of his or her demands and recognize the necessity of sacrifice on your own part to secure a joint decision.

◄ Concession Making in Different Situations ►

Now that you know *why* we need to make concessions, just exactly what is the best way to do so? Once again, it depends on the situation in which you find yourself. Let's look at each of the four quadrants in the Situational Matrix and see which concession-making strategy works best. I have reprinted the Situational Matrix from Chapter 7 here for your reference.

TACIT COORDINATION (QUADRANT IV)

The concession-making practice for Tacit Coordination situations need not detain us. As the driving-at-the-intersection example in Chapter 7 showed, avoiding needless disputes and accommodating when conflict cannot be avoided is the best practice.

If accommodation is not possible (the other side refuses to go first and you are stuck in a "mutual accommodation" impasse) don't worry about concession tactics. Just try to solve the problem in a genuine, helpful way. Go first if you must.

RELATIONSHIPS (QUADRANT II)

When the relationship counts more than the issue in dispute, the best concession strategy is accommodation. As the example of Albert Einstein's negotiation with the Institute for Advanced Study showed, the goal is to find out what the other party wants and *give it to him or her with*

FIGURE 9.1
The Situational Matrix: A Strategy Guide

Perceived Conflict over Stakes

		High	Low
Perceived Importance of Future Relationship Between Parties	High	**I: Balanced Concerns** (Business partnership, joint venture, or merger) *Best strategies:* Problem solving or compromise	**II: Relationships** (Marriage, friendship, or work team) *Best strategies:* Accommodation, problem solving, or compromise
	Low	**III: Transactions** (Divorce, house sale, or market transaction) *Best strategies:* Competition, problem solving, or compromise	**IV: Tacit Coordination** (Highway intersection or airplane seating) *Best strategies:* Avoidance, accommodation, or compromise

interest. Money is not the issue. If accommodation is impractical for some reason (the other party will not tell you what he or she wants), propose some simple and self-sacrificing compromise. Try to make the other party feel appreciated.

As simple as all this sounds, supercompetitive people have a "tin ear" for this advice. Because they treat most interactions as games and have trouble trusting others, they have no instinct for accommodation. They butt into line to get their seat on the airplane, and they haggle too hard when they should be more concerned with the relationship.

Some useful advice for competitive people who find themselves in situations calling for diplomacy: Get help from someone with better people skills. For those of us stuck negotiating with competitive people who do not understand that in some situations the stakes don't matter, keep your sense of humor, accommodate, and consider whether you want to continue dealing with a person who doesn't understand the value of relationships.

TRANSACTIONS (QUADRANT III)

When the stakes are all that matter, research shows that a firm concession strategy works best. In simple, price-only negotiations (what scholars call "distributive bargaining" situations), classic haggling is the rule: Open optimistically, hold for a bit, show a willingness to bargain, then make a series of progressively smaller concessions as you close in on your expectation level. Cooperative people may not be very good at the haggling game, but they must nevertheless learn to play it in competitive situations.

Note carefully: Hagglers' concessions initially converge on their expectation levels—not their absolute bottom lines. Why? Because the declining size of hagglers' concessions (in either percentage or absolute money terms) sends a powerful signal that they are getting close to a resistance point. *They want you to think that their expectation level is their "bottom line."* This is a bluff.

If you resist at their initial target level, hagglers will reluctantly continue making concessions toward their real bottom line—the point at which they would really rather walk away than do the deal.

Try this test sometime at a used-furniture store, bazaar, or other place of business where haggling is expected. Identify something you want and make a very low, but not outrageous offer. Let the seller make a concession and make another small move of your own. Then make a display of your cash or checkbook—in other words, identify yourself as a serious buyer. Keep insisting on your price until you hear the storekeeper say, in so many words, "no."

When you hear the "no," politely but firmly head for the door. As often as not, the seller will stop you before you leave the store and make a further concession. At that point it is your choice whether to keep bargaining or close the sale. Do not expect too many more concessions, however. Sellers do have their pride.

In more important, high-stakes deals, you should also be careful not to make big concessions too early. Start slowly. Why? Because big moves made early in bargaining can confuse the other side.

Let's say you are in a negotiation with a big chain to sell your small video store business. You will have no future role in the venture—it is a straight buyout. You have several issues before you: the price, the "currency" (whether you will take the price in cash or the acquiring firm's stock), and the closing date for the deal. The larger firm opens with an aggressive bid that covers all three issues: a low price, an all-stock deal, and a delayed closing date (which we'll assume favors the buyer in this deal).

What happens if, in your response, you move straight to your bottom line, hoping to conclude negotiations quickly and amicably? You propose a medium valuation (which is where you want to end up), accept the all-stock proposal, and ask for closing in two months (a reasonable time). You are surprised when the buyer's next offer moves just inches off its low valuation and keeps the far-off closing. The buyer does not even mention your agreement to the all-stock aspect of its offer. You begin to feel angry.

What is the problem here? When you make large concessions early in high-stakes transactional bargaining, you send a set of messages. One message is: *I really want this deal.* That message has leverage implications, and the other side may develop high expectations regarding the final price. It will want to test that hypothesis. If you suddenly dig in and refuse to move after being extremely flexible at the start, the other side may have trouble adjusting its expectations in light of the first impression you gave. You may even lose the deal.

The second message you send is: *The issues I conceded were not important to me.* By agreeing completely to the all-stock idea right away, you signaled your satisfaction with that term. But guess what? The other party may give you zero credit for this concession because you gave it up so easily. You have now told them, in effect, "I did not want cash."

Consider the other side's point of view. The acquiring firm may have been deeply worried that you would demand cash. It might have been willing to raise its price significantly or pay you some cash on the side for a consulting contract to induce you to use its stock as currency. But now you will get nothing for this concession.

Negotiation teachers call this phenomenon "concession devaluation." This is a fancy name for the truth contained in an old saying: "What we obtain too cheaply, we esteem too lightly." Competitive opponents will naturally take advantage of everything you give them, but even accommodating people will alter their expectations in the light of your off-handed concession behavior. If you give up something without even a comment, the other side's estimate of the value of your concession actually goes down because of your casual treatment of the issue. "I guess we valued this item incorrectly in our planning," the other side's negotiators say to themselves. "She didn't really care about getting cash. If the issue isn't worth anything to her, it isn't worth anything to us, either."

◄ Issue Trading Versus Haggling in ► Transactions: Integrative Bargaining

If many issues are on the table, concession making in high-stakes negotiations often takes the form of "issue trading" and "package bargaining" instead of simple haggling. Negotiation scholars use the term "distributive bargaining" to describe simple haggling (people are "dividing the pie") and the term "integrative bargaining" to describe the more complex process of trading off between issues (people are "making the pie bigger" by matching or "integrating" their interests, priorities, and differences). Many deals contain elements of both concession-making strategies.

How do classic hagglers handle a high-stakes negotiation with many different issues? Simple: They attack each issue one at a time and use the distributive procedure I described above to reach their desired expectation level on each issue. They start high, concede slowly, and close on issue 1. Then they repeat the process for issue 2. And so on.

But this simple strategy carries a higher risk of impasse than does the alternative method of issue trading. There may be some issues on which the other party cannot compromise at all. The haggling procedure also ignores the likelihood that different issues will be worth more to one party than the other. I care more about the closing date; they care more about the cash-or-stock issue. Pure haggling when there are differences to exploit leaves money on the table.

How does one engage in integrative bargaining? By identifying the issues, fears, and risks that are most important to each side and then "logrolling"—accommodating each other's most important interests and priorities in exchange for reciprocal accommodations.

If the concession rule for haggling is "Start high and concede slowly," the rule of thumb for integrative bargaining is to *make big moves on your "little" (less important) issues and little moves on your "big" (most important) issues.* But remember the danger of concession devaluation and never give up anything (even a "little" issue) without a demonstration that the concession is meaningful to you.

When both sides open at their highest defendable position on all their issues—but then show flexibility on the ones that have less urgency for them—they communicate important information about their respective priorities. As the parties observe where they are making headway and where they are encountering strong resistance, they "chart" the other side's needs and desires. This gives them guidelines on how integrative concession making should proceed.

After a discussion of all the issues (without making any concrete opening offers on any of them), issue trading often proceeds through package bargaining. One side proposes a total package, including a demand on each issue. The other side responds with a total package of its own, reflecting its aspirations. Up to this point, this procedure looks just like haggling, but it changes after the openings.

In their next move, the side that opened may make concessions on one or two of its "little" issues, making a display of its sacrifices, but hold firm on its more important priorities. The other side reciprocates, and after several rounds each side begins to figure out which issues are more important to the other.

By dealing with entire packages and agreeing that no issue is closed until all issues have been decided, both parties retain a high degree of flexibility. If, later in the process, they find themselves at an impasse over an issue both consider vital (such as price), they have the option of going back to earlier packages and exploring different combinations without being locked in to any particular concession on any particular issue.

Parties often trade issues in clusters, using a formulation well known to negotiation experts: *IF you give us what we want on issues A and B, THEN we might consider concessions on issues X and Y.* The "if . . . then" formula ensures that you never make a concession without linking it to a mutual concession from the other party. And of course, issues A and B are the most important ones to the party making the offer while issues X and Y tend to be lesser priorities. The parties may eventually need to haggle and fight over some of the issues that both think are important, but they have "issue-traded" on the ones that each can concede at relatively low cost.

Let's go back to the example in which you are selling your video store to a big chain and see how you might proceed using integrative bargaining. First, you would be better off opening with an aggressive demand: a high price for your company, an all-cash deal, and a rapid closing. As the negotiations progress, you might then hold to your high price and use your flexibility on the cash-or-stock issue to trade for more money: *"IF you can raise your price to meet my needs, THEN I will consider forgoing cash for part of the price and could agree to a closing within two months."*

The buyer might respond as follows: "We appreciate your flexibility on the currency issue, but we cannot pay the price you are asking and still do the deal. However, *IF you will agree to accept our stock as currency for the whole transaction, THEN we can offer you an increase of 5 percent on the price and we may be able to discuss a consulting contract with you that will pay you a little cash over the next six months."* And so it would go.

Integrative bargaining is more skillful than haggling, but it is no less competitive. In Transactions, therefore, don't be surprised if the other side resorts to firm tactics such as insisting you make two concessions before it makes one and stalling the negotiations at an impasse even as it uses integrative bargaining techniques.

Firm tactics in support of high expectations help each party test the other's leverage and see if the other side is inclined toward accommodation and compromise. Any investment banker or other professional deal maker will tell you that high-stakes negotiations can go through many tense episodes before each side is satisfied that it has tested the other party's limits and is ready to close.

➤ Making Concessions in ➤
Balanced Concerns Situations

In a Balanced Concerns situation, where both the future relationship and the stakes are roughly equal in importance for both sides, a variety of different bargaining and problem-solving procedures work. The goal is to address as many priorities as possible, make sure that each side gets its "fair share" on such issues as price, and maintain good working relationships between the parties going forward.

Because the stakes matter, you should still come to the table with high expectations. You will want to move slowly on your least important issues first and use the conditional "if . . . then" formulation for concession making. All trades should be reciprocal.

Because the relationship matters to both sides, more imaginative kinds of bargaining tactics are both possible and desirable than is the case in Transactions. Aggressive, hardball moves and transparent gambits do not work well. They are too bruising to personal feelings and usually obscure the shared interests the parties bring to the table. Instead, each party needs to probe more deeply into the real needs underlying the other side's demands and seek imaginative solutions.

Suppose we face the same video store acquisition as I discussed above, but the acquiring firm desperately needs you to stay with the company after the deal and run your store for at least another year. The acquiring company still wants to pay no more than a fair price, but now it wants a relationship with you, not just your store. How might this change its approach to concession making?

First, the buyer will want to avoid a bruising tug-of-war over price that might ruin the prospects for a good working relationship. It will be less likely to open by "talking to the mountain," and, if it does, it might very well explicitly describe its opening as merely "a way to get us started" or as "fully negotiable based on your needs."

The buyer's negotiators should also be more interested in developing or maintaining trust for the future relationship. This means giving you more (though by no means complete) information on their priorities and needs during the information exchange stage.

Once the opening round is over, they may begin proposing several different packages *at the same time,* asking you to identify the one that you prefer. You may get to evaluate a medium-price, all-stock, delayed-closing proposal next to a deal involving a low-price, fifty-fifty cash-and-stock structure with an early closing. This procedure helps you see how the issues trade off against one another from their point of view. You might adjust one of the proposals as you see fit and pass it back across the table. That proposal would then be the baseline from which you both move forward.

Finally, they will very likely get creative in their effort to bridge your mutual interests. Moving "outside the box" of the term sheet, they may offer you stock options with vesting rights at some future date and give you bonuses for hitting new, profitable sales targets. These ways of paying you are designed to encourage you to stay with the firm long enough to cash in on the bonuses while you introduce their people to your customers and show them the ins and outs of your business.

Interest-based, problem-solving approaches to bargaining work well in a Balanced Concerns situation. Why? Because they give parties a chance to "make the pie bigger" both within the context of the transaction at hand (by using integrative bargaining techniques) and the larger framework of the parties' ongoing relationship (by creatively exploiting their ability to help each other in the future).

Indeed, if the parties have a high degree of trust in each other, a problem-solving approach to bargaining may not involve concessions at all in the usual back-and-forth sense. Rather, the parties may spend much of their time dreaming up new ideas that might meet everyone's needs. Research suggests that the more options people develop in this sort of brainstorming process, the more likely they will be to stumble over something that works far better than a simple compromise.

Reseach suggests that genuine conflict between people over their legitimate goals, which many well-meaning people try to avoid or minimize in the name of harmonious human relations, actually helps energize the collaborative problem-solving process in a Balanced Concerns situation. A clash between two people with well-considered high expectations can motivate creative thinking as both sides strive to solve their problem, maintain their principles, keep their relationships in working order, and hit their targets. People with a problem-solving style have a talent for using conflict to keep the bargaining process going without letting the conflict degenerate into a personal battle.

◄ A Brief Note on the ►
"Good Guy/Bad Guy" Routine

There is one concession-making ploy that competitive negotiators use so often in high-stakes deals that it deserves a special mention. This is the "good guy/bad guy" routine. You know you are up against this when you find yourself liking one of the other side's negotiators and wishing another one would jump off a cliff. Another sign: The other side's representative tells you that your demands sound reasonable to *her*—but that someone else who isn't there (the bad guy) would never agree.

The good guy/bad guy gambit draws its effectiveness from a number of psychological phenomena we have met before. The good guy opens the negotiation with some friendly rapport-building chatter about shared interests and goals. The good guy appeals to our tendency to like people who agree with us and who are familiar and similar, as discussed in Chapters 4 and 8.

The bad guy then takes over when it comes to the opening. He opens at an outrageous level or attacks our proposal, as the case may be. This aggressive, confrontational moment startles us, creating a vision of potential loss as we see the deal disappearing and begin thinking about the further compromises we may need to make. The bad guy wants to lower our expectations and anchor us at his end of the bargaining range so we will make our adjustments from there.

Just about when we are ready to quit because the bad guy is not moving on anything, the good guy steps back in and insists that the bad guy make a concession. This makes the good guy an advocate for the norm of reciprocity and we like him even more. We start looking at the good guy as a champion of reasonableness and begin taking his advice about what needs to be done to bridge the gap between our side and the bad guy.

In this way, the good guy/bad guy routine takes advantage of the contrast effect we discussed in connection with optimistic openings. The good guy—who might appear demanding if viewed alone—looks reasonable, if not saintly, when seen sitting next to Godzilla. You are more likely to make concessions to the good guy because he seems so much nicer and his demands look so comparatively attractive.

The way to counter the good guy/bad guy routine is simple: Name the tactic publicly at the table and demand clarification on the issue of authority. Fight fire with fire.

"It looks as if one of you is playing the good guy and the other is playing the bad guy," you might say. "I had hoped we could use a more straightforward process to reach a fair deal. Before we proceed further, I would like to know who has authority to agree to what. I cannot negotiate with people who lack authority to close."

If the bad guy is a lawyer or other adviser, throw him or her out. Insist on trading directly with the decision maker. Let the "deal makers" take over from the "deal breakers."

◄ Summary ►

As you move through the opening and concession-making stage, remember that your strategy and tactics should be determined by three main elements: the *situation* (Transaction, Relationship, or Balanced Concerns?), your *leverage* (who has the most to lose?), and your own and your counterpart's *style* (are you or the other person predictably competitive or cooperative?).

Each of the four quadrants in the Situational Matrix carries its own presumed best concession strategy: competitive for Transactions, accommodating for Relationships, and interest-based problem solving for Balanced Concerns. Compromise is a useful tool—though not a preferred strategy—in all three situations.

As your leverage goes down, your need to soften your approach rises. And as your leverage rises, your need to accommodate goes down—regardless of the situation you are in.

Opening and Concession-Making Summary

Tactical Decision

		Should I Open?	*How to Open?*	*Concession Strategy*
Situation	Trans-actions	When in doubt, don't. But OK if you have good information.	Optimistically (highest or lowest figure supported by presentable argument).	Firmness: Concede slowly in diminishing amounts toward expectation level.
	Balanced Concerns	Same as above.	Fairly (highest or lowest figure supported by solid argument).	Big moves on little issues, little moves on big issues; brainstorm options, present several packages at once.
	Relation-ships	Yes.	Generously.	Accommodation or fair compromise.
	Tacit Coordina-tion	Yes, but avoid conflict if possible.	Do whatever it takes to solve the problem.	Accommodation.

10

Step 4: Closing and Gaining Commitment

Make every bargain clear and plain
That none may afterwards complain.
—ENGLISH RHYME

The master is not he who begins but he who finishes.
—SLOVAKIAN FOLK SAYING

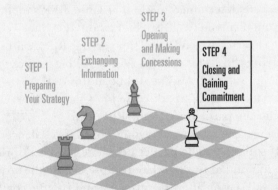

STEP 1
Preparing
Your Strategy

STEP 2
Exchanging
Information

STEP 3
Opening
and Making
Concessions

STEP 4
Closing and
Gaining
Commitment

The negotiation process concludes with an endgame: closing and gaining commitment. Closing can be smooth and simple or a time of high anxiety. People who like to negotiate relish the fast-paced tactics that can surround this stage. Those who do not like bargaining sometimes feel uncomfortable and pressured.

And if closing gambits such as splitting the difference, walkouts, and ultimatums do not raise your blood pressure, there is always the problem of securing commitment to actual performance. Is the other side's word enough to cement the deal? Perhaps. But what other steps may be necessary to ensure that the other party will keep its promise?

◄ Calling the Barbarians ►

To start, let's examine the final stage of bargaining in one of the biggest, most hotly contested deals of the twentieth century: the 1988 sale of American tobacco and food giant RJR Nabisco (RJR). The full story of this remarkable transaction is chronicled in *Barbarians at the Gate*.

RJR Chairman Ross Johnson set the sale in motion by proposing a management-led leveraged buyout (LBO) with financial backing from the upstart investment banking department of Shearson Lehman Hutton. Johnson's initial offer: a record-breaking $17.6 billion, or $75 per share for stock that had been trading in the forties prior to Johnson's bid. Johnson's stunning move sparked interest from several possible buyers, but the contest came down to a test between two rival teams: Johnson and his friends from Shearson versus Henry Kravis and Wall Street powerhouse Kohlberg Kravis Roberts and Company (KKR).

Both sides were determined to win this battle. KKR's reputation as the premier buyout firm on Wall Street was on the line. When he first learned that Shearson intended to finance the RJR deal without KKR, Kravis reportedly said, "This deal is so visible, so big . . . I can't lay off. We have to be in on this deal. And we will be in this deal."

Using the Situational Matrix discussed in Chapter 7, exactly what sort of situation did the parties face in the RJR deal?

Many business mergers and acquisitions are Balanced Concerns (Quadrant I) situations. The parties negotiate hard over price, but they must also be mindful of future relationships because the acquired firm's management will stay on after the purchase and run the company. These conflicting incentives somewhat soften the bargaining tactics parties use.

Johnson and his group had wanted a "cozy," relationship-based negotiation with Johnson's handpicked board. But Kravis spoiled that by entering with his own bid. With two potential buyers, the board put RJR up

for sale in a hotly contested and legally regulated "auction." Personal relationships mattered little. Money—a lot of it—was the sole issue. The
RJR deal became a pure Transaction (Quadrant III). Competitive bargaining tactics were the order of the day.

"WE NEED AN EXTENSION"

We enter the scene near the end of the story. It is 12:30 P.M. on November 30, 1988. Kravis has made a "final," mind-boggling $24 billion
bid for RJR: $106 per share. He has given the board only thirty minutes
to make a decision. Thirty minutes from now the bid will be considered
withdrawn and Kravis will walk away.

Kravis is sitting with his partner George Roberts and several advisers in
a cramped office at a New York law firm. The two men are tense but
optimistic.

Down the hall, a special committee of "outside" directors from RJR's
board (members who are not employed as executives by RJR) is meeting.
They are considering Kravis's $106-per-share offer and have managed to
keep the auction going without letting either the Shearson side or the
KKR side know the other side's latest bid. The negotiations have been going on for days. The pressure for a final decision is enormous.

Unbeknownst to Kravis, Ross Johnson's team has just submitted a last-
minute bid made up of both cash and a substantial component of "junk
bonds" and other fancy securities. The bid totals $108 per share, slightly
more than Kravis's $106. The bid has placed the board in a quandary.

If the board sells to Kravis for $106 with Johnson's bid for $108 in
hand, it faces lawsuits from RJR shareholders. The board's legal duty is
to sell RJR to the highest bidder. But the board is not sure if Johnson's
bid is really worth $108. The high-risk junk bonds make this uncertain.

So the board needs time to analyze Johnson's bid—and time is exactly
what Kravis's deadline has taken away from them. The board sends its
lawyer, Peter Atkins, down the hall to negotiate with Kravis for an extension to KKR's 1 P.M. deadline.

At twenty minutes to one, Atkins knocks at Kravis and Roberts's
door. The two men look up in anticipation. This is the moment they
have waited for. They are about to do the biggest deal in the history of
capitalism.

"We have received something," Atkins says cryptically, "and we can't
live with your one o'clock deadline. We need an extension."

Kravis and Roberts both bristle. They know exactly what the "something" must be—an offer from their rivals. They had imposed their deadline to block just this move.

"Absolutely not," says Kravis.

Let's push "pause" on the replay at this point. Kravis has imposed a deadline, the RJR board has attempted to wiggle out of it, and Kravis has responded. What are the parties up to? What psychological triggers lie behind this fast-paced maneuvering? Let's look at two key psychological factors that often play a role in the closing stage of negotiation, the "scarcity effect" and "overcommitment." As we do so, we'll continue to follow the RJR story to see what happened.

◄ Closing Factor 1: ►
Injecting Urgency by Using the Scarcity Effect

One of the most primal and powerful psychological levers in every negotiation is what psychologists call the scarcity effect. This label refers to our human tendency to want things more when we think the supply is running out. As discussed in Chapter 6 on leverage, your ability to get what you want in negotiation often depends on the other side's perception that it has something to lose from a "no deal" result. You can and often should appeal to scarcity arguments from the very beginning of the information exchange stage. But it is usually at the closing stage that these arguments are tested most strenuously.

As stated in the research, "Scarcity enhances the value of anything that can be possessed, is useful to its possessor, and is transferable from one person to another." When we think something we want is or is about to become scarce, we push an imaginary panic button labeled "Act Now" to avoid feeling regret that we missed an opportunity.

When the weather report calls for heavy snow, it is the scarcity effect that sends people racing to grocery stores to buy up all the milk and other perishable necessities. Place a single cookie on the dining room table in front of two young, hungry, and otherwise preoccupied kids and then say, "There's a cookie on the table. Who wants it?" The ensuing scramble is living proof of the scarcity effect. Lease new office space for your company with only three windowed offices and six senior executives, and you may see a grown-up version of the same behavior.

Clever negotiators use many devices to exploit the scarcity effect and bring the bargaining to a crisis. Several of them were on display in the RJR negotiation story.

SCARCITY CAUSED BY MANY PEOPLE
WANTING THE SAME THING: COMPETITION

First, astute negotiators try to emphasize that what they have is in great demand, and the supply is dwindling fast. They discuss their other offers or competing opportunities, hoping their opponents will feel the added pressure of the scarcity response and push the "Act Now" panic button to beat the competition.

In the RJR case, the board constantly emphasized its other offers, trying to get both sides to raise their price. Indeed, it was the auction atmosphere that prompted Kravis to inject his own note of urgency, the 1 P.M. deadline.

There really *was* another offer in the RJR case, so the scarcity was real. Only one firm would get RJR. But in many competitive situations the other side will try to bluff about scarcity, creating a vision of competition even when yours is the only real offer on the table.

Bluffs are a common event in negotiation, particularly in Transactions. I will discuss the ethics of bluffing in the next chapter. For now, it is enough to know why people bluff about things like competition: They do it to trigger the scarcity effect in the other party.

SCARCITY CAUSED BY TIME
RUNNING OUT: DEADLINES

A second tactic that triggers a sense of scarcity is a deadline. Kravis used this technique to match the board's use of the competitive auction. The goal of a deadline is simple: to create the sense that time is running out on the opportunity. Here today, gone tomorrow.

Henry Kravis was one of only a few people in the world with the financial clout and credibility needed to raise the $20 billion-plus to buy RJR. His rivals in the RJR deal were untested. By setting a firm deadline, Kravis sent a signal to the board that his participation should not be taken for granted. His goal? To stop the auction and obtain a quick, favorable decision.

Deadlines are most effective when they are linked to events in the outside world that the parties do not control. In many corporate merger negotiations, one of the firms may have a quarterly reporting deadline to disclose "material corporate developments" to securities regulators. Neither side wants to disclose the merger talks in this regulatory filing because disclosure might tip off others that the target firm is for sale. This would raise the price to the buyer and cause the seller's management to lose control of the deal. The regulatory deadline thus becomes a highly credible deal deadline.

The scarcity effect is doubled if a credible deadline combines in the other party's mind with scarcity based on high demand. The combination of competition and a deadline sounds like this: "You have until noon tomorrow to accept our offer, after which time we will sell to [or buy from] the other party who has expressed interest." Research shows that concession rates skyrocket in both amount and frequency as the negotiating parties perceive that they are under a deadline imposed by stiff competition.

Kravis was not able to get this double-whammy effect from his deadline both because there was no credible outside event dictating his deadline and because he did not have another company he planned to buy for his $20 billion-plus if he walked away from the RJR deal. The RJR board, on the other hand, did have another buyer. It could have maximized the effect of this leverage by imposing a deadline of its own, but it realized that a deal of this unprecedented size required more rather than less time to manage effectively.

A final way negotiators introduce a vision of scarcity through deadlines is to set time limits on certain elements of an existing offer. When the time runs out, these terms "explode," leaving a less attractive offer on the table. Firms recruiting at business and other professional schools sometimes give the students deadlines for accepting employment offers that include favorable terms such as cash bonuses or priority in selecting job sites if students accept right away.

The overall offer of employment is still good after these "exploding" terms disappear, but students short on cash take the extra benefits very seriously. They see real money disappearing if they delay their decision. In more complex deals, "exploding" terms can include favorable interest or financing rates, preferential delivery terms, and so on.

The overall effect of threats to withdraw special benefits is the same induced by a deadline for the whole deal: Here today, gone tomorrow. You had better "Act Now."

SCARCITY CAUSED BY WALKOUTS

Perhaps the most dramatic method of inducing a scarcity effect is to give the other side a "take it or leave it" ultimatum and then, when the other party protests, get up from the table and walk away. Nothing quite matches the emotional punch of watching a deal you want literally walk out the door.

All walkouts look spontaneous, but many are pure theater. If the other side is relatively naive and eager to do the deal, an experienced, competitive negotiator can use a walkout to play on its fears, dramatizing the need for quick capitulation. Walkouts also underline the importance of especially important issues.

There were no walkouts at the end of the RJR deal, but examples are easy to find elsewhere. Donald Trump has walked out of deals so often that the "Trump walkout" is a trademark of his style. Deal maker Wayne Huizenga's colorful career, chronicled in *The Making of Blockbuster*, is also littered with walkout stories.

In the early 1980s, for example, Huizenga and his partner Steven Berrard were about to pay $4 million for a company owned by a family in New Orleans. The closing was at a law office. The last issue on the table was $100,000 in cash residing in a company bank account. Huizenga told the family that the $100,000 would be his after the closing, and they replied just as emphatically that the money would stay with them.

"OK boys, let's go home," said Huizenga, packing his briefcase. No one moved. "Let's go, I said!" Huizenga barked and led his team out of the room and down the hall.

"Wayne, are you crazy? Over one hundred thousand dollars?" pleaded Berrard as they walked away.

"They're never going to let us get to the elevator," said Huizenga. Just then, the family's lawyer popped his head out of the door and called for them to return. Huizenga got his money.

To summarize, the scarcity effect is an emotional response, not a rational one. Manipulative negotiators use it to inject urgency and even panic into an otherwise reasoned process. Sometimes they are telling the truth—there really are other offers, a lot of demand, and a real deadline. Other times they are bluffing, hoping you will push the panic button and close the deal. It is always a matter of judgment—informed by your understanding of the leverage situation—that tips the balance in the tense moments when you must decide to yield or stand up to an attempt to push your panic button.

⊷ Back to the Barbarians ⊶

With our knowledge of the scarcity effect, let's return to the law office where Henry Kravis is negotiating with the RJR board over his deadline. Should Kravis stick to his deadline or grant an extension? There is no outside force dictating the deadline, so the answer depends heavily on Kravis's analysis of his leverage. Which side, Kravis or the RJR board, has the most to lose if Kravis walks away at this point?

Let's reason it out. If Kravis sticks to his deadline and walks out, he keeps his money but loses his chance to win the "deal of the century." The board, on the other hand, still has a buyer and the deal can still be done at a record-setting price. So Kravis faces scarcity, but the board does not.

At 1:15 P.M. (fifteen minutes after their original "drop-dead" deadline) Kravis's group called in Atkins as well as a member of the board's special committee, Charles Hugel. Kravis agreed to extend his deadline to 2 P.M. if the board would agree to pay KKR $45 million. This money, $1 million per minute, would cover part of KKR's expenses if it failed to win the contest.

The board was consulted. It agreed. The advisers scribbled the terms on a yellow pad. Everyone signed. The board had until 2 P.M. to consider KKR's $106 offer.

⊷ Closing Factor 2: ⊶
Overcommitment to the Bargaining Process

Before we press on to see what finally happened to Kravis in the RJR case, let's look at a second psychological phenomenon that came into play that day in 1988. Psychologists call it overcommitment.

Overcommitment derives from our human desire to avoid admitting failure or accepting loss when we have invested heavily in a prior course of action or decision. The more time someone invests in an initially sensible activity, the more committed he or she becomes to seeing it through, even though the decision may no longer make sense.

Let's begin with a simple, nonnegotiation illustration of overcommitment. Imagine you are at an amusement park and hear about a popular "splash and crash" ride. When you arrive at the ride there is a line, but you decide to give it a try. You have stood there two or three minutes, not moving much, when a park employee announces that the waiting time will be an hour and a half. Do you stay in line or go do something else?

Now imagine the same situation, *but this time the employee announces the news after you have stood in line for forty-five minutes.* The employee tells you that the line will take an hour and half to clear for people just entering it and for you it will take an additional forty-five minutes. Do you stay in line for the extra forty-five minutes or drop out and do something else?

Research on overcommitment suggests you are more likely to quit the line in case 1 than in case 2, even though the total waiting time is identical. Why? Because in case 2, you have invested a full forty-five minutes that you will "lose" by dropping out of line. In case 1, you "lose" only a few minutes. Once you have made an initial, significant investment in waiting, you are inclined to invest more time to achieve a realizable goal.

◄ Leveraging Loss Aversion ►

Psychologists, casino owners, and Wall Street stockbrokers have all profited for years from this well-documented human quirk of loss aversion. People who play slot machines often feel an urge to "get back to even" once they start to lose money. They keep pouring in tokens, throwing good money after bad. Inexperienced investors are reluctant to sell their losing stocks, hoping that these unlucky investments will turn around and bounce back to the break-even point. So they sell their winners and hold their losers, exactly the opposite of what many professional portfolio managers do.

How does this self-defeating psychological quirk apply to negotiation? As we invest increasingly significant amounts of time, energy, and other resources *in the actual negotiation process,* we become more and more committed to closing just the way the person in the amusement park line becomes increasingly determined to get to the ride as more and more time passes.

The overcommitment phenomenon can occur spontaneously even when the other side is acting in good faith. But manipulative opponents can string negotiations out solely for the purpose of getting us overcommitted. They spring their trap just before the closing by apologetically introducing a last-minute demand that is "essential" to the agreement. "We've come so far," they plead. "Don't let all this time and effort be wasted." Rather than face the loss of an unsuccessful negotiation, we may be more inclined to give them at least some of what they want and save the deal.

Overcommitment, in combination with the contrast effect discussed in Chapter 9, explains another common closing tactic used by slick negotiators that is called the nibble. The "nibbler" modestly requests small favors just before a deal closes. In the context of a lengthy and complicated negotiation, most people do not want to spoil either the deal or the relationship by quibbling over such small items. They often make the requested concessions. By nibbling at all their contracts, however, professional negotiators can add as much as 3 to 5 percent in additional value to their deals over a year's time.

The antidote to overcommitment and nibbling is obvious. If you know you are negotiating with a nibbler, hold something back to give away at the end. If the other party is less familiar to you, keep your eye on your goals, make sure the other party is just as invested in the negotiation process as you are, and do not respond sympathetically to last-minute demands. We would be outraged if someone tried to charge us extra money to get on the amusement park ride after we had patiently waited for an hour with our ticket in hand. You should have the same attitude about last-minute requests in negotiation. At the very least you should insist on a reciprocal concession.

◄ A Final Look at Kravis and RJR ►

Now back to Kravis. Just prior to the 2 P.M. deadline, Shearson submitted a new junk bond bid, this time for an astronomical $112 per share. Kravis responded by waiving his deadline and submitting a final cash bid of $108. During the next seven hours, the parties jockeyed for position and measured the ever-increasing risks of bidding at levels no investment banker had ever seen before. And time took its toll on the KKR team, which became increasingly committed, some would say overcommitted, to closing the deal.

In the end, the board gave Kravis one last chance to top Johnson's $112 junk bond bid. After tense consultations with his team, Kravis placed his highest and last offer of $109 per share (more than $25 billion in all) on the table. The board ultimately determined that Johnson's speculative junk bond bid for $112 and Kravis's more reliable bid for $109 were essentially equal. At 9:15 P.M., the board decided in favor of KKR based on KKR's greater credibility and experience in raising money of this magnitude.

It was a sweet victory for a fierce competitor. But you can now be the judge of whether Kravis played his hand wisely. Which factor played the greater role in determining the final price—bargaining dynamics or business analysis? The combination of Kravis's competitive spirit, the scarcity effect, and overcommitment had a lot to do with the way the deal worked out. The conventional wisdom today is that Kravis paid too much for RJR.

◄ Softer Closing Tactics: ► Shall We Split the Difference?

The closing tactics we have covered arise in a number of consumer and business settings, but let's be honest—they are the exception in most of our lives. By far the largest number of our negotiations relate to people and firms with which we have ongoing relationships. Competitive tactics such as deadlines and other scarcity effect ploys may have a role in relational negotiations, but "softer" closing techniques are the rule when the relationship matters. We don't tell people we want to work with to take it or leave it and then walk away.

In true Relationship situations, closing is simple. Your goal is to assure the other party of your goodwill. Accommodate; then close quickly and amiably.

In a Balanced Concerns situation in which both the stakes and the relationship matter, closing is more complicated. You want to leave the other side feeling good, but you must also be careful to achieve your fair share of the substantive benefits from the deal.

In either case, there are some reliable, softer tactics that can help you close most relationship-sensitive negotiations. Let's look at them.

Perhaps the most frequently used closing technique is splitting the difference. Bargaining research tells us that the most likely settlement point in any given transaction is the midpoint between the two opening offers. People who instinctively prefer a compromise style like to cut through the whole bargaining process by getting the two opening numbers on the table and then splitting them right down the middle.

Even in cases in which the parties have gone through several rounds of bargaining, there often comes a time when one side or the other suggests that the parties meet halfway between their last positions. In situations in which the relationship between the parties is important, this is a perfectly appropriate, smooth way to close.

Why is splitting the difference so popular? First, it appeals to our sense of fairness and reciprocity, thus setting a good precedent for future dealings between the parties. A split is very much like the fifty-fifty sharing of money in the ultimatum game discussed in Chapter 4. Each side makes an equal concession simultaneously. What could be fairer than that?

Second, it is simple and easy to understand. It requires no elaborate justification or explanation. The other side sees exactly what you are doing.

Third, it is quick. For people who do not like to negotiate or are in a hurry, splitting the difference offers a way out of the potentially messy interpersonal conflict that looms whenever a negotiation occurs.

Splitting the difference is such a common closing tactic that it often seems rude and unreasonable to refuse, regardless of the situation. This is taking a good thing too far, however. There are at least two important situations in which I would hesitate to split the difference.

First, you should be careful that the midpoint being suggested is genuinely fair to your side. If you have opened at a reasonable price and the other party opened at an aggressive one, the midpoint is likely to favor the other party by a big margin. So don't split the difference at the end if there was a lack of balance at the beginning.

Second, when a lot of money or an important principle is on the line and relationships matter, quickly resorting to splitting may leave opportunities for additional, creative options on the table.

Think back to Benjamin Franklin's meal deal in Chapter 7. How would a split-the-difference solution have looked? Ben would have eaten some vegetarian meals and some nonvegetarian meals; ditto for the apprentices. Both would have been unhappy half the time. Instead of this "nobody wins" outcome, Ben took half the cook's fee and started preparing all his own meals, and everyone was happy all the time.

When the gap between offers is too wide to split, another friendly way to close is to obtain a neutral valuation or appraisal. If the parties cannot agree on a single appraiser, they can each pick one and agree to split the difference between the two numbers given by the experts.

Another innovative closing technique is something called a postsettlement settlement. Howard Raiffa of Harvard University has advocated that parties try to move from good agreements to better deals in which they seek that bit of extra value they may have left on the table.

Under Raiffa's approach, the parties reach an agreement that works for everyone. They then agree—with or without the help of an expert—to continue searching for trade-offs and ideas that might make one or both sides better off without making either one worse off. If they cannot agree on an improvement to their agreement, they return to their original deal.

My own research suggests that this technique, which sounds good in theory, is hard to implement in practice. I was so taken with Raiffa's idea that I helped to develop a computer program that would assist parties search for better deals after they concluded a negotiation. I was surprised by what I discovered: People showed little interest in the postsettlement settlement phase we offered them.

Why did Raiffa's appealing idea not interest them? First, by the time they finished a hotly contested, complex deal, they were tired and wanted to stop. Enough is enough, they seemed to say. Second, during the negotiation process, they changed their views about what was important to them, and it was hard for our postsettlement settlement system to keep up with these rapidly changing preferences. Finally, they worried that the other side might back out of the original deal based on what happened during the postsettlement settlement process. Best to leave well enough alone, they told us.

My experimental subjects taught me something. Good, solid deals and amiable working relationships are hard to come by. Most people who finish a negotiation with both are wise to value the fruits of their hard work and get on with their lives.

◄ What Happens if Negotiations Break Down? ►

The concession-making stage of bargaining sometimes ends with no deal rather than an agreement. The parties reach an impasse. In fact, a no deal result is sometimes the right answer. No deal is better than a bad deal, after all. In addition, sometimes people deliberately trigger an impasse to test the other side's resolve or push them to think more creatively.

But many bargaining breakdowns are regrettable mistakes. In some cases, negotiators escalate their commitment to their prior positions and pride gets in the way of continuing with bargaining. My favorite impasse story of this sort comes out of the Korean War.

In 1969, two negotiators representing, respectively, the U.N. Command (an American general named James B. Knapp) and North Korea (General Yi Choon Sun) met in a small hut in the demilitarized zone between North and South Korea. The North Koreans had called the meeting. And under the rules set by the Korean Military Armistice Commission, used hundreds of times since the war had ended in stalemate in 1953, meetings continued until the side calling the meeting declared them formally adjourned. *In addition, neither side was permitted to leave the room until a formal adjournment had been declared.*

Seven hours into this meeting, General Knapp proposed a plan to de-escalate the Korean conflict. Among other things, Knapp demanded that North Korea immediately stop all "polemic, bellicose, war-mongering public statements."

General Yi took issue with this demand, fell silent, then sat there, arms folded, staring at General Knapp in steely disapproval. Knapp returned the hostile glare. And there the two men remained *for four and a half hours—without saying a word.* Like two tigers sizing each other up, neither could blink first (or go to the bathroom) without admitting weakness.

As the meeting reached its eleventh hour and thirty-fifth minute, General Yi abruptly rose and departed without saying a word. Knapp then declared, "In view of North Korea's conduct, I consider this meeting to be terminated." History does not record the speed with which he left the room.

In addition to escalation problems, the parties may start too far apart to close the gap. Many times there are miscommunications, misunderstandings, and simple bad chemistry that the parties fail to overcome. Now what?

◄ Jump-starting the Negotiation Process ►

Perhaps the easiest way to overcome impasse is to leave yourself a back door through which to return to the table when you get up to leave it. "In light of the position you have taken," you might say as you pack your bags, "we are unable to continue negotiations at this time." An attentive opponent will pick up on your use of the words "at this time" and tactfully ask you later if the time has come to reinitiate talks. This back door also allows you to contact the other side at a later date without losing face.

If the other negotiator leaves in a genuine fit of anger, he may not be very careful about leaving a back door open. If so, you should consider how you can let him back in without unnecessary loss of face. You must, in one expert's phrase, build him a "golden bridge" across which to return to the table. Such bridges include "forgetting" that he made his ultimatum in the first place or recalling his last statement in a way that gives him an excuse for returning.

When miscommunication is the problem, a simple apology may be enough to get the parties back on track. If the relationship has deteriorated beyond apologies, changing negotiators or getting rid of intermediaries altogether may be necessary.

In America, the sport of professional baseball lost nearly two full seasons in the 1990s because of an impasse in negotiations between the players' union and the club owners. The team owners from the big cities wanted to limit the size of team payrolls. The team owners from smaller cities wanted the team owners from big cities to subsidize their franchises. The players wanted more money. It was a three-ring circus. The breakthrough came when the owners hired a new negotiator—a lawyer named Randy Levine—to represent them at the table. Levine acted in the role of mediator as much as advocate and brought a high degree of both credibility and creativity to the process that, according to one participant, "broke the dam of mistrust" that had built up between the parties. Another move that helped move the talks beyond impasse was getting all parties to agree to stop talking to the press and taking public positions that made it hard for them to compromise at the table. Chapter 2 discussed how public commitments can help you stick to your goals, but there comes a time when it is in everyone's interest to get unstuck from their positions. In a high stakes negotiation such as a labor strike, this often means getting the parties out of the spotlight so they can work in private.

The worst impasses are the products of emotional escalation that builds on itself: My anger makes you angry, and your response makes me even angrier. The 1969 standoff between General Knapp and General Yi falls into this category.

The solution to this sort of collision, in business deals as well as wars, is what I call the "one small step" procedure. One side needs to make a very small, visible move in the other side's direction, then wait for reciprocation. If the other party responds, the two can repeat the cycle again, and so on. Commentator Charles Osgood, writing about the Cold War in the early 1960s, created an acronym for this process: GRIT (Graduated and Reciprocated Initiatives in Tension Reduction).

Egypt's late prime minister, Anwar Sadat, used the "one small step" technique to deescalate the Arab-Israeli conflict when he flew to Jerusalem on November 19, 1977 and later met with Prime Minister Menachem Begin. By simply getting off a plane in Israel—a very small step indeed—Sadat demonstrated his willingness to recognize Israel's existence. This move eventually led to the Camp David peace accords and Israel's return of the Sinai Peninsula to Egypt.

An executive once told me a bargaining story that nicely sums up how the "one small step" process can work in everyday life. Two parties were in a complex business negotiation. Both were convinced that they had leverage, and both thought that the best arguments favored their own view of the deal. After a few rounds, neither side would make a move.

Finally one of the women at the table reached in her purse and pulled out a bag of M&M's. She opened the bag and poured the M&M's into a pile in the middle of the table.

"What are those for?" asked her counterparts.

"They are to keep score," she said.

Then she announced a small concession on the deal—and pulled an M&M out of the pile and put it on her side of the table.

"Now it's your turn," she said to the men sitting opposite.

Not to be outdone, her opponents put their heads together, came up with a concession of their own—and pulled out *two* M&M's. "Our concession was bigger than yours," they said.

The instigator of the process wisely let the other side win this little argument and then made another concession of her own, taking another M&M for herself.

It wasn't long before the parties were working closely together to close the final terms of the deal. Call this the M&M version of the GRIT process. Any similar mechanism that restarts the norm of reciprocity within the bargaining relationship will have a similar, helpful effect.

Overall, when parties reach an impasse, it is usually because each sees the other's demands as leaving it below its legitimate expectations. Eventually, if the parties are to make any progress, they must change their frame of reference and begin seeing that they will be worse off with no deal than they would be accepting a deal that falls below their original expectations.

Sometimes this transition takes time. The impasse must be allowed to last long enough that one or both parties actually alter their expectations. A final agreement must be seen as a gain compared with available alternatives.

If all else fails, you may need to call in a neutral third party such as a facilitator, mediator, or arbitrator to assist both sides in reframing the negotiation. Such professionals are specialists at helping people focus on what they stand to lose if there is no agreement. If even these people cannot unblock the impasse and the dispute is one in which legal rights play a role, the parties may have to go to court to resolve their dispute.

◄ Don't Be Satisfied with an Agreement— ►
Get a Commitment

When two of the largest firms on Wall Street, Dean Witter Discover & Co. and the Morgan Stanley Group, announced in 1997 that they had agreed to merge their businesses, they included an interesting footnote: Each firm promised to pay the other $250 million if it backed out of the deal.

When Boston College football star Doug Flutie landed a spectacular, six-year $8.3 million contract to play for Donald Trump's old United States Football League team, the New Jersey Generals, Flutie's agent got Trump to announce the agreement to the press immediately, before the parties had even formalized the deal with a written contract. Flutie's agent was delighted to see his client's name in print next to that $8.3 million figure.

What do these stories have in common? They are about gaining commitment, the last step in closing a deal. In each case, the parties bound themselves to each other by taking actions that gave them extra incentives to close the deal as promised.

The goal of all negotiations is to secure commitment, not merely agreement. You want a deal that sticks under which the other side will reliably perform. Sometimes a mere handshake will be enough to secure performance, particularly if the parties have a long-standing relationship and trust each other. Other times, more elaborate commitment devices, such as contracts, public ceremonies, and explicit penalties, are required.

A student of mine once told a story in class that illustrates the difference between agreements and commitments better than most academic discussions I have heard. Her story also shows how knowledge of negotiation dynamics can help you improve others' lives as well as your own.

My student—let's call her Theresa—was helping to run a volunteer organization that took inner-city children out to the country on Saturdays for recreational activities. She and others in her group chartered buses, got athletic equipment, arranged for adult volunteers to chaperone, brought food enough for all, and gave the kids a day away from the stress and hardship of life on the streets.

Everything was working fine except the adult volunteers. These well-meaning people were easy enough to persuade when she and others in the organization solicited their help. But many failed to appear on their assigned Saturday. Worse still, they were usually too embarrassed to call and let Theresa know they would not be there. This left the buses short on chaperones and the games short on supervisors.

Theresa faced a commitment problem that was threatening the whole program. How could she get volunteers to show up on their assigned day?

Then she and her organization hit on an idea. When she called volunteers to clear their schedule and assign them a day, she gave them each an important additional assignment: to bring an essential item for the day's lunch—hamburger meat, rolls, salad, charcoal for the fire, and so on. With this simple, additional promise, the number of volunteers who showed up skyrocketed. Why? People who had previously failed to show had apparently comforted themselves with the thought that one less volunteer would not matter on the trip. But now that they had a concrete image of what their participation meant (hamburgers are useless without charcoal, and vice versa), each person saw that his or her contribution mattered. Each was part of a team. A failure by one would mean a loss for all. The volunteer's self-esteem and sense of responsibility, which had led him or her to volunteer in the first place, now prompted actual performance.

As the Dean Witter, Doug Flutie, and Theresa stories make clear, the big difference between mere agreements and genuine commitments is the risk of loss faced by parties for nonperformance. An agreement to do something carries little risk; it merely signals that a person is willing, for the moment at least, to do something as promised. A commitment alters this state by making it costly for the promisors to back out of their agreements.

◄ Four Degrees of Commitment ►

There are many devices that help guarantee performance of an underlying promise. Such things as security bonds, deposits, and down payments are all examples. Within an organization, compensation systems often link raises, bonuses, or pension vesting periods to promises to stay with a firm for a specified period of time. This gives employees something to lose if they fail to live up to their agreement to work for the agreed number of years.

Different kinds of negotiating situations call for different forms of commitment. If you agree to baby-sit for a neighbor, your promise is the only commitment anyone expects. Your relationship secures your agreement. But a multibillion-dollar business acquisition usually involves legally binding contracts, teams of accountants, and a formal closing at which specific documents and assets simultaneously change hands.

There is more at stake and less trust, so people take extra steps to protect their expectations.

In virtually every negotiation, the commitment process begins with a simple **social ritual**. In the West, the favored ritual is a handshake. Other cultures use bows or similar signs of respect and trustworthiness.

In relatively closed social groups, shaking hands (or its equivalent) and giving your word are usually taken very seriously. A failure to perform after giving these social signals may threaten both the self-esteem of the promise giver and his or her membership in the group.

As the promise being made increases in gravity, the social rituals supporting it also increase in complexity. Many of these more complex rituals include some form of **public announcement** or disclosure.

Think back to the "talking to the mountain" story in Chapter 1, the story of the Arusha people and the boundary dispute between the two farmers. The parties concluded their negotiation by sharing a ritual meal of goat and beer while publicly announcing their agreement before the entire community. The witnesses to the agreement provided a collective memory for the terms of the deal and made it less likely that either side would renege.

Donald Trump's press conference to announce the Doug Flutie deal may have featured French champagne instead of Tanzanian beer, but the announcement served some of the same social purposes as the Arusha ceremony. Both Trump and Flutie were more committed as a result of having told the world about their deal.

Accountability also enhances commitment. If the promisor's personal reputation is at risk when his or her performance falls short, he or she is more likely to perform as promised.

Theresa's "bring the hamburger" ploy was a subtle accountability device. Under the old regime, when Theresa had brought all the food, the volunteers had thought of themselves as anonymous and interchangeable parts of the program. Under the new regime, when the volunteers each brought a part of the lunch, they now thought of themselves as "the hamburger" or "the drinks." A failure to show up was immediately noticeable.

One common way to enhance commitment that also improves accountability is to memorialize an agreement in writing. By writing down what was agreed to in explicit terms, people naturally pay more attention to the content of their promises. This act also sets into motion the psychological consistency principle discussed in Chapters 2 and 3. Remember how door-to-door salespeople are taught to secure a sale? They get the customer to personally fill in the blanks of the order form. The act of memorializing what they have agreed to makes customers feel a greater sense of commitment.

Many written agreements have the added benefit of being legally enforceable. The Dean Witter–Morgan Stanley merger's $250 million penalty clause for failure to close was part of a legal contract. As such, it could be enforced in court by either side and thus made backing out of the agreement extremely costly.

Because the word "contract" has legal significance, it is wise to know exactly what steps are required to make one. Many contracts become legally enforceable on the basis of verbal agreements and exchanges of promises alone. One side calls the other and makes an offer, the other side accepts, they both promise to perform, and bingo, there is a legal contract. This is the legal norm in most of the world, although the terms of such contracts, being verbal, are hard to prove in court.

However, in the United States an agreement for the sale of a good such as a car worth more than $500, a multiyear contract for such things as employment, or a contract to sell an item of real estate such as a home *must normally be in writing and signed by the party against whom performance is sought*. Without this formal writing, no court will enforce the agreement. And a party—even one who has made a verbal agreement and sworn to perform on a stack of holy books—is contractually free to change his or her mind and sell the car or home to someone else tomorrow.

In some transactions, no device, legal or otherwise, is solid enough to fully secure a commitment. In these cases, it is often both prudent and efficient to use a **simultaneous exchange** to close the deal. In the case of a car or home sale, for example, parties typically exchange the title to the property and a check for the required payment at the same time. Their preliminary agreement may be secured by a nonrefundable deposit, but the actual transfer of title does not take place until the seller receives the money.

◄ Summary ►

The final stage of negotiation, closing and gaining commitment, poses some significant challenges. In competitive situations a number of strong psychological levers, including the scarcity effect and overcommitment to the process, can cause one side to panic when it would be better off making a calmer, more rational decision.

Yet holding out poses risks, too. The other side may have genuine leverage and take its business elsewhere. Firmness can also lead to impasse. Although disagreement often prompts parties to become more creative in their search for solutions, it can also put deals and relationships in jeopardy. How you close therefore requires a measure of judgment, not just passionate commitment to your goals.

Finally, negotiations are not over until the parties have secured commitments to performance. Agreements alone are not enough unless the relationships and trust between the parties are deep and stable. The secret of making commitments is simple: Set the situation up so the other party has something to lose if it fails to perform. And be willing to take a similar step yourself.

This chapter concludes our tour of the bargaining process, but there is one final topic to cover before you can go to the bargaining table with confidence: ethics. Can you bargain with the devil without losing your soul? I think so, but it's not easy.

Bargaining and Closing Summary

Tactical Decision

Situation		Should I Open?	How to Open?	Concession Strategy	Closing Strategy
	Transactions	When in doubt, don't. But OK if you have good information.	Optimistically (highest or lowest figure supported by presentable argument).	Firmness. Concede slowly in diminishing amounts toward expectation level.	Deadlines; walkouts; final offer; split the difference; appraisal.
	Balanced Concerns	Same as above.	Fairly (highest or lowest figure supported by solid argument).	Big moves on little issues, little moves on big issues; brainstorm options, present several packages at once.	All of the above; postsettlement settlement.
	Relationships	Yes.	Generously.	Accommodation or fair compromise.	Split the difference; accommodation.
	Tacit Coordination	Yes, but avoid conflict if possible.	Do whatever it takes to solve the problem.	Accommodation.	Accommodation.

11

Bargaining with the Devil
Without Losing Your Soul:
Ethics in Negotiation

> The market is a place set apart where people may de-
> ceive each other.
>
> —ANACHARSIS (600 B.C.)

> Most people I play cards with I trust, but I still want to cut
> the cards.
>
> —JOHN K. O'LOUGHLIN, ALLSTATE INSURANCE COMPANY

I have reserved the discussion of ethics for the end of our study of bargaining because ethical questions suffuse every aspect and stage of the
negotiation process. Now that we have fully explored the intricacies of
preparation, information flow, explicit bargaining, and commitment, we
have the background knowledge we need to probe the tough ethical
questions all negotiators confront.

Let's start with a story. It comes from the life of the late Darrell Sifford, a Philadelphia newspaper columnist. Sifford was a fatherly figure
to those who admired him. He often urged people to be honest and
straightforward with each other. But when it came to his first real haggling encounter, he felt it necessary to take a different path. He wrote
about the subject in one of his newspaper columns.

Sifford and his wife were living in Minneapolis, Minnesota, in a
large high-rise apartment complex. Sifford decided to go shopping for

something to decorate their TV room. As he was walking by a discount furniture store display window, he spied an elegant world globe illuminated by a light inside. The globe sat atop an attractive cherry stand. He immediately fell in love with it.

As he entered the store, an elderly, enthusiastic salesman greeted him. "What can I do for you?" the salesman said.

"That globe in the window," said Sifford. "I want to look at it."

The salesman led Sifford to the window, where Sifford looked at the globe more closely and turned over the price tag. It was a shocker: $495.

"That's more than I wanted to pay," said Sifford, shaking his head.

The salesman sympathized and began showing Sifford a variety of other globes, but none had the charm of the first he had seen. After looking at a few alternatives, Sifford said he wanted the globe in the window but did not want to pay $495 for it. The salesman asked Sifford if he lived in the area, and Sifford pointed to his apartment building in the distance.

"Then you don't have a problem," the salesman said. "The store automatically gives a discount to people in the neighborhood. How does four hundred and fifty dollars sound?"

"That sounds high," Sifford replied.

At this point, as Sifford told the story to his readers, an inner voice told him that he should bargain for this globe. He had never haggled in a store before and had always thought that bargaining was slightly degrading, a practice for people who either did not have money or were too cheap to spend it. But he was far from his native Philadelphia, so he decided to go for it. No more Mr. Nice Guy.

Sifford considered for a moment whether it was OK for him to stretch the truth a little and quickly decided that it was. He pushed on.

"I saw a globe just like this in a discount catalog for three hundred and twenty-five dollars," Sifford lied. "How can you call yourself a discount store if you're that much higher than the catalog?"

"It cost us more than that," the salesman responded, "but I tell you what I'll do. I'll sell you this globe for four hundred dollars. That's a steal. You can't find a better price in any store."

"Then I'll buy it from the catalog," said Sifford firmly. "Thanks for your time." And he headed for the door.

The salesman jumped. "I'll talk to my manager," he said. He returned less than a minute later. "My manager is in an especially good mood today. He says you can have the globe for three hundred and fifty dollars," he reported.

"That's not good enough," Sifford replied, walking back to the globe and looking carefully at it. "Look at this! There's a nick down at the bottom. This is damaged merchandise."

The salesman looked at the stand. There was a barely noticeable mark. "I don't understand this," he said. Sifford reported that the salesman was actually *smiling* as he said this, suggesting a certain admiration for Sifford's tactic. "We don't deal in damaged merchandise. Let me talk to my manager again."

A minute later the salesman returned. "You drive a hard bargain," the salesman said. He gave Sifford the globe for $325. Sifford proudly carried the globe, no longer just an ornament, home to his wife.

◄ The Core Ethical Problem for Negotiators ►

Sifford got a bargain. But he made up a lie about a catalog price to get it. Did he act ethically? He clearly thought so, and millions of people around the world would be astonished to learn that such a lie is in any way morally troublesome. People say all kinds of things to position their demands when they are buying and selling, and, as the ancient Greek quotation from Anacharsis that led the chapter suggests, people have behaved this way for thousands of years. Lies are indisputably a feature of everyday social life in every culture.

A study done in the 1990s at the Harvard Business School asked more than 750 MBA students, who came from all over the world, to rate a long list of questionable bargaining tactics. The tactics ranged from bluffing in opening demands and lying to strengthen a bargaining position to bribing someone to provide information about an opponent's bargaining position. Students were quite comfortable with what the investigators called traditional competitive bargaining tactics, such as bluffing about bottom lines, opening demands, time constraints, and other offers. They even approved promising (contrary to their real intent) that a future relationship would develop in return for concrete concessions.

Sifford's conduct seems to fall comfortably within the zone of traditional competitive bargaining tactics as defined in the Harvard study. Isn't that the end of the matter?

Perhaps. Yet many people of good conscience would see an obvious problem with Sifford's choice: He told an outright lie for the purpose of gaining an advantage for himself. And among the most effective of what Professor Gerald Williams has called "cooperative" negotiators, a scrupulous desire to "conduct oneself ethically" in negotiations is a major motivational objective. These negotiators do not see bargaining as a game and generally do not think of lies as legitimate moves in the process.

So Sifford's lie might make some people feel, if not outraged, at least uncomfortable. They would ask some hard questions.

If Sifford's lie is OK, when are such lies not OK? Would it be ethical for the salesman to lie to Sifford, inventing a fictional "interested buyer" who was planning to purchase the globe later that day for $350 (or more) if Sifford did not?

Perhaps most compelling, isn't lying a habit that can become addictive if used regularly? The CEO of an executive search firm in New York estimated that roughly 25 percent of the businesspeople he interviews are "persistent liars." It does not seem farfetched to suggest that these people may have become liars in their professional lives in part through developing a habit of lying to achieve their less important personal goals. Telling a lie is easy. If a lie works well in small consumer matters, why not lie in situations where the stakes matter a bit more, such as employment? Pretty soon, a measurable portion of a person's success may depend on using lies. Truth telling becomes an optional, expensive luxury.

Sifford's lie was trivial, but it raises the core problem we face if we try to act ethically in negotiations. Professor James J. White, a negotiation teacher at the University of Michigan Law School, summed up the problem this way: "The negotiator's role is at least passively to mislead his opponent about his settling point while at the same time to engage in ethical behavior."

White's statement embodies the contradictions many people encounter when they start thinking about bargaining ethics. Is it really possible to speak coherently about ethical ways of misleading someone for a selfish purpose? What does White mean by "passive" deception? Might not active deception about a little issue such as Sifford's catalog price be more ethical than passive deception about something really important in a multibillion-dollar deal? There are no easy answers to these questions. And the problems become even tougher when you add professional ethical duties such as those imposed on lawyers, physicians, accountants, and others into the mix.

◄ Ethics Come First, Not Last ►

This subject comes at the end of the book, but your attitudes about ethical conduct are *preliminary* to every bargaining move you make. Your ethics are a vital part of your identity as a person, and, try as you may, you will never be able to successfully separate the way you act in negotiations from the person you are in other parts of your life. That is "you" at the bargaining table as well as "you" in the mirror every morning.

Your personal beliefs about ethics also come with a price tag: The stricter your ethical standards, the higher the cost you must be willing to pay to uphold them in any given transaction. The lower your ethical standards, the higher the price may be in terms of your reputation. And the lower the standards of those with whom you must deal, the more time, energy, and prudence are required to defend yourself and your interests.

I'll give you my bias on this subject right up front. I think you should aim high where ethics are concerned. I count myself in the camp that wishes Sifford had found a better way to get his bargain. As I noted in Chapter 1, personal integrity is one of the four most important effectiveness factors for the skilled negotiator. Research on effective negotiation affirms that not only Williams's "effective cooperative" negotiators but also a wide range of professionals—from accountants to contract managers, and from bankers to professional buyers and sellers—list personal integrity among the important traits of a skilled negotiator.

Fine. But what does personal integrity mean? Am I saying that Sifford lacked personal integrity because he lied to a shopkeeper about having seen a better price elsewhere?

No. Let me repeat what I said in Chapter 1 about what personal integrity means where negotiation is concerned. I said that negotiators who value "personal integrity" can be counted on to "negotiate consistently, using a thoughtful set of personal values that they could, if necessary, explain and defend to others." This definition puts the burden on you as an individual—not me as a judge—to construct your own ethical framework. I learned long ago that the best way to teach others about values is to raise tough questions, give people tools to think about them, then get out of the way.

Although I wish Sifford had not lied, he passed my test with flying colors. He published an article candidly discussing his behavior. The article was read by thousands and debated by many. If your own negotiation behavior can withstand scrutiny like that, you have "personal integrity" in my book. I may disagree with your choices, but we will have an honest, principled disagreement.

My goal in this chapter is not to preach to you about ethics but rather to give you some tools for making choices like the one Sifford made. Reasonable people will differ on ethical questions, but you will have personal integrity in my estimation if you can pass my "explain and defend" test after making a considered, ethical choice. After we have examined some ways of thinking about your own duties, we will look at how you can defend yourself when others use ethically questionable tactics against you.

◄ The Minimum Standard: Obey the Law ►

Regardless of how you feel about ethics, everyone has a duty to obey the laws that regulate the negotiation process. Of course, bargaining laws differ between countries and cultures, but the normative concerns underlying these different legal regimes share important characteristics. I will look briefly at the American approach to the legal regulation of deception as an example of the way law works in negotiations, but basic principles of fairness and prudence in bargaining conduct are global, not national.

American law disclaims any general duty of "good faith" in the negotiation of commercial agreements. As an American judge once wrote: "In a business transaction both sides presumably try to get the best deal . . . . The proper recourse [for outrageous conduct] is to walk away from the bargaining table, not sue for 'bad faith' in negotiations." This general rule assumes, however, that no one has committed fraud. As we shall see, the law of fraud reaches deep into the complexities of negotiation behavior.

There are six major elements of a fraud case. A bargaining move is fraudulent when a speaker makes a (1) knowing (2) misrepresentation of a (3) material (4) fact (5) on which the victim reasonably relies (6) causing damages.

A car dealer commits fraud when he resets a car odometer and sells one of his company cars as if it were brand new. The dealer knows the car is not new; he misrepresents its condition to the buyer; the condition of the car is a fact rather than a mere opinion, and it is a fact that is important ("material") to the transaction; the buyer is acting reasonably in relying on the mileage as recorded on the odometer when she buys the car, and damages result. Similarly, a person selling her business commits fraud when she lies about the number and kind of debts owed by the business.

Lies about important facts that go to the core of a deal are not unknown in business negotiations. But most negotiators don't need a lawyer or an ethicist to tell them that such misrepresentations ought to be avoided. These are cases of fraud, pure and simple. People who try to cheat you are crooks.

More interesting questions about lying come up on the margins of the law of fraud. What if the dealer says you had better buy the car today because he has another buyer ready to snatch the car away tomorrow? That may be a statement of fact, but is it material? It looks like Sifford's little lie about his catalog price. Assuming Sifford is innocent of legal fraud in the globe case, should we hold a professional car dealer to a different legal standard? Is the car dealer's lie about the other buyer fraudulent or just a form of creative motivation?

Suppose the seller does not state a fact but instead gives an artfully phrased opinion? Perhaps the person selling her business says that a large account debt "could probably be renegotiated" after you buy the firm. Could this opinion be deemed so misleading as to be fraudulent if the seller knows for a fact that the creditor would never consider renegotiation?

Let's look briefly at each element in the law of fraud and test where the legal limits lie. Surprisingly, though we would all prefer to see clear black and white rules outlining our legal duties, staying on the right side of the law often requires a prudent respect for the many gray areas that inevitably color an activity as widespread and multifaceted as negotiation. Knowing what the law is helps you stay within its boundaries, but this knowledge does not eliminate the need for a strong sense of right and wrong.

ELEMENT 1: "KNOWING"

To commit fraud, a negotiator must have a particular state of mind with respect to the fact he or she misrepresents. The misstatement must be made "knowingly." One way of getting around fraud, therefore, might be for the speaker to avoid direct contact with information that would lead to a "knowing" state of mind.

For example, a company president might suspect that his company is in poor financial health, but he does not yet "know" it because he has not seen the latest quarterly reports. When his advisers ask to set up a meeting to discuss these reports, he tells them to hold off. He is about to go into negotiations with an important supplier and would like to be able to say, honestly, that so far as he knows the company is paying its bills. Does this get him off the hook? Perhaps. But many courts have stretched the definition of "knowing" to include statements that are, like the executive's in this case, made with a conscious and reckless disregard for their truth.

Nor is reckless disregard for truth the limit of the law. Victims of misstatements that were made negligently or even innocently may obtain relief in certain circumstances. These kinds of misstatements are not deemed fraudulent, however. Rather, they are a way of recognizing that a deal was based on a mistake.

ELEMENT 2: "MISREPRESENTATION"

In general, the law requires a negotiator to make a positive misstatement before a statement is judged fraudulent. A basic legal rule for commercial negotiators is "Be silent and be safe."

As a practical matter, of course, silence is difficult to maintain if one's bargaining opponent is an astute questioner. In the face of inconvenient questions, negotiators are often forced to resort to verbal feints and dodges such as "I don't know about that" or, when pressed, "That is not a subject I am at liberty to discuss." When you choose to lie in response to a pointed question probing the strength of your bargaining position, you immediately raise the risk of legal liability. As we shall see below, however, some lies are not "material" and the other party may be charged with a duty to discount the truth of what you tell them.

Surprisingly, there are circumstances when it may be fraudulent to keep your peace about an issue *even if the other side does not ask about it.* When does a negotiator have a duty to voluntarily disclose matters that may hurt his bargaining position? American law imposes affirmative disclosure duties in the following four circumstances:

1. *When the negotiator makes a partial disclosure that is or becomes misleading in light of all the facts.* If you say your company is profitable, you may be under a duty to disclose whether you used questionable accounting techniques to arrive at that statement. You should also update your prior statement if you show a loss in the next quarter and negotiations are still ongoing.

2. *When the parties stand in a fiduciary relationship to each other.* In negotiations between trustees and beneficiaries, partners in a partnership, shareholders in a small corporation, or members of a family business, parties may have a duty of complete candor and cannot rely on the "be silent and be safe" approach.

3. *When the nondisclosing party has vital information about the transaction not accessible to the other side.* In general, sellers have a greater duty to disclose hidden defects about their property than buyers do to disclose "hidden treasure" that may be buried there. A home seller must disclose termite infestation in her home, but an oil company need not voluntarily disclose that there is oil on a farmer's land when negotiating to purchase it. This is a slippery exception; the best test is one of conscience and fairness.

4. *When special codified disclosure duties, such as those regarding contracts of insurance or public offerings of securities, apply.* Legislatures sometimes impose special disclosure duties for particular kinds of transactions. In the United States, for example, many states now require home sellers to disclose all known problems with their houses.

If none of these four exceptions applies, neither side is likely to be found liable for fraud based on a nondisclosure. Each party can remain silent, passively letting the other proceed under its own assumptions.

ELEMENT 3: "MATERIAL"

Suppose that an art gallery owner has been given authority by an artist to sell one of the artist's paintings for any price greater than $10,000. Is it fraud for the gallery owner, as part of a negotiation with a collector, to say, "I can't take less than $12,000"? In fact, she *does* have authority to sell the painting for anything above $10,000, so there has been a knowing misrepresentation of fact. Suppose the buyer says, "My budget for this purchase is $9,000," when she is really willing to spend $11,000? Same thing. The legal question in both cases is whether these facts are "material."

They are not. In fact, lies about demands and bottom-line prices are so prevalent in bargaining that many professional negotiators do not consider such misstatements to be lies, preferring the term "bluffs."

Why? Such statements allow the parties to assert the legitimacy of their preferences and set the boundaries of the bargaining range without incurring a risk of loss. Misleading statements about bottom-line prices and demands also enable parties to test the limits of the other side's commitment to their expressed preferences.

The American legal profession has gone so far as to enshrine this practice approvingly in its Model Rules of Professional Conduct. These rules provide that "estimates of price or value placed on the subject of a transaction and a party's intention as to an acceptable settlement of a claim" are not "material" facts for purposes of the ethical rule prohibiting lawyers from making false statements to a third person.

There are thus no legal problems with lying about how much you might be willing to pay or which of several issues in a negotiation you value more highly. Demands and bottom lines are not, as a matter of law, "material" to a deal.

As one moves from bluffs about how much one wants to spend or charge toward more assertive, specific lies about *why* one price or another is required, the fraud meter goes up. One common way to back up a price demand, for example, is Sifford's "I can get it cheaper elsewhere" argument, used by consumers the world over. Negotiators often lie about their available alternatives. Is this fraudulent?

When a shopper lies to a storekeeper that she can get an item cheaper across town, the statement is not "material." After all, the seller presumably knows (or should know) at least as much about the value of what he is selling as the buyer does. If the seller wants to sell it for less than the asking price, who knows better than the seller what the right price is?

But suppose we switch roles. Suppose the seller lies about having another offer that the buyer has to beat? For example, take the following older, but still important legal case from Massachusetts.

A commercial landlord bought a building and negotiated a new lease with a toy shop tenant when the tenant's lease expired. The proprietor of the toy shop bargained hard and refused to pay the landlord's demand for a $10,000 increase in rent. The landlord then told the shop owner that he had another tenant willing to pay the $10,000 amount and threatened the current tenant with immediate eviction if he did not promptly agree to the new rate. The tenant paid but learned later that the threat had been a bluff; there had been no other tenant. The tenant successfully sued for fraud.

In another case, this time from Oklahoma, a real estate agent was held liable for fraud, *including punitive damages*, when she pressured a buyer into closing on a home with a story that a rival buyer (the contractor who built the house) was willing to pay the asking price and would do so later that same day.

What makes these lies different in a legal sense from the "I can't take less than $12,000" statement by the art gallery owner or the "I can get it cheaper elsewhere" comment by a shopper? I think the difference has to do with the fact that the victims in these cases were "little people"—small businesses and consumers—who were being pressured unfairly by professionals. The made-up offers were "material" facts from the buyers' point of view. They were specific, factual, coupled with ultimatums, and impossible to investigate.

But I do not think a court would have reached the same result if both parties had been consumers or both sophisticated professionals. Nor would I expect to see results like this outside a wealthy, consumer-oriented country such as the United States. Still, it is worth noting that such cases exist. They counsel a degree of prudence on the part of professional sellers or buyers when dealing with the public.

ELEMENT 4: "FACT"

On the surface, it appears that only misstatements of objective facts are occasions for legal sanctions. Businessmen seeking to walk close to the legal line are therefore careful to couch their sales talk in negotiation as opinions, predictions, and statements of intention, not statements of fact. Moreover, a good deal of exaggeration or puffing about product attributes and likely performance is viewed as a normal aspect of the selling process. Buyers and sellers cannot take everything said to them at face value.

The surface of the law can be misleading, however. Courts have found occasion to punish statements of intention and opinion as fraudulent when faced with particularly egregious cases. The touchstone of the law of fraud is not whether the statement at issue was one of pure fact but rather whether the statement succeeded in concealing a set of facts the negotiator preferred to keep out of sight.

Suppose you are borrowing money from your uncle and tell him that you plan to spend the loan on college tuition. In fact, you are really going to buy a fancy, new sports car. Fraud? Possibly.

In the memorable words of a famous English judge, "The state of a man's mind is as much a fact as the state of his digestion." Lies regarding intention even have a special name in the law: promissory fraud. The key element in a promissory fraud case is proof that the speaker knew he could not live up to his promise *at the time the promise was made*. In other words, he made the promise with his fingers crossed behind his back. If

you are the victim, you must also show that the other side's intention going into the deal went to its very heart—that is, that the statement of intention was "material."

What about statements of opinion? Self-serving statements about the
value of your goods or the qualifications of your product or company are
the standard (legal) fare of the negotiating table. However, when negotiators offer statements of opinion that are flatly contradicted by facts
known to them about the subject of the transaction, they may be liable
for fraud. In one New York case, for example, the seller of a machine
shop business opined to a prospective buyer that the buyer would have
"no trouble" securing work from his largest customer. In fact, the seller
was in debt to his customer, intended to pay off this debt from the proceeds of the sale to the buyer, and had virtually no work there due to his
reputation for poor workmanship. The buyer successfully proved that
the sale had been induced by the seller's fraudulent statement of opinion and collected damages.

What seems to matter in these cases is unfairness. If a statement of
intention or opinion so conceals the true nature of the negotiation proposal that a bargaining opponent cannot accurately assess an appropriate range of values or risks on which to base the price, then it may be
fraudulent.

ELEMENT 5: "RELIANCE"

Negotiators who lie sometimes defend themselves by saying, in effect,
"Only a fool could have believed what I said. The other party had no
business relying on me to tell him the truth—he should have investigated
for himself."

As we saw in our discussion of lies about other offers, this defense
works pretty well when both sides are on roughly the same footing. But
when one side has a decided advantage, as does a professional buyer or
seller against a consumer or small business, American courts are more
sympathetic to the idea that the victim reasonably relied on the lie.

In addition, courts are sympathetic to those who, in good faith, rely on
others to treat them fairly in the negotiation process and who have that
trust violated by more powerful firms trying to steal their trade secrets
and other information. There have been a number of cases, for example,
allowing recoveries to independent inventors and others who disclosed
trade secrets in the course of negotiations to sell their discoveries. The
prospective buyers in these cases are typically big companies that at-

tempted to use the negotiation process as a way of getting something for nothing. The prudent negotiator, however, always secures an express confidentiality agreement if secret information or business plans must be disclosed in the course of the information exchange process.

One trick that manipulative negotiators use to avoid liability after they have misstated important facts or improperly motivated a transaction is to write the true terms and conditions into the final written agreement. If the victim signs off on the deal without reading this contract, he will have a hard time claiming reasonable reliance on the earlier misstatements in a fraud case later on.

For example, suppose you negotiate the sale of your company's principal asset, an electronic medical device, to a big medical products firm. During the negotiations, the company assures you that it will aggressively market the device so you can earn royalties. The contract, however, specifically assigns it the legal right to shelve the product if it wishes. After the sale, it decides to stop marketing your product and you later learn the company never really intended to sell it; it was just trying to get your product off the market because it competed with several of its own.

In a case like this, a court held that the plaintiffs were stuck with the terms of the final written contract. The lesson here is clear: *Read contracts carefully before you sign them, and question assurances that contract language changing the nature of the deal is just a technicality or was required by the lawyers.*

ELEMENT 6: "CAUSATION AND DAMAGES"

You cannot make a legal claim for fraud if you have no damages caused by the fraudulent statement or omission. People sometimes get confused about this. The other negotiator lies in some outrageous and unethical way, so they assume the liar's conduct is illegal. It may be, but only if that conduct leads directly to some quantifiable economic loss for the victim of the fraud. If there is no such loss, the right move is to walk away from the deal (if you can), not sue.

◄ Beyond the Law: A Look at Ethics ►

As you may have noticed, the legal rules that govern bargaining are suffused with a number of ethical norms. For example, professionals with a big bargaining advantage are sometimes held to a higher standard when negotiating with amateurs and consumers than they are when they approach others as equals. Parties that stand in special relationships to each other, such as trustees or partners, have heightened legal disclosure duties. Lies protecting important factual information about the subject of the transaction are treated differently from lies about such things as your alternatives or your bottom line. Silence is unacceptable if an important fact is inaccessible to the other side unless you speak up.

Did Sifford commit legal fraud when he lied to the salesman about the price he could get from a catalog? Clearly not. He told a lie, but it was not a material fact within the context of his transaction. And the shop had no right to rely on Sifford for this sort of information. It could easily have investigated this information had it thought catalog prices were important.

Yet we saw above that the same lax legal standard might not apply had the store lied to Sifford about having another buyer. The real estate broker, recall, had to pay damages when she lied to a customer about having another bid when there was none.

Conclusion: Sifford is legally in the clear; the salesman might be on slightly thinner ice. Are your legal obligations the end of the story as far as ethics are concerned? The answer to that question depends on your attitude to bargaining as an activity in your life.

Sifford put bargaining into a special category, one that included allowable lies. He wrote that "stretching the truth" was "the way to play this game." With more experience (remember, this was his first haggle), he might have taken a different view. He might have decided that lying was OK in some situations but not others. Or he might have determined that an honest life requires a single set of ethical standards across the board.

I want to challenge you to identify what *your* beliefs are. To help you decide how you feel about ethics, I will briefly describe the three most common approaches to bargaining ethics I have heard expressed in conversation with literally hundreds of students and executives. See which shoe fits—or take a bit from each approach and construct your own.

As we explore this territory, remember that nearly everyone is sincerely convinced that they are acting ethically most of the time, whereas they often think others are acting either naively or unethically, depending on their ethical perspective and the situation. Thus, a word of warning is in order. Your ethics are mainly your own business. They will help you increase your level of confidence and comfort at the bargaining table. But do not expect others to share your ethics in every detail. Prudence pays.

◄ Three Schools of Bargaining Ethics ►

The three schools of bargaining ethics I want to introduce for your consideration are (1) the "It's a game" Poker School, (2) the "Do the right thing even if it hurts" Idealist School, and (3) the "What goes around, comes around" Pragmatist School.

Let's look at each one in turn. As I describe these schools, try to decide which aspects of them best reflect your own attitudes. After you figure out where you stand today, take a moment and see if that is where you ought to be. My advice is to aim as high as you can, consistent with your genuinely held beliefs about bargaining. In the pressured world of practice, people tend to slide down rather than climb up when it comes to ethical standards.

THE "IT'S A GAME" POKER SCHOOL

The Poker School of ethics sees negotiation as a "game" with certain "rules." The rules are defined by the law, such as the legal materials we covered above. Conduct within the rules is ethical. Conduct outside the rules is unethical.

The modern founder of the Poker School was Albert Z. Carr, a former Special Consultant to President Harry Truman. Carr wrote a book in the 1960s called, appropriately enough, *Business as a Game.* In a related article that appeared in the *Harvard Business Review,* Carr argued that bluffing and other misleading but lawful negotiating tactics are "an integral part of the [bargaining] game, and the executive who does not master [these] techniques is not likely to accumulate much money or power."

People who adhere to the Poker School readily admit that bargaining and poker are not exactly the same. But they point out that deception is essential to effective play in both arenas. Moreover, skilled players in both poker and bargaining exhibit a robust and realistic distrust of the other fellow. Carr argues that good players should ignore the "claims of friendship" and engage in "cunning deception and concealment" in fair, hard bargaining encounters. When the game is over, members of the Poker School do not think less of a fellow player just because that person successfully deceived them. In fact, assuming the tactic was legal, they may admire the deceiver and vow to be better prepared (and less trusting) next time.

We know how to play poker, but how exactly does one play the bargaining "game"? Stripped to its core, it looks like this: Someone opens, and then people take turns proposing terms to each other. Arguments supporting your preferred terms are allowed. You can play or pass in each round. The goal is to get the other side to agree to terms that are as close as possible to your last proposal.

In the bargaining game, it is understood that both sides might be bluffing. Bluffs disguise a weak bargaining hand, that is, the limited or unattractive alternatives you have away from the table, your inability to affect the other side's alternatives, and the arguments you have to support your demands. Unlike poker players, negotiators always attempt to disclose a good hand if they have one in the bargaining game. So the most effective bluffs are realistic, attractive, difficult-to-check (but false) alternatives or authoritative (but false) supporting standards. Experienced players know this, so one of the key skills in the bargaining game is judging when the other party's alternatives or arguments are really as good as he or she says. If the other side calls you on your bargaining bluff by walking away or giving you a credible ultimatum, you lose. Either there will be no deal when there should have been one, or the final price will be nearer to their last offer than to yours.

As mentioned above, the Poker School believes in the rule of law. In poker, you are not allowed to hide cards, collude with other players, or renege on your bets. But you are expected to deceive others about your hand. The best plays come when you win the pot with a weak hand or fool the other players into betting heavily when your hand is strong. In bargaining, you must not commit outright, actionable fraud, but negotiators must be on guard for anything short of fraud.

The Poker School has three main problems as I see it. First, the Poker School presumes that everyone treats bargaining as a game. Unfortunately, it is an empirical fact that people disagree on this. For a start, neither the idealists nor the pragmatists (more on these below) think bargaining is a game. This problem does not deter the Poker School, which holds that the rules permit its members to play even when the other party disagrees about this premise.

Second, everyone is supposed to know the rules cold. But this is impossible, given that legal rules are applied differently in different industries and regions of the world.

Finally, as you now know (having read about the legal treatment of fraud), the law is far from certain even within a single jurisdiction. So you often need a sharp lawyer to help you decide what to do.

THE "DO THE RIGHT THING EVEN IF IT HURTS" IDEALIST SCHOOL

The Idealist School says that bargaining is an aspect of social life, not a special activity with its own unique set of rules. The same ethics that apply in the home should carry over directly into the realm of negotiation. If it is wrong to lie or mislead in normal social encounters, it is wrong to do so in negotiations. If it is OK to lie in special situations (such as to protect another person's feelings), it is also OK to lie in negotiations when those special conditions apply.

Idealists do not entirely rule out deception in negotiation. For example, if the other party assumes you have a lot of leverage and never asks you directly about the situation as you see it, you do not necessarily have to volunteer information weakening your position. And the idealist can decline to answer questions. But such exceptions are uncomfortable moments. Members of the Idealist School prefer to be candid and honest at the bargaining table even if it means giving up a certain amount of strategic advantage.

The Idealist School draws its strength from philosophy and religion. For example, Immanuel Kant said that we should all follow the ethical rules that we would wish others to follow. Kant argued that if everyone lied all the time, social life would be chaos. Hence, you should not lie. Kant also disapproved of treating other people merely as the means to achieve your own personal ends. Lies in negotiation are selfish acts designed to achieve personal gain. This form of conduct is therefore unethical. Period. Many religions also teach adherents not to lie for personal advantage.

Idealists admit that deception in negotiation rarely arouses moral indignation unless the lies breach a trust between friends, violate a fiduciary responsibility, or exploit people such as the sick or elderly, who lack the ability to protect themselves. And if the only way you can prevent some terrible harm like a murder is by lying, go ahead and lie. But the lack of moral outrage and the fact that sometimes lying can be defended does not make deception in negotiations right.

Idealists strongly reject the idea that negotiations should be viewed as "games." Negotiations, they feel, are serious, consequential communication acts. People negotiate to resolve their differences so social life will work for the benefit of all. People must be held responsible for all their actions, including the way they negotiate, under universal standards.

Idealists think that the members of the Poker School are predatory and selfish. For its part, the Poker School thinks that idealists are naive and even a little silly. When members of the two schools meet at the bargaining table, tempers can flare.

Some members of the Idealist School have recently been trying to find a philosophical justification for bluffs about bottom lines. There is no agreement yet on whether these efforts have succeeded in ethical terms. But it is clear that outright lies such as fictitious other offers and better prices are unethical practices under idealist principles.

The big problem for the idealists is obvious: Their standards sometimes make it difficult to proceed in a realistic way at the bargaining table. Also, unless adherence to the Idealist School is coupled with a healthy skepticism about the way other people will negotiate, idealism leaves its members open to exploitation by people with standards other than their own. These limitations are especially troublesome when idealists must represent others' interests at the bargaining table.

Despite its limitations, I like the Idealist School. Perhaps because I am an academic, I genuinely believe that the different parts of my life are, in fact, a whole. I aspire to ethical standards that I can apply consistently. I will admit that I sometimes fall short of idealism's strict code, but by aiming high I hope I am leaving myself somewhere to fall that maintains my basic sense of personal integrity.

I confess my preference for the Idealist School so you will know where I am coming from in this discussion. But I realize that your experience and work environment may preclude idealism as an ethical option. That's OK. As I hope I am making clear, idealism is not the only way to think about negotiation in ethical terms.

THE "WHAT GOES AROUND COMES AROUND" PRAGMATIST SCHOOL

The final school of bargaining ethics, the Pragmatist School, includes some original elements as well as some attributes of the previous two. In common with the Poker School, this approach views deception as a necessary part of the negotiation process. Unlike the Poker School, however, it prefers not to use misleading statements and overt lies if there is a serviceable, practical alternative. Uniquely, the Pragmatist School displays concern for the potential negative effects of deceptive conduct on present and future relationships. Thus, lying and other questionable tactics are bad not so much because they are "wrong" as because they cost the user more in the long run than they gain in the short run.

As my last comment suggests, people adhere to this school more for prudential than idealistic reasons. Lies and misleading conduct can cause serious injury to one's credibility. And credibility is an important asset for effective negotiators both to preserve working relationships and to protect one's reputation in a market or community. This latter concern is summed up in what I would call the pragmatist's credo: What goes around comes around. The Poker School is less mindful of reputation and more focused on winning each bargaining encounter within the rules of the "game."

What separates the Pragmatist School from the Idealist School? To put it bluntly, a pragmatist will lie a bit more often than will an idealist. For example, pragmatists sometimes draw fine distinctions between lies about hard-core facts of a transaction, which are always imprudent (and often illegal), and misleading statements about such things as the rationales used to justify a position. A pragmatic car salesman considers it highly unethical to lie about anything large or small relating to the mechanical condition of a used car he is selling. But this same salesman might not have a problem saying "My manager won't let me sell this car for less than $10,000" even though he knows the manager would sell the car for $9500. False justification and rationales are marginally acceptable because they are usually less important to the transaction and much harder to detect as falsehoods than are core facts about the object being bought and sold.

Pragmatists are also somewhat looser within the truth when using so-called blocking techniques—tactics to avoid answering questions that threaten to expose a weak bargaining position. For example, can you ethically answer "I don't know" when asked about something you *do* know that hurts your position? An idealist would refuse to answer the question or try to change the subject, not lie by saying "I don't know." A pragmatist would go ahead and say "I don't know" if his actual state of knowledge is hard to trace and the lie poses little risk to his relationships.

What would the pragmatists make of Sifford's lie about his catalog price? My guess is that they would not consider this move an ethical problem. There were no relationship risks involved in Sifford's fib. There was no question of constructing a good working relationship, no reputational interests at stake, and the salesman seemed to know exactly what Sifford was up to. He did not violate the salesman's trust. An idealist, by contrast, would object to Sifford's tactic on ethical grounds because it involved a lie designed to gain selfish advantage. Case closed.

◄ The Ethical Schools in Action ►

As a test of ethical thinking, let's take a simple example. Assume you are negotiating to sell a commercial building and the other party asks you whether you have another offer. In fact, you do not have any such offers. What would the three schools recommend you do?

A Poker School adherent might suggest a lie. Both parties are sophisticated businesspeople in this deal, so a lie about alternatives is probably legally "immaterial." But a member of the Poker School would want to know the answers to two questions before making his move.

First, could the lie be easily found out? If so, it would be a bad play because it wouldn't work and might put the other side on guard with respect to other lies he might want to tell. Second, is a lie about alternatives the best way to leverage the buyer into making a bid? Perhaps a lie about something else—a deadline, for example—might be a better choice.

Assuming the lie is undetectable and will work, how might the conversation sound?

Buyer: Do you have another offer?
Poker School Seller: Yes. A Saudi Arabian firm presented us with an offer for $____ this morning, and we have only forty-eight hours to get back to it with an answer. Confidentiality forbids us from showing you the Saudi offer, but rest assured that it is real. What would you like to do?

How would an idealist handle this situation? There are several idealist responses, but none would involve a lie. One response would be the following.

Buyer: Do you have another offer?
Idealist Seller 1: An interesting question—and one I refuse to answer.

Of course, that refusal speaks volumes to the buyer. Another approach would be to adopt a policy on "other buyer" questions.

Buyer: Do you have another offer?
Idealist Seller 2: An interesting question, and one I receive quite often. Let me answer you this way. The property's value to you is something for you to decide based on your needs and your own

sense of the market. However, I treat all offers with the greatest confidence. I will not discuss an offer you make to me with another
buyer, and I would not discuss any offer I received from someone
else with you. Will you be bidding?

Of course, this will work for an idealist only if he or she really and truly
has such a policy—a costly one when there is another attractive offer he
or she would like to reveal.

A final idealist approach would be to offer an honest, straightforward
answer. An idealist cannot lie or deliberately mislead, but he is allowed
to put the best face he can on the situation that is consistent with the
plain truth.

> *Buyer:* Do you have another offer?
> *Idealist Seller 3:* To be honest, we have no offers at this time. How-
> ever, we are hopeful that we will receive other offers soon. It might
> be in your interest to bid now and take the property before com-
> petition drives the price up.

How about the pragmatists? They would suggest using somewhat more
sophisticated, perhaps even deceptive, blocking techniques. These techniques would protect their leverage in ways that were consistent with maintaining working relationships. Once again, assume that the buyer has asked
the "other offer" question and there are no other offers. Here are five ways
a pragmatist might suggest you block this question to avoid an out-and-out
factual lie about other offers while minimizing the damage to your leverage. Some of these blocking techniques would work for idealists, too.

- *Declare the question out of bounds.* ("Company policy forbids any discussion of other offers in situations like this"—note that, if untrue, this is a lie, but it is one that carries less risk to your
  reputation because it is hard to confirm. If there really is such
  a company policy, an idealist could also use this move to block the
  question.)
- *Answer a different question.* ("We will not be keeping the property
  on the market much longer because the market is moving and our
  plans are changing." Again, if untrue, this statement is a mere lie
  about a "rationale" that troubles pragmatists less than idealists.)
- *Dodge the question.* ("The more important question is whether we
  are going to get an offer from you—and when.")

- *Ask a question of your own.* ("What alternatives are you examining at this time?")
- *Change the subject.* ("We are late for our next meeting already. Are you bidding today or not?")

Blocking techniques of this sort serve a utilitarian purpose. They preserve some leverage (though not as much as the Poker School) while reducing the risk of acquiring a reputation for deception. Relationships and reputations matter. If there is even a remote chance of a lie coming back to haunt you in a future negotiation with either the person you lie to or someone he may interact with, the pragmatists argue that you should not do it.

So—which school do you belong to? Or do you belong to a school of your own such as "pragmatic idealism"? To repeat: My advice is to aim high. The pressure of real bargaining often makes ethical compromisers of us all. When you fall below the standard of the Poker School, you are at serious risk of legal and even criminal liability.

◄ Bargaining with the Devil: ► The Art of Self-defense

Regardless of which school of bargaining ethics you adopt, you are going to face unscrupulous tactics from others on occasion. Even members of the Poker School sometimes face off against crooks. Are there any reliable means of self-defense to protect yourself and minimize the dangers? This section will give you some pointers on how to engage in effective self-defense against unethical tactics at the bargaining table.

First, let me relate a couple of stories of questionable bargaining behavior to see what the potential victims did to avert disaster. Then we will see how they could have perhaps done better. After that, I will list and describe some of the more common unethical gambits so you can recognize them when someone uses one against you.

◄ "That Was Just My Personal Price" ►

The first story involves a used-car purchase. A St. Louis newspaper reporter named Dale Singer went out to buy his daughter a used car. After some shopping, he found a perfectly suitable vehicle on the used-car lot

of a luxury-car dealership. The sticker price: $9,995. Singer haggled with
the salesman, and the price quickly dropped to $9,000. Singer haggled a
little more, and the salesman excused himself to visit with the sales manager. The salesman returned after a few minutes with a question.

"Would you buy it today for $8,500?" the salesman asked.

Singer liked the sound of that, but he was still shopping. He said he
would get back to the salesman after he had looked around a bit more.

A full day of car shopping turned up nothing more attractive than the
first car. That evening Singer called the salesman back and offered
$8,300. "I figured he probably wouldn't budge from his $8,500 offer, but
I knew that this was how the game was played," he later explained.

The salesman coolly replied that the price was now $8,900. When
Singer protested, the salesman explained that the $8,500 figure had
been his "personal offer" but that price had not been approved by the
sales manager. Singer reminded him that the $8,500 figure had been
mentioned just after a visit to the manager, and the salesman was sympathetic. He could sell the car for $8,700, but that was the best he could do.

Outraged, Singer demanded to speak with the sales manager himself.
The sales manager came on the line and explained that $8,500 was his
cost, so $8,700 was his final price. Singer asked for the name of the gen-
eral manager of the dealership, received it, and hung up.

A few minutes later the telephone rang again. It was the sales manager. Because there had been a genuine misunderstanding over the
price, he said, Singer could have the car for $8,500.

Singer bought the car, but the dealership later balked at giving him
full warranty service on the vehicle because of the low price he had paid.
Singer ended up with a fully functioning car at the price he wanted to
pay, but he was left wondering "Why should a customer have to work so
hard to be treated fairly?" He felt abused and bitter.

Singer did not know it, but the dealer "lowballed" him, tricking him
into becoming committed to the car at a bargain price, then nudging the
price up to exploit Singer's rising interest in the vehicle. Lowballing is a
classic, proven manipulative sales technique based on a hidden psychological premise. Singer was alert enough to reject it, but it works against
many customers.

◄ The Bidding War ►

My second story comes from a boom year in the New York City residential real estate market: 1997. A three-bedroom co-op apartment on Park Avenue went on the market, priced to sell at $1.7 million. Bonnie Chajet of Ashforth Warburg Associates had the exclusive listing.

As Ms. Chajet tells the story, the listing had not been on long when a man showed up with his own broker, looked at the apartment, and placed an all-cash bid for $1.4 million. The seller rejected the bid, telling the buyer he wasn't even close. Nothing more was heard from him.

Four days passed with no interest being shown in the unit. Finally, a second potential buyer looked the apartment over in the company of a different broker. He placed a bid of $1.3 million, which the seller also rejected. Chajet was at least pleased that so many different brokers were picking up on the listing.

Finally, after another three days with no takers, a third buyer with yet another broker appeared and bid $1.275 million. The seller rejected the third bid, too, but he began to wonder if Chajet had priced the apartment correctly.

When her client questioned the list price, Chajet did some investigating. It soon turned out that the second and third bidders were friends of the first one. "They were all in it together," explained Chajet, "trying to give the seller the signal that he'd better take the 'high' offer." The apartment sold a few days later—for the full price.

Chajet and her client were the victims of bid rigging, a blatant form of deception. Like lowballing, phony bids are designed to exert subtle psychological pressure on people who do not suspect they are being conned.

◄ Techniques for Coping with ► Unethical Tactics

What do these two stories tell us about "bargaining with the devil"? Let's see if we can make a list of effective self-defense moves.

WATCH OUT FOR "TRANSACTIONS"

Certain situations pose a higher risk of unethical conduct than othe
It is no coincidence that these two stories (as well as Darrell Siff

were Transaction events (see Chapter 7). When the price is the primary issue and there are limited prospects for future dealings between the parties, there is a higher risk of ethical problems.

One might have hoped that the car dealership in Singer's story would have seen the sale as part of a potential relationship rather than simply a transaction, but the used-car segment of even a luxury-car business is sometimes staffed with people paid on commission who couldn't care less about customer relations. Be on guard whenever the stakes matter and the relationship does not.

The risk of unethical conduct rises even higher when competition is "hot." Research shows that leverage imbalances at the bargaining table encourage unethical behavior. Interestingly, both the stronger and the weaker parties have incentives to lie and cheat. One set of authors concluded after their experiment that "it is to the advantage of those who possess little power to use deceit against those of greater power when they do not wish to comply with the latter's demands." Another set of scholars found that the more powerful party in an unbalanced situation can become "intoxicated" with his leverage. They offer the opinion that "in general, negotiators with more power are more likely to abuse that power by using less ethical tactics."

RELY ON RELATIONSHIPS
WHENEVER POSSIBLE

When seeking bargaining partners, use your relationship network (see Chapter 4) to advantage. Try to get recommendations, referrals, and introductions that will show the other side that the relationship with you matters. This move somewhat mitigates the incentives to behave unethically that would otherwise apply.

Singer might have saved himself some grief by shopping for a dealership rather than a car. He could have checked with friends and gotten the names of dealers with a high reputation for service and fair dealing. He could have approached the dealership with these referrals from known, valued customers as partial protection from exploitative conduct.

Relationships could not have helped Chajet because in the real estate market one has to take all comers. But it is worth noting that the seller was saved in this deal by his professional relationship with his broker, Chajet herself. Without a broker, the seller might well have fallen for this con game.

Research shows that, in general, the prospect of an ongoing relationship raises people's ethical standards. As one scholar has put it, "When a negotiator does not anticipate having to 'live with' the consequences of using ethically marginal tactics, she is far more willing to use them."

PROBE, PROBE, PROBE

Be alert to the potential for deception in negotiation. Most people tend to give others the benefit of the doubt when judging whether lies have been told. This bias is fine for most of our social interchanges and for Relationship and Tacit Coordination situations involving negotiation. But it can be costly when the stakes matter in bargaining.

If your suspicions are aroused, as they were in both Singer's and Chajet's cases, don't rest until you discover what is going on. Chajet saved her client by conducting an investigation into the fake bids, probably by checking with her network, that is, the brokers who had innocently accompanied the phony buyers. As an astute negotiator, Sir Frances Bacon, put it in an essay called "Of Negotiating" he wrote in 1597, "In dealing with cunning people, we must ever consider their needs to interpret their speeches."

Singer could have done much better on this score. The car salesman misled him about the price, but Singer was a victim as much of his own assumptions as of the salesman's guile. The salesman spoke clearly and carefully: "Would you buy it today for $8,500?" Singer might have fleshed out this curiously phrased question before drawing his conclusion that the car was available at that price. "Are you making me a concrete offer at that price?" he could have asked.

Probing will help you gain insight into whether the other side's story holds together, but do not expect the other party to come right out and admit he is acting unethically. You will have to rely on your judgment as well as his conduct. Research suggests that it is very difficult to detect when others are lying and, even when you do, to discern what they are lying about. You should check as many sources of information as possible before you draw a firm conclusion.

If you discover that the other side is acting unethically, should you call him or her on it? Perhaps—if that advances your goals. But I would wait to see if direct embarrassment is really necessary. For example, suppose the buyer in Chajet's case turned out to be the only interested party. His check for $1.4 million is good and the offer is all cash. Should you take his money or confront him with his unethical conduct? I think I would take the cash. But I would wait until the check cleared before I gave him the deed.

BE ASSERTIVE AND PERSISTENT

When other people are acting unethically, it is up to you to insist on fairness. Singer ultimately got his price by pushing back, persevering, and refusing to be lowballed. Chajet's seller also pushed back. He was not stampeded into a sale based on the sequence of declining bids.

MAINTAIN YOUR OWN STANDARDS— DON'T SINK TO THEIRS

It is tempting to engage in tit for tat when the other side uses unethical tactics. We get angry. We lose perspective and start down the unethical path ourselves.

Avoid this trap. First, no matter what school of bargaining ethics you adhere to, you need to keep your record clean both to maintain your self-respect and to avoid gaining a reputation for slippery dealing. Second, as soon as you begin acting unethically, you lose the right to protest other people's conduct. Their behavior may give you a legitimate claim to extract concessions, or it may form the basis for a legal case. Once you join them in the gutter, you forfeit your moral and legal advantage.

Figure 11.1 is a tool to keep yourself out of trouble with deception. You'll have to decide for yourself whether the advice on the chart passes muster under your personal ethical standards. So far as I know, all of the alternatives are legal, so Poker School adherents who find themselves in a tight spot in which a lie will not work should feel free to use them. Pragmatists usually prefer to avoid lies if relationships matter, so these will be helpful to them, too. Idealists can use any of these that involve telling the truth in a way that does not mislead or deflecting a question with an obvious, transparent blocking maneuver.

Remember, there is no commandment in negotiation that says "Thou shalt answer every question that is asked." And as an aspiring idealist, I have found it useful to follow this rule: *Whenever you are tempted to lie about something, stop, think for a moment, and then find something—anything—to tell the truth about.* If the other side asks you about your alternatives or your bottom line, deflect that question and then tell the truth about your goals, expectations, and interests.

FIGURE 11.1

Alternatives to Lying

Instead of Lying About	*Try This*
1. Bottom line	Blocking maneuvers: *Ask about their bottom line. *Say, "It's not your business." *Say, "I'm not free to disclose that." *Tell the truth about your goal. *Focus on your problems/needs.
2. Lack of authority	Obtain only limited authority in the first place. Require ratification by your group.
3. Availability of alternatives	Initiate efforts to improve alternatives. Stress opportunities and uncertainties. Be satisfied with the status quo.
4. Commitment to positions	Commit to general goals. Commit to standards. Commit to addressing the other side's interests.
5. Phony issues	Inject new issues with real value or make a true wish list.
6. Threats	Use cooling-off periods. Suggest third-party help. Discuss use of a formula.
7. Intentions	Make only promises you can and will keep.
8. Facts	Focus on uncertainty regarding the facts. Use language carefully. Express your *opinion*.

◄ A Rogue's Gallery of Tactics ►

As my final offering on this topic, here is a list of the more common manipulative tactics you will encounter at the bargaining table. We have seen some of these before, but I will summarize them again for ease of reference. Note that only some of them involve overt deception.

I do not label these "unethical" because most of them are well within the boundaries of the Poker School and some can work even for pragmatists when there is no relationship problem in view.

LIES ABOUT BOTTOM LINES
AND ALTERNATIVES

We've talked about these. They are the most common lies of all. Take any statements of this sort with a big grain of salt unless you know and trust the other party, or you have all the leverage and the other party's claims about its alternatives don't matter.

LOWBALLING

This is the "too good to be true" offer the car dealership tried to use on Singer. The other side gets you committed to the deal before revealing the full, true cost to you. After you say "yes," they know you want what they are peddling and they work the price back in their favor by adding terms.

Don't think this technique works only in sales. Have you ever met a children's soccer coach who got you to agree to let your child play on his team, only to find out that the team practices every evening at dinnertime and plays on Sundays at 6 A.M.? That's a lowball encounter.

PHONY ISSUES

Negotiation guru Roger Dawson calls this the "Decoy" or "Red Herring" technique. One side lists four or five issues as being very important or even vital, when, in fact, only one or two matter. The rest are phony issues. That side pushes hard on the whole agenda, creating a serious risk of impasse, then relents on all the phony issues in exchange for major concessions on the issues that really matter.

Here is an example of the phony issues ploy involving some people we have met before in this book. When Akio Morita's Sony Corporation was in the middle of its $5 billion purchase of Columbia Pictures in 1989, it negotiated a $200 million side deal with Jon Peters and Peter Guber for Guber-Peters Entertainment to run Sony's new movie division. There was just one problem: Guber and Peters were already under contract with Warner Bros. and Warner's boss, Steve Ross.

Guber and Peters assured Sony that they had an oral agreement that Ross would release them from their existing contract if the Sony-Columbia deal went through, but they were secretly worried that Ross might cause trouble (and they were right—Ross subsequently sued Sony for $1 billion over this issue). The Guber-Peters team needed to negotiate as much time as possible to fix the release.

Guber and Peters threw three issues onto the table in the final round of bargaining over their proposed contract with Sony: two phony issues and the issue of the time they would get after the Sony-Columbia deal closed to obtain their release from Warner. They negotiated all night on all three issues. At 7 A.M., the Guber-Peters team made its final move: "On point number one, we give up," said their attorney. "On point number two, we give up. On point number three—the timing—you should give up." Sony relented and gave them a full month to get their release.

FAKE AUTHORITY PLOYS

Lies about authority take two forms. First, people will lie and say they have authority when they do not. That was essentially what the car salesman did when he mentioned the $8,500 price to Singer just after visiting the sales manager. These lies are usually in the service of a lowball maneuver. They are hard to combat. In general, when in any doubt, it pays to ask for proof of authority when the other side makes an offer.

The second kind of lie involves people saying they have no authority when in fact they do. Lawyers and other agents and brokers do this a lot. If you make an offer that is within their authority, they will lie and say that they are not authorized to accept your offer because it is not high or low enough. The solution to this problem is to avoid dealing with agents if you can. Make your offers directly to the people who have the power to say "yes" or "no."

Finally, watch out for authority ploys such as the ones discussed in Chapter 3 in which the other side presents you with a dense contract of "standard terms" or claims the boss is asking everyone to agree. Defer to authority if you must, but make sure the authority is real.

OVERCOMMITMENT

This tactic was discussed in detail in Chapter 10. Essentially, the other negotiator drags out the negotiation process and/or gets you to make an investment based on an assumption that it will go through. Then he raises or lowers the price or adds new terms at the last minute, trusting that you have too much invested to lose and so will say "yes." The best antidote is to monitor your commitment and ask yourself if the other party is as invested as you are.

GOOD GUY/BAD GUY

This tactic was covered in Chapter 9. It uses the contrast effect to make otherwise unreasonable terms and conditions look reasonable. The bad guy introduces outrageous and demanding terms. His teammate, the good guy, becomes your advocate and argues the bad guy down to a merely aggressive level. You and the good guy bond against the bad guy. In the end, you win the argument and lose the negotiation. The best way to fight this is to recognize it, name it, and refuse to go along with it.

CONSISTENCY TRAPS

Chapter 3 discusses this tactic. A consistency trap works as follows: The other negotiator gets you to agree to an innocent-sounding standard or norm. Then he springs the trap by showing you that his proposal is the logical consequence of your admission. The solution to a consistency trap is to see it coming before you agree to the standard and hedge your commitment to the standard.

RECIPROCITY PLOYS

When we negotiate, we take turns exchanging questions and answers and making concessions. Watch out for people who either refuse to reciprocate in the process or who only appear to do so without giving substantive answers. The norm of reciprocity entitles you to tit-for-tat treatment in bargaining. Insist on it.

THE NIBBLE

Chapter 10 mentions this one. Parties nibble at an agreement just before closing. They raise an extra issue or demand that in and of itself is so small it does not seem worthy of debate. But they get this issue without trading for it, so it is pure profit. The dedicated nibbler can add 3 to 5 percent of value to his or her contracts this way. This tactic gains power from both the contrast effect and the overcommitment phenomenon. The antidote? Just say no. Or require something in trade for every concession requested by the nibbler.

◄ Summary ►

Ethical dilemmas are at the center of many bargaining encounters. There is no escaping the fact that deception is part of negotiation. And there is no escaping the importance people place on personal integrity in their dealings with others at the bargaining table. One ethical slip and your credibility is lost not just for one but for many deals. Effective negotiators take the issue of personal integrity very seriously. Ineffective negotiators do not.

How do you balance these two contradictory factors? I have presented three frameworks for thinking about ethical issues: the Poker School, the Idealist School, and the Pragmatist School. I personally think you are better off sticking to the truth as much as possible. I sometimes lose leverage as the price of this scruple, but I gain a greater measure of ease and self-respect as compensation.

Where you come out on bargaining ethics, of course, is a matter for you to decide. My only injunction to you is the one I started out with in Chapter 1 and repeated earlier in this chapter: Negotiators who value personal integrity can be counted on to behave consistently, using a thoughtful set of personal values that they could, if necessary, explain and defend to others.

◄ ETHICS: A CHECKLIST ►

✓ Decide which school of bargaining ethics you belong to.

✓ Determine whether you can use your relationships to offset the dangers of unethical conduct by others involved in the transaction.

✓ Probe, probe, probe. Don't take what you hear at face value.

✓ Pause. Remember that you don't have to answer every question.

✓ Don't lie. Instead, find a way to use the truth to your advantage.

12

Conclusion: On Becoming an Effective Negotiator

Do not be so sweet that people will eat you up, nor so bitter that they will spit you out.

—Pashto folk saying

Everyone lives by selling something.

—Robert Louis Stevenson

When we hear the word "negotiations," most of us think about formal, even dramatic events involving diplomats, politicians, sports and entertainment personalities, CEOs, Wall Street deal makers, and labor lawyers. These negotiations are the "blockbusters" of bargaining: staged affairs conducted by trained, experienced professionals for the benefit of specific audiences.

These high-profile bargaining contests are important, but they are relatively rare occasions even for the experts involved in them. The real negotiating work most of us do takes place in a myriad of ordinary events that happen every day, mainly out of view except to ourselves and those closest to us. These less visible negotiations include those between medical staffs and patients' families in hospital corridors over care for loved ones; closed-door battles over control and power between feuding business partners; tense bargaining sessions among corporate executives over which divisions and employees will face downsizing at their firm;

and the back-and-forth discussions that take place at kitchen tables as parents and children give operational meaning to words such as "independence" and "responsibility."

These negotiations matter just as much as the "big deals" do. And the people involved in them—reasonable people trying to do their jobs and make their lives work—need reliable, expert knowledge about the negotiation process to help them become more effective. That is why I wrote this book—to help you make negotiation a ready tool for achieving goals in every facet of your business, community, and personal life.

I once received a letter from a former executive negotiation student of mine, a man I'll call Bill Siegel. Bill, who owns his own small company in the northeastern United States, was a participant in our Wharton Executive Negotiation Workshop a couple of years ago. He had been a genuinely anxious negotiator when he came through the Wharton program—uncertain of his skills and convinced that visiting the dentist was to be preferred to bargaining. Siegel was writing to give me an update on how his negotiation skills were progressing.

"My ten-year-old still has me against the wall," he joked, "but business negotiations have actually become challenging and fun." After commenting on some marketing alliances and partnerships he was putting together, he told an interesting story that illustrates many of the points I have tried to make in the book.

As a member of a nonprofit organization concerned with revitalizing his community, Siegel had heard that his city was about to spend $450,000 to demolish an ornate, 125-year-old downtown building.

Bill thought this was a waste, and negotiation training kicked in immediately.

His first step, of course, was to prepare clear, specific goals. Bill determined that he wanted to save the building, put it to productive use, and, if possible, make a profit for himself in the process. He investigated and found out that, although the city placed a high priority on restoring its commercial tax base, no one in city hall had the time or imagination to salvage this building.

With this preliminary step behind him, Bill made his first move. He used his relationship network to gain access to the city official in charge of demolishing the building. Siegel convinced this official that, provided Siegel could put together a deal at minimal cost to the city, it would make more sense to give Siegel $450,000 to renovate the building than to spend the money destroying the property.

With $450,000 in his pocket, Siegel started looking for interested parties who might help him raise further funds. A friend told him there might be state grants available for a downtown renewal project like this, and he soon located $270,000 of state money from a program designed to help preserve historic downtown buildings. Finally, he persuaded city tax officials to provide a generous tax abatement from the city for any commercial tenants he could line up. With the tax abatement as leverage, he landed three prospective commercial tenants and a historical group interested in relocating to the building after it was renovated.

His last step was to ensure that he achieved his own personal goal for this project—a profit. He negotiated a ninety-nine-year lease on the building from the city for the grand sum of $1. He then sold the whole package to a professional real estate developer for a substantial sum. There was enough money in the deal to make everyone happy.

The remarkable thing about Siegel's story is the way his negotiation skills made *everyone* better off: city, state, tenants, the developer, and him. And he negotiated this deal in his spare time—he is in the consulting, not real estate, business.

Siegel's story gives you a sense of what can happen once you learn the basics of how negotiations work and start making a difference in the world. As a teacher, I am constantly reminded of the powerful boost that negotiation skills give people who are trying to achieve their goals, often against major odds. With confidence in your bargaining abilities, obstacles become opportunities.

◄ A Final Look at Effectiveness ►

Let's see how Bill Siegel's story can help us review what we have learned about negotiation. To improve the way you negotiate, the first step is to make a commitment to work on this area of activity. Once you have formulated your resolve, there is no substitute for concentrating on the four effectiveness factors I discuss in Chapter 1—a willingness to prepare, high expectations, the patience to listen, and a commitment to personal integrity. These are the best practices of the best negotiators and will improve your results no matter what negotiation situation you face and no matter who you are. Siegel exhibited all four factors in his downtown renewal project.

The Six Foundations also provide basic, all-purpose touchstones for good execution: Know your style, survey your goals and focus on your expectations, look for the applicable standards, attend to and use your relationships, probe the other side's interests, and work on your leverage before getting started. Finally, perform a good situational analysis using the Situational Matrix in Chapter 7 and chart your course through the information exchange, opening and concession-making, and closing and commitment stages of each encounter. Choosing the right strategy for the situation and people you face is critical to your success. Have a confident attitude based on high ethical standards throughout the process.

Before we conclude, I want to put a final item into your negotiator's "toolbox": a tailored, operational checklist to raise your bargaining potential to its peak performance. There are two separate performance checklists below: one for people who are basically cooperative and one for those who are more competitive. Pick the one that applies to you, then carry it with you as you go into your next bargaining session.

━ Seven Tools for Highly Cooperative People ━

If you are basically a cooperative, reasonable person, you need to become more **assertive, confident,** and **prudent** in negotiations to become more effective. How can you do this? It is sometimes the hardest thing in the world to gear up for a potentially confrontational negotiating situation.

Here are seven specific tools to improve your bargaining performance.

1. *Avoid concentrating too much on your bottom line—spend extra time preparing your goals and developing high expectations.* As a cooperative person, you often worry about other people's needs first. You focus on your bottom line and try to do just a little better than that. And guess what? Your bottom line is exactly what you get. Research confirms that people who expect more get more. Refocus your thinking on your goals and expectations. Spend extra time considering carefully what you want and why you want it.

2. *Develop a specific alternative as a fallback if the negotiation fails.* Too often, cooperative people leave themselves without choices at the bargaining table. They have no alternatives planned if negotiations fail.

Take note: If you can't walk away, you can't say "no."

Remember the story about "Janie Rail" in Chapter 6. A Houston utilities buyer built her own railroad when the rail company she was doing business with refused to give her a competitive price for delivering coal. Lesson: There is always an alternative. Find out what it is and bring it with you to the bargaining table. You will feel more confident.

3. *Get an agent and delegate the negotiation task.* If you are up against competitive negotiators, you will be at a disadvantage. Find a more competitively oriented person to act as your agent or at least join your team. This is not an admission of failure or lack of skill. It is prudent and wise.

4. *Bargain on behalf of someone or something else, not yourself.* Even competitive people feel weaker when they are negotiating on their own behalf. Cooperative people think they are being selfish to insist on things coming out their way.

Fine. Don't negotiate for yourself. Stop for a moment and think about other people and causes—your family, your staff, even your future "retired self"—that are depending on you to act as their agent and "bring home the bacon" in this negotiation. Then bargain on *their* behalf. Research shows that people bargain harder when they act as agents for others' interests.

5. *Create an audience.* Research reveals that people negotiate more assertively when other people are watching them. That is why labor negotiators are so tough—they know the union rank and file is watching their every move.

Take advantage of this effect. Tell someone you know about the negotiation. Explain your goals and how you intend to proceed. Promise to report to them on the results when the negotiation is over.

6. *Say, "You'll have to do better than that, because . . ."* Cooperative people are programmed to say "yes" to almost any plausible proposal someone else makes. To improve, you need to practice pushing back a little when others make a bargaining move.

A simple phrase that works is "You'll have to do better than that, because . . ." (fill in a reason). The better the reason, the better you will feel about it *but any truthful reason will do.*

Research shows that many people will respond favorably if you make a request in a reasonable tone of voice and accompany it with a "because" statement. In one famous study, a Harvard psychologist increased the compliance rate for requests by 50 to 100 percent just by giving a "dummy" reason when she made a request. She set up an experiment at a photocopy machine in the library and had her experimenters wait for a line to form, then try to cut into the line to make copies.

When the requester had just five pages to copy, about 60 percent of the people said "yes" to the question "Excuse me, I have five pages. May I use the Xerox machine?" When the requestor had twenty pages to copy, the "yes" rate understandably dropped to 24 percent.

Then the requestor added the phrase "because I'm in a rush" to the end of the request. Now it went like this: "Excuse me, I have five [or twenty] pages. May I use the Xerox machine because I'm in a rush?" The success rate leaped to 94 percent for the five-page request and a remarkable 42 percent for the twenty-page request.

Try this technique at the store, at school, in the airport, on the telephone, everywhere. Then use it at the bargaining table. Remember, the better the reason, the better you will feel about it and the more likely you will be to achieve your goal. And try doing this the idealist way: Make the reason truthful.

7. *Insist on commitments, not just agreements.* Cooperative people think others are as good-hearted as they themselves are. They trust others more than is good for them, and they think an agreement is all that is needed to ensure that performance will take place as promised.

Don't be so trusting. Agreements are fine if you have a solid basis for believing that the other party's word is its bond. But be sure you have that foundation before risking all the work you have invested in a negotiation. If you don't know the people on the other side well or suspect that they may be untrustworthy, set the agreement up so they have something to lose if they fail to perform.

◄ Seven Tools for Highly Competitive People ►

If you are basically a competitive but still reasonable person, you need more than anything to become **more aware of other people and their legitimate needs.** How can you do this? It is sometimes the hardest thing in the world to overcome your inherent suspicion of others' motives. And it is difficult to resist temptation when you are dealing with a cooperative person who is naively handing things to you.

Here are seven specific tools you can use to improve your bargaining performance.

1. *Think win-win, not just win.* I know I said at the beginning of the book that win-win is an empty idea. It is—for accommodating and cooperative people. For competitive people, win-win is an excellent reminder that the other party matters. Go for deals in which both sides do better but you do the best of all.

2. *Ask more questions than you think you should.* Competitive people like to get enough information to see where an advantage might lie, then pounce and try to exploit the opening. Don't be in such a hurry. Other

people have a variety of needs; they do not always want the same things you do. If you can understand what is really important to them, they will give you more of what is important to you.

3. *Rely on standards.* Reasonable people respond well to arguments based on their standards and norms. Don't be too quick to use a leverage-based approach to negotiation when a standards-based approach will work just as well. Reasoned arguments also work better than power plays when future relationships are important.

4. *Hire a relationship manager.* You will do better when the relationship matters if you delegate the relationship management aspect of the deal to someone who is better with people than you are. This is not a sign of failure; it is prudent and wise.

5. *Be scrupulously reliable. Keep your word.* You may have a tendency to cut corners when you see victory just ahead. But other people notice if you break your promises, even over little things. And they have memories like elephants.

Establish a record of scrupulous reliability, and others will trust you more. A lot of money can be made when people trust each other.

6. *Don't haggle when you can negotiate.* You are tempted to haggle over every issue and try to win each one. That is a sure way to leave money on the table in complex negotiations.

Try integrative bargaining in complex situations: Make big moves on your little issues and little moves on your big ones. Manage your priorities. Package your trade-offs using the "If . . . Then" formulation discussed in Chapter 9.

7. *Always acknowledge the other party. Protect his or her self-esteem.* People are proud. They like to hear you say they have some leverage, even when they do not.

Don't gloat when you are the more powerful party. Treat people on the other side with appropriate respect. This does not cost much, and they will appreciate it. Someday they will have the leverage, and they will remember you more kindly.

➤ A Final Word ➤

In the Introduction, I said my goal in writing this book was to show you how to negotiate realistically and intelligently, without giving up your self-respect. You are now in a position to judge if I have achieved that goal.

Effective negotiation is, in my judgment, 10 percent technique and 90 percent attitude. To acquire the right attitude, you need all three of the elements mentioned above: realism, intelligence, and self-respect.

You will not succeed unless you approach the negotiation process realistically. It is best to be prudent and prepared. Unscrupulous people will try to take advantage of you. Don't let them.

Bargain smart. Remember that the key to success in negotiation is *information*. Use the information you gather to negotiate intelligently. Formulate adaptive strategies that fit both the situation and the people you confront. Don't go into a negotiation with the idea that a single one-size-fits-all strategy will get you through. Use your planning tools and think about what you will do in advance.

Finally, take the high road. Without self-respect, you lose the will to succeed as well as the respect of others. It requires hard work to maintain your integrity in bargaining but that work is well worth it.

I study negotiation because it is a fascinating aspect of human social life. It keeps surprising me. I teach it because I feel tremendous satisfaction when I see people like Bill Siegel take negotiation knowledge, make it their own, and start achieving their goals. This book has been part of that effort. Join me in using the laboratory of your everyday life to keep learning more about this remarkable process. You have the tools to improve.

Now, practice using them.

Appendix A:
Bargaining Styles
Assessment Tool

<-->

Follow this four-step process to determine your personal bargaining style preferences.

1. Without giving the matter too much thought (and without revising your answers for any reason!), please select ONE STATEMENT in each pair of statements below. Select the statement you think is *more accurate* for you when you face a negotiation or disagreement with someone else—even if you think neither statement is very accurate or both are very accurate. Think about such situations in general—not just ones at work or at home. And don't pick the statement you "ought" to agree with—pick the one your gut tells you is more accurate for you most of the time. Some statements repeat, but do not worry about answering consistently. Just keep going. All answers are equally "correct."

2. After selecting a statement from every pair, go back and add up the total number of As, Bs, Cs, Ds, and Es you recorded. Put the totals in the "Results" space at the end of the survey.

3. Plot your total scores on the Evaluation Grid provided. Connect each of the numbers you circle with lines to make a simple graph. Your strongest inclinations will plot at the top of the graph while your weakest inclinations will plot near the bottom.

4. Return to the Chapter 1 text, or continue reading in this Appendix for a more in-depth explanation of your scores and the general subject of bargaining styles.

STEP 1: STYLE SURVEY

1. **E. I work hard to preserve the relationship with my counterpart**
   B. I try to identify the underlying issues   I select _E_

2. D. I work to defuse tense situations
   A. I gain concessions by being persistent   I select _A_

3. **E. I focus on solving the other party's problem**
   D. I try to avoid unnecessary conflicts   I select _E_

4. C. I search for a fair compromise
   E. I work hard to preserve the relationship   I select _E_

5. **C. I suggest fair compromises**
   D. I avoid personal confrontations   I select _C_

6. C. I seek the midpoint between our positions.
   B. I search for the problems underlying our
      disagreements   I select _B_

7. **D. I tactfully resolve many disagreements**
   C. I expect "give and take" in negotiations   I select _C_

8. A. I clearly communicate my goals
   B. I focus my attention on the other side's needs   I select _A_

9. **D. I prefer to put off confrontations with other people**
   A. I win my points by making strong arguments   I select _A_

10. C. I am usually willing to compromise
    A. I enjoy winning concessions   I select _C_

11. **B. I candidly address all the problems between us**
    E. I care more about the relationship than
       winning the last concession   I select _E_

12. D. I try to avoid unnecessary personal conflicts
    C. I search for fair compromises   I select _C_

13. **C. I give concessions and expect some concessions in return**
    A. I strive to achieve all my goals in negotiations   I select _A_

14. A. I enjoy getting concessions more than making them
    E. I strive to maintain the relationship   I select _E_

15. **E. I accommodate their needs to preserve the relationship**
    D. I leave confrontational situations to others if I can   I select _E_

16. E. I try to address to the other person's needs
    A. I work hard to achieve all my goals   I select _E_

17. **A. I make sure to discuss my goals**
    D. I emphasize areas on which we agree   I select _A_

18. E. I am always looking out for the relationship
    C. I give concessions and expect the other side to
       do the same   I select _E_

19. **B. I identify and discuss all of our differences**
    D. I try to avoid confrontations   I select _B_

20. A. I obtain my share of concessions
    E. I strive to maintain relationships   I select _E_

21. **B. I identify and discuss all of our differences**
    **C. I look for the compromises that might bridge
       the gap**   I select _B_

22. E. I develop good relations with the other party
    B. I develop options that address both of our needs   I select _B_

23. **C. I seek the middle ground**
    A. I strive to achieve my goals in negotiations   I select _A_

24. B. I identify all of our differences and look for solutions
    D. I try to avoid unnecessary conflicts   I select _B_

25. **E. I try to preserve the relationship with my counterpart**
    C. I search for fair compromises   I select _E_

26. D. I emphasize the issues on which we agree
    B. I uncover and address the things on which we
       disagree   I select _D_

27. **A. I work hard to achieve my goals**
    B. I pay attention to the other person's needs   I select _A_

28. C. I look for the fair compromise
    B. I try to identify all of the underlying problems   I select _C_

29. **D. I avoid unnecessary disagreements**
    E. I focus on solving the other person's problem   I select _D_

30. A. I strive to achieve my goals
    B. I work to address everyone's needs   I select _B_

STEP 2: RECORD RESULTS

Add up all your A, B, C, D, and E answers on the previous pages and put those totals below:

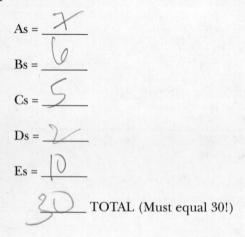

As = 7

Bs = 6

Cs = 5

Ds = 2

Es = 10

30 TOTAL (Must equal 30!)

STEP 3: PLOT YOUR SCORES

Find and circle the numbers on the following grid that correspond to your scores for each of the five letters. Circle your A score in the first vertical column on the left side of the grid marked "Competing—A." Circle your B score in the next vertical column marked "Collaborating—B," and so on over to the last vertical column on the right, which is for your E or "Accommodating" score.

Once you have one circle in each column of the grid, connect these five circles with straight lines so you have created a simple graph. Scores at the top of the graph (usually those above the 70th percentile) are your strongest bargaining style inclinations. Scores at the bottom of the graph (usually below the 30th percentile) are your weaker bargaining style inclinations. All scores between the 30th and 70th percentiles represent moderate, functional bargaining style inclinations. And the higher or lower the percentile, the stronger the inclination to use that move in ordinary negotiations.

For deeper insight into bargaining styles, their origins and their meanings, continue reading in Appendix A. First-time readers may want return to Chapter 1 and pick up the theme of bargaining styles there, leaving the further study of this subject for later.

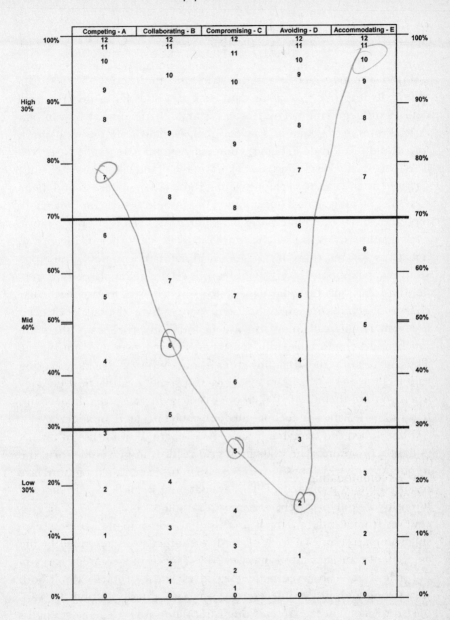

FURTHER ANALYSIS OF YOUR PERSONAL BARGAINING STYLES

Interest in personal bargaining styles and the use of assessment instruments to probe this factor date back almost as far as do organized courses on negotiation. The reason is simple: bargaining styles can play crucial roles in negotiation. Entrepreneur Donald Trump is well known to be (and takes pride in being) competitive to his core. Cable News Network personality Larry King is well known to be (and takes pride in being) empathetic and easy to get along with. If these two men were to find themselves negotiating against one another, both would be wise to think about their own and their counterpart's bargaining styles before making a move.

Bargaining styles, as I see them, are relatively stable, personality-driven behaviors and reactions that arise in negotiating encounters. These patterns reappear because we are, for reasons related to family, culture, gender, and early professional experience, predisposed toward particular courses of action in negotiation. Some people have a broad set of styles they can readily call upon to solve negotiation problems. Others are much more comfortable with some bargaining moves and not others. The true test of your bargaining styles is your emotional reaction to using various strategies—which strategies give you genuine satisfaction, even joy when you use them well? Which ones repeatedly cause you anxiety and frustration, leaving you feeling uncomfortable, irritated, or angry?

I developed the Bargaining Styles Assessment Tool for use in my negotiation programs. The evaluation grid records in percentile form the frequency with which business executives in my executive programs have reported their various scores. This evaluation grid allows you to plot the intensity of your preferences against a sample of over 1,500 global executives from a wide variety of professional fields. Below, I present capsule summaries of what each of the five conflict styles described by the assessment translates into when viewed as aspects of a complex bargaining style. I have observed many executives whose profiles exhibit both very strong and, just as interestingly, very weak predispositions for various strategies. These extremes often translate into systematic strengths and weaknesses as negotiators, depending on the situation they face.

SOME CHARACTERISTICS OF NEGOTIATORS
EXHIBITING THE FIVE BARGAINING STYLES

Over the years, I have discussed bargaining style profiles with thousands of executives and other professionals. In these conversations, I have tested various style-based hypotheses with them for confirmation or disconfirmation. Below I summarize this experience by commenting on the bargaining strengths and weaknesses that may be exhibited by negotiators in a relatively high (70th or higher) percentile or relatively low (30th or lower) percentile for each conflict mode. For shorthand, I refer to people with each trait by the name of the bargaining style itself (e.g., "high accommodator" or "low compromiser"). I am thus assuming in these comments that the person is "high" or "low" in the subject conflict style *only*—and "in the middle" for all other modes. This is a convenient rather than a realistic assumption, but it permits me to discuss some important implications of each trait. Individuals may exhibit strong or weak preferences for several strategies, and the interaction of these preferences will, of course, affect the way they experience and manage their bargaining behavior in any given situation.

ACCOMMODATING

Negotiators Strongly Predisposed toward Accommodating. Negotiators with a strong predisposition toward accommodation derive significant satisfaction from solving other peoples' problems. They often have good relationship-building skills and are relatively sensitive to others' emotional states, body language, and verbal signals. This is a great trait to summon when working on negotiating problems within teams, bargaining in sales-based "relationship management" roles, or providing many types of customer services.

In terms of weaknesses, high accommodators sometimes place more weight on the relationship aspect of negotiations than the situation may warrant. In such cases, they are vulnerable to more competitively oriented people. High accommodators who feel taken advantage of in such situations may then experience resentment, further impeding their effectiveness.

Weakly Predisposed toward Accommodating. Negotiators with low accommodation scores have a tendency to hold out for their view of the "right" answer to a negotiating problem. They stay within their own frame of reference, seeing their solution as *objectively* correct. In short, low accommodators are sometimes more concerned with being "right" than with being persuasive. Where the low accommodator is an expert who understands the negotiation problem better than others at the table, this trait will assure that a group spends plenty of time considering the objectively "best" outcome. However, others may perceive the low accommodator as stubborn to the point of being unreasonable. This perception can interfere with effective group decision making. In addition, more accommodating people may mistake the low accommodator's preoccupation with the "right" answer (and associated lack of attention to other people's feelings and emotions) as a signal that the low accommodator does not care about them as individuals. Again, this can lower people's willingness to cooperate.

COMPROMISING

Negotiators Strongly Predisposed toward Compromising. People with a strong predisposition toward compromising are usually eager to close the deal by "closing the gap" in negotiations. They scan the environment for fair standards and formulae that can help them achieve closure as quickly as possible. When time is short, or when the stakes are small, a predisposition toward compromise can be a virtue. Others will see the high compromiser as a relationship-friendly "reasonable person." However, high compromisers often rush the negotiation process unnecessarily and make concessions too quickly. They do not question their own assumptions and rarely ask enough questions of the other side. They may also be satisfied with the first fair standard that presents itself as the basis for concluding the deal when other, equally fair standards might support a more advantageous deal.

Weakly Predisposed toward Compromising. People with a weak predisposition for compromise are, almost by definition, men and women of principle. Their great strength is their ability to summon passion and commitment when serious matters of principle and precedent are at stake in a negotiation. Their great weakness is their tendency to "make an issue" of everything—finding issues of principle where others see only issues relating to money or relative convenience. By arguing at length about things others see as secondary, the low compromiser risks being seen by others as stubborn—a person who is more concerned with winning an argument than closing a deal. Their distaste for such arbitrary allocation norms as splitting the difference can also make it more difficult for the low compromiser to close a deal when time is short.

A comparison between low accommodators and low compromisers is instructive. Low accommodators can (more quickly than most) become attached to their own preferred "correct" solutions. Low compromisers, by comparison, become attached to their own preferred "correct" principles and fairness arguments. In both cases, they may irritate other people, acquiring reputations for being stubborn.

AVOIDING

Negotiators Strongly Predisposed toward Avoiding. High avoiders are adept at deferring and dodging the confrontational aspects of negotiation. As a positive attribute, avoidance can be experienced by others as graceful tact and diplomacy. It can also permit groups to function better in the face of dysfunctional, hard-to-resolve interpersonal differences. High avoiders are skilled at using such conflict-reducing methods as clear rules, unambiguous decision-making authority, and hierarchies to substitute for negotiations. High avoiders are also at home using techniques like e-mail, memos, hired agents, and other intermediaries that minimize the need for face-to-face confrontation. When interpersonal conflict is a *functional* aspect of organizational or group life, high avoiders can be a bottleneck in the flow of important information about the intensity of people's preferences. And when interpersonal conflicts fester, they sometimes get worse, leading to all manner of problems. Finally, high avoiders pass up many opportunities to ask for things that would make them better off when others would be perfectly happy to accommodate their need. This may result in their becoming dissatisfied with a situation when a solution to meet their needs is only a question away.

Weakly Predisposed toward Avoiding. Low avoiders have little fear of interpersonal conflict. Indeed, they may in some cases enjoy it. As negotiators, they have a high tolerance for assertive, candid bargaining. They can fight hard against their bargaining counterpart all day and share drinks and stories with the same person in the evening. Low avoidance scores are helpful in such professions as labor-management relations, litigation, and mergers and acquisitions work. But beware: People with low scores in avoiding sometimes lack tact, and are often viewed as overly confrontational. In bureaucratic settings, low avoiders may be seen as troublemakers who refuse to leave well enough alone. The low avoider is characteristically frustrated by bureaucracy and office politics, which are alien settings to him or her.

COLLABORATING

Negotiators Strongly Predisposed toward Collaborating. High collaborators enjoy negotiations because they enjoy solving tough problems in engaged, interactive ways. They are instinctively good at using negotiations to probe beneath the surface of conflicts to discover basic interests, perceptions, and new solutions. They relish the continuous flow of the negotiation process and encourage everyone to be involved. They are assertively and honestly committed to finding the best solution for everyone. By the same token, people with a strong predisposition for collaborating sometimes needlessly create problems by transforming relatively simple situations into more complex (and interesting) occasions to practice their skills. This can irritate other people who want closure, who lack time to invest in a matter, or who do not wish to risk triggering interpersonal conflict over a small, albeit nagging, issue. High collaborators also need other, less collaborative skills to claim their fair share of the gains they help create. A high collaborator with a very low competing score can be at risk against a highly competitive counterpart.

Weakly Predisposed toward Collaborating. Low collaborators dislike using the bargaining process as a forum for creativity. These negotiators prefer having problems clearly specified before the negotiation begins and like to stick to the agenda and their preset goals once a meeting starts. They often bring a methodical pace, solid planning, and a need for clarity to their practice. When the matters being negotiated are so inherently complex that real-time brainstorming is the best way to proceed, low collaborators may become a bottleneck, slowing the process down. One way for low collaborators to compensate for this weakness is to make liberal use of breaks in the bargaining process to gather their thoughts and reset their strategy.

COMPETING

Negotiators Strongly Predisposed toward Competing. Like high collaborators, high competitors also enjoy negotiating. But they enjoy it for a different reason: Negotiating presents an opportunity for winning and losing, and they like to win. For this reason, high competitors prefer to frame negotiations as games with moves that can result in gains or losses, depending on one's relative skill. Highly competitive negotiators have strong instincts about such matters as leverage, deadlines, how to open, how to position final offers, ultimata, and similar aspects of traditional negotiations. Competitors have energy and motivation in transactional negotiations in which the stakes are high. However, because their style can dominate the bargaining process, competitive people can be hard on relationships. The "loser" in a negotiating game, for example, may feel taken, coerced, or abused. This can affect future dealings. In addition, competitive negotiators instinctively focus on the issues that are easiest to count in terms of winning and losing—like money. They may overlook nonquantitative issues that can also yield value.

Weak Predisposition toward Competing. People with a weak predisposition for competing do not think that negotiations are simply about winning and losing. They see negotiations as a dance, not a game. It is a dance in which the goal is for the parties to treat each other fairly, avoid needless conflict, solve problems, or create trusting relationships. Others often view people with low competing scores as especially nonthreatening. This can be a strength in many professional settings in which the ability to gain trust is a critical skill. However, when there are large stakes on the table, the low competitor will be at a disadvantage.

SOME QUESTIONS PEOPLE FREQUENTLY ASK REGARDING BARGAINING STYLES

In using the Bargaining Styles Assessment Tool, I have encountered a number of reoccurring questions from students and executives. Below, I share some of the more common questions, along with some suggested answers.

1. *Is there an "optimal" score for negotiators?*

No. There is no "right" set of style preferences for negotiation effectiveness. Rather, people with instincts or aversions for each of the five styles tend to display certain systematic strengths and weaknesses. These strengths and weaknesses, in turn, either help or hurt, depending on the situation and who is sitting across the table. For people who engage in transactional negotiations as a profession, higher competitive and collaborative scores will be an indication that they enjoy their work. For people who do a lot of relationship-based sales or consulting, higher accommodating and compromising scores may be a sign that they feel comfortable in their jobs. Professional diplomats, by contrast, sometimes report higher-than-usual scores for avoiding conflict.

In other words, your scores may be one indication of how naturally your style "fits" the professional setting in which you negotiate. But there is no single profile that works best for all negotiators.

2. *What does it mean if a person prefers several styles?*

Each person has a unique combination of preferences. Many have strong predispositions toward several styles. People tend to assess their counterparts, analyze the situation they face, check to see if their most preferred (and therefore familiar) style is appropriate, and proceed. If their most preferred style is inappropriate (e.g., they are a high avoider and they are selling their used car), they tend to shift to their next most preferred style. This shifting of approaches can also occur in the middle of a negotiation if the preferred style is not working to advance the process.

Some style combinations yield characteristic results. For example, someone high in both *competing* and *collaborating* tends, as noted earlier, to be comfortable in many negotiating situations in which the stakes are large. Someone high in both *competing* and *avoiding*, meanwhile, is somewhat one-dimensional as a negotiator and tends to project a "we're-doing-this-my-way-or-I'm-hitting-the-road" attitude. If this person cannot use his or her competitive tactics, they tend to exit the situation or delegate the bargaining to someone else. Those with high scores in both *accommodating* and *compromising*, by contrast, are very relationship-oriented and will tend to be seen as relatively easy to get along with as they move fluidly between an orientation toward solving the other person's problem and an orientation toward simple, fast, fair allocations.

3. *What if a person's scores are all in the middle percentiles—i.e., he or she has no strong preferences?*

Scores in the midrange percentiles often indicate that the style in question is relatively accessible and can be called out as the occasion demands. Some people score in this middle range for all five attributes, indicating that they have a very adaptable style that can serve them well in most situations. These negotiators may still be at a relative disadvantage, however, when facing off against equally experienced people who have much more definite preferences. For example, "moderately" competitive negotiators facing highly competitive counterparts in a situation that rewards a competitive approach may need to summon all their energies and instincts to stay even with their counterparts' moves. The counterparts will experience less stress and "stretch" in this situation.

4. *Does my bargaining style affect the way I perceive other negotiators?*

Unquestionably. Research shows that most of us believe that other people are like ourselves. As one old saying puts it, "The thief thinks everybody steals." And cooperative people assume that others are cooperative. Thus, when a competitive person meets a cooperative person at the bargaining table, each is likely to assume the other is someone other than he or she actually is—leading to significant confusion. The cooperative person may share information, make a fair opening offer, and engage in other efforts to be open and reasonable, assuming that these efforts will be reciprocated. The competitive person, thinking that these moves are either evidence of naivety or designed to trick him into giving up leverage, takes advantage of the situation to secure a favorable position and then pounces, sweeping his or her money off the table. The cooperative person now feels betrayed and reacts angrily. And this behavior confirms the competitive person's initial hypothesis that the opponent was, in fact, in it for herself all along. Things go downhill from there.

In other words, the competitive person's belief that others are competitive sometimes acts as a self-fulfilling prophesy. And the same process can sometimes work in reverse, with a cooperative person's belief in cooperativeness allowing his or her counterpart to drop their guard and behave in a more reasonable, helpful way. Whether this works, of course, depends on what type of person is actually sitting on the other side of the table.

By contrast, when two people displaying similar styles meet, the rapport can be instant. As the super-competitive Donald Trump notes in his 1987 book, The *Art of the Deal,* "When [a competitive person] says no, sometimes you can talk him out of it. You rant and rave; and he rants and raves back, and you end up making a deal." The same sort of "style match" occurs when two cooperative people negotiate against one another.

In general, my advice is to take a minute at the beginning of a negotiation to size up your counterpart and see which styles he or she is bringing to the table. You can do this by negotiating some smaller items before you get to the main event and gauge the other person's reactions. Are they careful to reciprocate your every move? That is a sign of cooperativeness. Do they seem to be holding on to information and jumping on chances to "stay ahead"? You may have a competitive person on your hands. Either way, don't waste time trying to convert the person to your preferred style. Just accept them as they are and work to achieve your goals.

5. *Do scores change over time?*

Scores are a function of the time and place in which one fills out the instrument. If one has had a recent, very bitter conflict that has ruined a relationship, there may be a tendency to regret this event and select more accommodating choices than would otherwise be the case. Similarly, if one has recently been taken advantage of in a tough negotiation, then one's scores might reflect a desire to correct this by selecting more competitive statements than would ordinarily be true.

If users can place their mind in "neutral" and simply do their best to select which of the statements in each pair better expresses their overall preferred attitude, however, the scores should be relatively stable over time. At the very least, the direction of these scores ought to remain relatively steady, with strongly preferred strategies maintaining their preferred positions—though by somewhat smaller margins. My own scores have not changed much over the years, for example. But the same may not be true for a younger or inexperienced negotiator who takes the assessment at one stage of a career and then, many years and experiences later, repeats it.

6. *How is the Bargaining Styles Assessment Tool different from the Thomas-Kilmann Conflict Mode Instrument referenced in the first edition of* Bargaining for Advantage?

The Bargaining Styles Assessment shares a common structure with the Thomas-Kilmann Conflict Mode Instrument (TKI), which I recommended in the first edition of this book. Both surveys feature a "forced choice" method of self-reporting that is used in many psychological assessments. Moreover, both tests incorporate the five style categories developed by Professors Blake and Mouton in the mid-1960s: competing, collaborating, compromising, accommodating, and avoiding.

However, the statements used in the Bargaining Styles Assessment (and sequence in which they appear) differ from those used in the TKI and are more directly related to negotiation than are many of the TKI statements. Readers are encouraged to compare the two self-assessment approaches for themselves by ordering a copy of the TKI from its owner, Consulting Psychologists Press, Inc. at its Web site CPP.com and comparing their results from the two surveys.

Appendix B:
Information-Based Bargaining Plan

I. The Problem

Problem Statement: I must negotiate with (*person*) to (*solve what problem*).

II. Goals and Decision Makers

My Specific, High Expectation:	Target decision-maker:
Bottom Line:	Influencers (Should I negotiate with these people first?):

III. Underlying Needs and Interests (Shared/Ancillary/Conflicting)

Mine	*Theirs*

IV. Leverage

What do I lose if there is no deal?	If no deal, what will they lose?
What steps or alternatives will reduce these losses?	Can I influence their alternatives or make their status quo worse?

Leverage Favors: ☐ Me ☐ Other Party ☐ About Even
(Who has the most to lose overall from "no deal"?)

V. Possible Proposals

Options: Build on Shared Interests/Bridge Conflicting Interests/Be Creative

VI. Authoritative Standards and Norms

Mine	Theirs	My Counter Arguments

VII. Third Party Moves

Can I use a third party as leverage? As an excuse? As an audience? Coalition partner?

VIII. Situation and Strategy Analysis

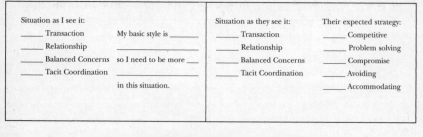

Situation as I see it:

_____ Transaction
_____ Relationship
_____ Balanced Concerns
_____ Tacit Coordination

My basic style is _____

_____

so I need to be more ___

_____

in this situation.

Situation as they see it:

_____ Transaction
_____ Relationship
_____ Balanced Concerns
_____ Tacit Coordination

Their expected strategy:

_____ Competitive
_____ Problem solving
_____ Compromise
_____ Avoiding
_____ Accommodating

IX. Best Modes of Communication

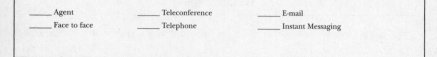

_____ Agent
_____ Face to face

_____ Teleconference
_____ Telephone

_____ E-mail
_____ Instant Messaging

X. Overall Positioning Theme

A short statement that sums up your underlying purpose in this negotiation:

Notes

<--->

INTRODUCTION: It's Your Move

xx **"You must actually negotiate":** James C. Freund, *Anatomy of a Merger* (New York: Academic Press, 1975), p. 10.

CHAPTER 1: The First Foundation: Your Bargaining Style

3 **Danish folk saying:** R.G.H. Siu, *Folk Wisdom and Management 3,333 Proverbs* (Washington, D.C.: Manuscript, 1994), p. 13.

4 **talking into the night:** Bettye H. Pruitt, *The Making of Harcourt General* (Boston: Harvard Business School Press, 1994), pp. 219–242.

4 **of large, shady trees:** This story is taken, with a few dramatic elaborations on my part, from the true story of a negotiation among the Arusha people described at length by anthropologist P. H. Gulliver. See. P. H. Gulliver, *Disputes and Negotiations: A Cross-Cultural Perspective* (New York: Academic Press, 1979), pp. 234–252.

8 **finally won a hand:** Connie Bruck, *Master of the Game: Steve Ross and the Creation of Time Warner* (New York: Penguin Books, 1994), p. 93.

8 **CNN's owner, Ted Turner:** Larry King's agent was Bob Woolf. See Bob Woolf, *Friendly Persuasion: How to Negotiate and Win* (New York: Berkley Books, 1990), pp. 147–148.

14 **using these two labels:** Gerald R. Williams, *Legal Negotiation and Settlement* (St. Paul, Minn.: West Publishing, 1983), p. 19.

14 **John Carlisle in England:** Neil Rackham and John Carlisle, "The Effective Negotiator—Part 1: The Behavior of Successful Negotiators," *Journal of European Industrial Training*, Vol. 2, No. 6 (1978), pp. 6–11; Neil Rackham and

John Carlisle, "The Effective Negotiator—Part 2: Planning for Negotiations," *Journal of European Industrial Training*, Vol. 2, No. 7 (1978), pp. 2–5.

15 **toward affirming their status:** Deborah Tannen, *You Just Don't Understand: Men and Women in Conversation* (New York: William Morrow, 1990); *Talking from 9 to 5: Women and Men at Work* (New York: William Morrow, 1994).

16 **a bit more cooperatively than men:** Amy E. Walters, Alice F. Stuhlmacher, and Lia L. Meyer, "Gender and Negotiator Competitiveness," *Organizational Behavior and Human Decision Processes*, Vol. 76 (1998), pp. 1–29; Alice Stuhlmacher and Amy E. Walters, "Gender Differences in Negotiation Outcomes: A Meta-analysis," *Personnel Psychology*, Vol. 52 (1999), pp. 653–677.

16 **a number of studies and contexts:** Linda Babcock and Sara Laschever, *Women Don't Ask: Negotiation and the Gender Divide* (Princeton, NJ: Princeton University Press, 2003). See also D. M. Kolb and J. Williams, *The Shadow Negotiation: How Women Can Master the Hidden Agendas that Determine Bargaining Success* (New York: Simon and Schuster, 2000).

17 **what scholars call "stereotype threat":** Laura J. Kray, Leigh Thompson, and Adam Galinsky, "Battles of the Sexes: Gender Stereotype Confirmation and Reactance in Negotiations," *Journal of Personality and Social Psychology*, Vol. 80, No. 6 (2001), pp. 942–958; Laura J. Kray, Adam Galinsky, and Leigh Thompson, "Reversing the Gender Gap in Negotiations: An Exploration of Stereotype Regeneration," *Organizational Behavior and Human Decision Processes*, Vol. 87, No. 2 (2002), pp. 386–409.

18 **cross-cultural issues can be showstoppers:** Catherine H. Tinsley, "How Negotiators Get to Yes: Predicting the Constellation of Strategies Used Across Cultures to Negotiate Conflict," *Journal of Applied Psychology*, Vol. 86, No. 4 (2001), pp. 583–593.

19 **people of equal rank:** John L. Graham, "The Japanese Negotiation Style: Characteristics of a Distinct Approach," *Negotiation Journal*, Vol. 9, No. 2 (April 1993), pp. 123–140.

19 **Latin America to negotiate a complex deal:** Laura-Ann Dooly, "Culture Clashes Hinder Deals," *The National Law Journal*, Vol. 22, No. 3 (September 13, 1999), pp. B1, B4.

20 **help you avoid cross-cultural meltdowns:** The best overall treatment of cross-cultural negotiating issues is Camille P. Schuster and Michael J. Copeland, *Global Business: Planning for Sales and Negotiations* (Fort Worth, TX: The Dryden Press, HarcourtBrace College, 1996). There are abundant resources in the business press and literature on specific cultures and the problems that can arise for negotiators. See, for example, Terri Morrison, Wayne A. Conaway, and George A. Borden, *Kiss, Bow and Shake Hands: How to Do Business in Sixty Countries* (New York: Adams Publishing, 1995); John L. Graham and N. Mark Lim, "The Chinese Negotiation," *Harvard Business Review*, October 2003, pp. 82–91.

21 **has confirmed its importance:** Arvind Rangaswamy and G. Richard Shell, "Using Computers to Achieve Joint Gains in Negotiation: Towards an Electronic Bargaining Table," *Management Science*, Vol. 43, No. 8 (1997), pp. 1147–1163.

22 **straightforward dealing very highly:** Gerald R. Williams, *Legal Negotiation and Settlement* (St. Paul, Minn.: West Publishing, 1983), pp. 20–40; Howard Raiffa, *The Art and Science of Negotiation* (Boston: Harvard University Press, 1982), pp. 119–122.

23 **all make a difference:** I have explored these and related questions in an article. See G. Richard Shell, "When Is It Legal to Lie in Commercial Negotiations?," *Sloan Management Review*, Vol. 32, No. 3 (1991), pp. 93–101.

CHAPTER 2: The Second Foundation:
Your Goals and Expectations

26 **King Ching of Chou (1100 B.C.):** Violina P. Rindova and William H. Starbuck, "Ancient Chinese Theories of Control," *Journal of Management Inquiry*, Vol. 6, No. 2 (June 1997), pp. 153–155.

26 **Sam Walton, founder of Wal-Mart:** Sam Walton, "Running a Successful Company: Ten Rules That Worked for Me," in *Sam Walton: Made in America* (New York: Doubleday, 1992), p. 246.

27 **"America wants big radios":** Akio Morita, *Made in Japan* (New York: E. P. Dutton, 1986), pp. 83–85.

28 **are to obtain it:** Several research studies have shown that people who set specific goals outperform those who set general or "do your best" goals. See G. Lathan and E. Locke, "Self-regulation Through Goal Setting," *Organizational Behavior and Human Decision Processes*, Vol. 50, No. 2 (1991), pp. 212–247. E. Locke and G. Latham, *A Theory of Goal Setting and Task Performance* (Englewood Cliffs, N.J.: Prentice-Hall, 1990), pp. 29–31; I. R. Gellately and J. P. Meyer, "The Effect of Goal Difficulty on Physiological Arousal, Cognition, and Task Performance," *Journal of Applied Psychology*, Vol. 77, No. 2 (1992), pp. 694–704.

28 **with others at risk:** For a good survey on the use of ambitious goals to raise performance, see Kenneth R. Thompson, Wayne A. Hochwater, and Nicholas J. Mathys, "Stretch Targets: What Makes Them Effective?" *Academy of Management Executive*, Vol. 11, No. 3 (1997), pp. 48–61.

28 **Cat replies, cutting her off:** Lewis Carroll, *Alice's Adventures in Wonderland* (New York: Penguin, 1960), p. 64.

29 **ought reasonably to accomplish:** Peter M. Blau, *Exchange and Power in Social Life* (New York: John Wiley & Sons, 1964), pp. 145–151.

29 **to obtain doctoral degrees:** U.S. Department of Education, *National Education Longitudinal Study 1988–1994* NCES 96-175 (May 1996), pp. 45–46.

29 **the firmer our expectations grow:** Scholars have identified these factors, and more, in a variety of empirical studies. See Reinhard Tietz, Hans-Jürgen Weber, Ulrike Vidmajer, and Christoph Wentzel, "On Aspiration-Forming Behavior in Repetitive Negotiations," in Heinz Sauermann, ed., *Bargaining Behavior* (Tübingen, Germany: J.C.B. Mohr, 1978), pp. 88–102; Steven R. Wilson and Linda L. Putnam, "Interaction Goals in Negotiation," *Communication Yearbook*, Vol. 13 (1989), pp. 374–406; Kristina A.

Diekmann, Ann Tenbrunsel, Pri Pradhan Shah, Holly A. Schroth, and Max Bazerman, "The Descriptive and Prescriptive Use of Previous Purchase Price in Negotiations," *Organizational Behavior and Human Decision Processes,* Vol. 66, No. 2 (1996), pp. 179–191.

30 **"What convinces is conviction":** Booz, Allen & Hamilton, *Strategy & Business* (New York: Fourth Quarter, 1997), p. 79.

30 **Florida Panthers (ice hockey):** Gail DeGeorge, *The Making of Blockbuster* (New York: John Wiley & Sons, 1996), pp. 17–43. A friend of Huizenga's notes that Huizenga "always keeps the carrot far enough out in front of him and he never really wants to catch it. That's his personality. He's never satisfied" (ibid., p. 42).

30 **a "positive bargaining zone":** Howard Raiffa, *The Art and Science of Negotiation* (Cambridge, Mass.: Harvard University Press, 1982), pp. 45–50. Raiffa prefers to speak of "reservation prices," but the "bottom line" concept is identical.

31 **with reference to their bottom line:** Sally Blount White, Kathleen L. Valley, Max H. Bazerman, Margaret A. Neale, and Sharon R. Peck, "Alternative Models of Price Behavior in Dyadic Negotiations: Market Prices, Reservation Prices, and Negotiator Aspirations," *Organizational Behavior and Human Decision Processes,* Vol. 57, No. 3 (1994), pp. 430–447.

31 **a powerful motivating force:** Russel Korobkin, "Aspirations and Settlement," *Cornell Law Review,* Vol. 88 (2002), pp. 1–49.

32 **all else being equal:** Sally Blount White and Margaret A. Neale, "The Role of Negotiator Aspirations and Settlement Expectancies in Bargaining Outcomes," *Organizational Behavior and Human Decision Processes,* Vol. 57, No. 2 (1994), pp. 303–317.

32 **negotiators have this ability:** Neil Rackham and John Carlisle, "The Effective Negotiator—Part 2: Planning for Negotiations," *Journal of European Industrial Training,* Vol. 2, No. 7 (1978), pp. 2–5 (reporting that skilled negotiators were significantly more likely to set both goals and limits in negotiation, whereas average negotiators set only a single-point objective).

33 **strategy earned him millions:** Michael Pye, *Moguls: Inside the Business of Show Business* (New York: Holt, Rinehart and Winston, 1980), pp. 88–89.

33 **of records in half:** Ibid., pp. 106–107.

33 **accept second-place status:** Bryn Burrough and John Helyer, *Barbarians at the Gate* (New York: Harper & Row, 1990), pp. 325–326.

34 **the modest $2.10 goal:** Sydney Siegel and Lawrence Fouraker, "The Effect of Level of Aspiration on Differential Payoff," in *Bargaining and Group Decision Making* (New York: McGraw-Hill, 1960), pp. 61–70.

34 **with more modest goals:** Arvind Rangaswamy and G. Richard Shell, "Using Computers to Achieve Joint Gains: Toward an Electronic Bargaining Table," *Management Science,* Vol. 43, No. 8 (1997), pp. 1147–1163.

35 **would care to admit:** Morris Rosenberg, *Conceiving the Self* (New York: Basic Books, 1979), p. 61.

35 **and lower their targets:** Peter M. Blau, *Exchange and Power in Social Life* (New York: John Wiley & Sons, 1964), p. 145; Kurt Lewin, Tamara Dembo,

Leon Festinger, and Pauline S. Sears, "Level of Aspiration," in J. McV. Hunt, ed., *Personality and the Behavior Disorders*, Vol. 1 (New York: Ronald Press, 1944), pp. 337–340.

36 **as specific as possible:** Vandra L. Huber and Margaret A. Neale, "Effects of Self- and Competitor Goals on Performance in an Interdependent Bargaining Task," *Journal of Applied Psychology*, Vol. 72, No. 2 (1987), pp. 197–203.

36 **self-confidence and commitment:** Visualization has been shown to enhance performance in a number of human activities, most notably athletics. See A. Bandura, *Social Foundations of Thought and Action* (Englewood Cliffs, N.J.: Prentice-Hall, 1986), pp. 61–62; Donald R. Liggett and Sadao Hamada, "Enhancing the Visualization of Gymnasts," *American Journal of Clinical Hypnosis*, Vol. 35, No. 3 (1993), pp. 190–197.

37 **improves salespeople's performance:** Robert B. Cialdini, *Influence: The Psychology of Persuasion* (New York: William Morrow, 1984), p. 79.

37 **to achieve a goal:** A number of studies have demonstrated that negotiators bargain somewhat harder when they think they are under the "surveillance" of a supporter or constituency. See Orly Ben-Toav and Dean G. Pruitt, "Accountability to Constituents: A Two-Edged Sword," *Organizational Behavior and Human Decision Processes*, Vol. 34, No. 3 (1984), pp. 283–295; Peter J. D. Carnevale, Dean G. Pruitt, and Scott D. Britton, "Looking Tough: The Negotiator Under Constituent Surveillance," *Personality and Social Psychology Bulletin*, Vol. 5, No. 1 (1979), pp. 118–121.

38 **for closing the purchase:** Steve Massey, "US Airways Reiterates Cost-Cutting Warning to Unions," *Pittsburgh Post Gazette*, April 11, 1997, p. A1 (describing US Airways CEO Steve Wolf's announcement of a September 30, 1997 deadline for the settlement of a dispute with his pilots' union because that was the date on which his contract with Airbus for $14 billion worth of planes would be canceled).

38 **winning a competition:** Cialdini, *Influence*, pp. 264–265.

38 **"escalation of commitment":** Max Bazerman, *Judgement in Managerial Decision-Making*, 4th ed. (New York: John Wiley & Sons, 1998), pp. 66–78.

39 **regret the "winner's curse":** Richard H. Thaler, *The Winner's Curse: Paradoxes and Anomalies of Economic Life* (New York: Free Press, 1992), pp. 1–5.

CHAPTER 3:   The Third Foundation:
Authoritative Standards and Norms

40 **Samuel Taylor Coleridge:** Michael R. Roloff, Frank E. Tutzauer, and William O'Daniley, "The Role of Argumentation in Distribution and Integrative Bargaining Contexts: Seeking Relative Advantage but at What Cost?" in M. Afzalur Rahim, ed., *Management Conflict: An Interdisciplinary Approach* (New York: Praeger, 1989), p. 109.

40 **J. P. Morgan:** Ron Chernow, *The House of Morgan* (New York: Simon & Schuster, 1990), p. 114.

42 **restoring the peace:** R. F. Barton, *The Halfway Sun: Life Among the Head-hunters of the Philippines* (New York: Brewer and Warren, 1930), pp. 65–86. This story is also retold in P. H. Gulliver, *Disputes and Negotiations: A Cross-Cultural Perspective* (New York: Academic Press, 1979), pp. 30–31.

43 **"the consistency principle":** Robert Cialdini, *Influence: The Psychology of Persuasion*, 2nd ed. (New York: William Morrow, 1987), p. 59.

48 *Experiments with Truth:* M. K. Gandhi, *The Story of My Experiments with Truth* (Ahmedabad, India: Jivanji Dahyabhai Desai, 1927), pp. 272–276.

49 **a frock coat and necktie:** Ibid.

50 **an otherwise negotiable issue:** P. H. Gulliver, *Disputes and Negotiations: A Cross-Cultural Perspective* (New York: Academic Press, 1979), pp. 191–94; Dean Pruitt, *Negotiation Behavior* (New York: Academic Press, 1981), pp. 4–5; P. J. DiMaggio and W. W. Powell, "The Iron Cage Revisited: Institutionalism, Isomorphism, and Collective Rationality in Organizational Fields," *American Sociological Review*, Vol. 48, No. 1 (1983), pp. 147–160.

50 **price of a home:** M. H. Bazerman, M. A. Neale, K. L. Valley, E. J. Zajac, and Y. M. Kim, "The Effect of Agents and Mediators on Negotiation Outcomes," *Organizational Behavior and Human Decision Processes*, Vol. 53, No. 1 (1992), pp. 53–73 (noting that real estate commissions in the United States were formerly set by regulation at 6 percent and have continued at that level for decades in the wake of deregulation).

51 **significantly affect negotiation results:** Sally Blount, Melissa C. Thomas-Hunt, and Margaret A. Neale, "The Price Is Right—Or Is It? A Reference Point Model of Two-Party Price Negotiations," *Organizational Behavior and Human Decision Processes*, Vol. 68, No. 1 (October 1996), pp. 1–12.

53 **"would've approached it differently":** Paul Magnusson, "A Wake-up Call for Business," *Business Week*, September 1, 1997, p. 29.

54 **our deference to authority:** Herb Cohen, *You Can Negotiate Anything* (New York: Lyle Stuart, 1980), pp. 58–60.

55 **eardrops into people's eyes:** Neil M. Davis and Michael R. Cohen, *Medication Errors: Causes and Prevention* (Philadelphia: George F. Strickley, 1981), p. 80.

55 **ultimately, negotiate effectively:** Connie J. G. Gersick and J. Richard Hackman, "Habitual Routines in Task-Performing Groups," *Organizational Behavior and Human Decision Processes*, Vol. 47 (1990), pp. 65–97.

56 **[Sound of impact.]:** This conversation is reprinted in Deborah Tannen, *Talking from 9 to 5* (New York: Avon Books, 1994), pp. 92–93, based on the actual transcript taken from Air Florida Flight 90's "black box" flight recorder. See Aircraft Accident Report NTSB-AAR-82-8, published by the U.S. Government National Transportation Safety Board, Washington, D.C. 20594.

CHAPTER 4: The Fourth Foundation:
Relationships

58 **Franklin D. Roosevelt:** I do not know the original source of this quotation. I found it in a book on negotiation by sports and entertainment agent Bob

Woolf. See Bob Woolf, *Friendly Persuasion: How to Negotiate and Win* (New York: Berkley Books, 1990), p. 37.

58 **Kenyan folk saying:** R.G.H. Siu, *Folk Wisdom and Management 3,333 Proverbs* (Washington, D.C.: Manuscript, 1994), p. 74.

59 **"have had with them":** Alvin W. Gouldner, "The Norm of Reciprocity: A Preliminary Statement," *American Sociological Review*, Vol. 25, No. 2 (April 1960), pp. 161–178; quote at pp. 170–171.

59 **Italy in 1935:** Robert Cialdini summarizes this research in his book. See Robert B. Cialdini, *Influence: The Psychology of Persuasion* (New York: William Morrow, 1984), pp. 17–57.

60 **can from every transaction:** Economist Matthew Rabin wrote a pathbreaking article in 1993 in which he modeled the effect of relationships on exchange. This article is considered somewhat radical within the economics profession. See Matthew Rabin, "Incorporating Fairness into Game Theory and Economics," *American Economic Review*, Vol. 83, No. 5 (December 1993), pp. 1281–1302. Of course, the entire discipline of social psychology assumes that relationships affect exchange in deep, pervasive ways.

60 **J. P. Morgan in his autobiography:** Andrew Carnegie, *Autobiography* (New York: Doubleday, 1920), pp. 165–166.

61 **"henceforth a firm friend":** Ibid., p. 166.

61 **called the "ultimatum game":** Ultimatum games provide data about our taste for fairness both with and without relationships as factors in decision making. For a review of the ultimatum game literature, see Werner Guth and Reinhard Tietz, "Ultimatum Bargaining Behavior: A Survey and Comparison of Experimental Results," *Journal of Economic Psychology*, Vol. 11 (1990), pp. 417–432.

62 **this patently unfair division:** Most ultimatum game studies reveal that people offer an average of 40 percent of the amount being divided and will usually reject amounts that fall below 20 percent. See George Lowenstein, Samuel Issacharoff, Colin Camerer, and Linda Babcock, "Self-serving Assessments of Fairness and Pre-trial Bargaining," *Journal of Legal Studies*, Vol. 22, No. 1 (1993), pp. 135–159.

66 **dating couples handled bargaining:** William R. Fry, Ira J. Firestone, and David L. Williams, "Negotiation Process and Outcome of Stranger Dyads and Dating Couples: Do Lovers Lose?," *Basic and Applied Social Psychology*, Vol. 4, No. 1 (1983), pp. 1–16.

67 **when it comes to bargaining:** Jennifer J. Halpern, "The Effect of Friendship on Personal Business Transactions," *Journal of Conflict Resolution*, Vol. 38, No. 4 (December 1994), pp. 647–664.

67 **between friends and strangers:** Edward H. Lorenz, "Neither Friends nor Strangers: Informal Networks of Subcontracting in French Industry," in *Trust: Making and Breaking Cooperative Relations* (New York: Basil Blackwell, 1988), p. 194.

68 **similarity to help him:** Two studies documenting the similarity principle from the early 1970s are discussed in Cialdini, *Influence*. In the first, re-

searchers dressed as "hippies" or as "straights" and roamed a college campus asking for small change (a dime). They discovered that their request was granted roughly two thirds of the time when they were dressed similarly to the person being asked but less than half the time when the target was dressed differently. See T. K. Emswiller and J. E. Willits, "Similarity, Sex and Requests for Small Favors," *Journal of Applied Social Psychology*, Vol. 1 (1971), pp. 284–291. The same result was achieved by similar means in a study seeking signatures on an anti-Vietnam War petition. See P. S. Suedfeld, S. Bochner, and C. Matas, "Petitioner's Attire and Petition Signing by Peace Demonstrators: A Field Experiment," *Journal of Applied Social Psychology*, Vol. 1 (1971), pp. 278–283.

69 **the HBJ example:** Colin Camerer, "Gifts as Economic Signals and Social Symbols," *American Journal of Sociology*, Vol. 94 (Suppl.) (1988), pp. S180–S214.

70 **do in the West:** Murray Weidenbaum, "The Bamboo Network: Asia's Family-Run Conglomerates," *Strategy and Business*, No. 10 (1998), pp. 59–65; Cynthia L. Kemper, "Russian business success is a long-term proposition," *The Denver Post*, June 8, 1997, p. 14.

70 **reciprocal signs of respect:** The ceremony can be quite elaborate; one business book takes three pages to describe it. See Jon P. Alston, *The Intelligent Businessman's Guide to Japan* (New York: Charles E. Tuttle, 1990), pp. 39–42.

70 **the issue of trust:** Ibid., pp. 49–53.

70 *guanxi* **(pronounced "gwang-chi"):** Eric W. K. Tsang, "Can *guanxi* be a source of sustained competitive advantage for doing business in China?," *Academy of Management Executive*, Vol. 12, No. 2 (1998), pp. 64–73.

70 **"simplest deals can disintegrate":** "The *'Guanxi'* List 1997," *International Business Asia*, Vol. 5, No. 12 (June 30, 1997), pp. 11–23.

71 **soon opened as planned:** See Evelyn Iritani, "On the Front Lines: A Handful of U.S. Entrepreneurs Are Battling Bureaucracy and Corruption to Establish Their Niches in China," *Los Angeles Times*, October 8, 1997, p. D1.

71 **"best business and political circles":** "The *'Guanxi'* List 1997," *International Business Asia*, pp. 11–21.

CHAPTER 5: The Fifth Foundation:
The Other Party's Interests

76 **Adam Smith (1776):** Adam Smith, *An Inquiry into the Nature and Cause of the Wealth of Nations* (Oxford: Oxford University Press, 1993), p. 22.

76 **Henry Ford:** I have not been able to find the original source of this quote but it is attributed to Henry Ford in Dale Carnegie, *How to Win Friends and Influence People*, rev. ed. (New York: Pocket Books, 1981), p. 37. The quote has an ironic twist, given Henry Ford's reluctance to alter his Model T car's basic design even when consumers began demanding variety from automobile manufacturers.

78 **"always another billion dollars":** Melissa Wahl, "1st Union chief's nerve-racking wait for CoreStates," *Philadelphia Inquirer*, November 26, 1997, p. D1.
78 **"thinking about the other side . . .":** Gail DeGeorge, *The Making of Block-buster* (New York: John Wiley & Sons, 1996), p. 48. I have altered this quotation to the present tense for clarity.
78 **having partisan perceptions:** Leigh A. Thompson, "They Saw a Negotiation: Partisanship and Involvement," *Journal of Personality and Social Psychology*, Vol. 68 (1995), pp. 839–853.
78 **are contributing to it:** Actually, most negotiators believe not only that others are like them but also that others are not quite as flexible, purposeful, competent, fair, honest, or cooperative—in short, that others are like them only not as "good." See Max H. Bazerman and Margaret A. Neale, *Negotiating Rationally* (New York: Free Press, 1992), p. 61.
79 **make the pie bigger:** Ibid., pp. 16–22.
79 **50 percent of the time:** Leigh Thompson, *The Mind and Heart of the Negotiator* (Englewood Cliffs, N.J.: Prentice-Hall, 1998), p. 49.
79 **real interests and motivations:** Walter Morley Balke, Kenneth Hammond, and G. Dale Meyer, "An Alternate Approach to Labor-Management Relations," *Administrative Science Quarterly*, Vol. 18 (1973), pp. 311–327.
80 **feasible options for settlement:** N. Rackham and J. Carlisle, "The Effective Negotiator—Part 1: The Behavior of Successful Negotiators," *Journal of European Industrial Training*, Vol. 2, No. 6 (1978), pp. 6–11; N. Rackham and J. Carlisle, "The Effective Negotiator—Part 2: Planning for Negotiations," *Journal of European Industrial Training*, Vol. 2, No. 7 (1978), pp. 2–5.
80 **price, power, or control:** Only 11 percent of the comments of the less skilled negotiators were focused on possible common ground. Rackham and Carlisle, Part 2.
81 **on their own goals:** Leigh Thompson, "Information Exchanged in Negotiation," *Journal of Experimental Social Psychology*, Vol. 27 (1991), pp. 161–179; Leigh Thompson and T. DeHarpport, "Social Judgment, Feedback, and Interpersonal Learning," *Organizational Behavior and Human Decision Processes*, Vol. 58, No. 3 (1994), pp. 327–345; Leigh Thompson and R. Hastie, "Social Perception in Negotiation," *Organizational Behavior and Human Decision Processes*, Vol. 47, No. 1 (1990), pp. 98–123.
84 **"Ask and It Shall Be Discounted":** "Ask and It Shall Be Discounted: Business-to-business bargains are becoming a way of life," *Business Week*, October 6, 1997, pp. 116–118.
85 **up to that time in U.S. history:** Wahl, "1st Union chief's nerve-racking wait," p. D1.
86 **California, and its garbage:** Jeff Bailey, "Arizona Has Plenty of What Oceanside Needs and Vice Versa," *The Wall Street Journal*, March 4, 1997, p. 1.

CHAPTER 6: The Sixth Foundation: Leverage

89 **I know those reasons:** Bob Woolf, *Friendly Persuasion: How to Negotiate and Win* (New York: Berkley Books, 1990), p. 129.

89 **Attributed to American gangster Al Capone:** Ibid., pp. 129–130.

90 **bargainers achieve their goals:** Chester L. Karrass, *The Negotiating Game*, rev. ed. (New York: HarperBusiness, 1992), pp. 20–22.

90 **faced a big problem:** This story comes from Matthew Lynn, *Birds of Prey, Boeing vs. Airbus: A Battle for the Skies*, rev. ed. (New York: Four Walls Eight Windows, 1997), pp. 120–122.

91 **turned-producer Peter Guber:** Nancy Griffin and Kim Masters, *Hit and Run: How Jon Peters and Peter Guber Took Sony for a Ride in Hollywood* (New York: Simon & Schuster, 1996), pp. 88–89.

91 **its giant generating station:** Daniel Machalaba, "Tired of Costs, Delays of Railroads, Firms Lay Their Own Tracks," *The Wall Street Journal*, February 6, 1998, p. A1.

93 **is dictating your moves:** Hostage situations have been the subject of extensive research in negotiation, particularly by scholars interested in human communication. See William A. Donohue and Anthony J. Roberto, "Relational Development as Negotiated Order in Hostage Negotiation," *Human Communication Research*, Vol. 20, No. 2 (December 1993), pp. 175–198, for a review of the literature.

95 **threat may lack credibility:** Thomas C. Schelling makes this point convincingly in his classic work. Thomas C. Schelling, *The Strategy of Conflict* (London: Oxford University Press, 1960), pp. 21–52.

95 **the use of force:** Before police and other authorities began using negotiation to help them resolve hostage situations, many more hostages died during police-led assaults to free them than were killed directly by hostage takers. See Abraham H. Miller, *Terrorism and Hostage Negotiations* (Boulder, Colo.: Westview Press, 1980), pp. 37–38.

96 **surviving are quite good:** Ibid., p. 42.

97 **"it for [many] hours":** Ibid.

97 **to meet his death:** Bruce W. Nelan, "How They Did It: In a Quick and Brutal Assault, Fujimori's Troops Rescue All But One of the 72 Hostages," *Time*, May 5, 1997, p. 67. This phenomenon works both ways. Hostages sometimes suffer from the "Stockholm syndrome," named for a famous 1973 bank robbery in Sweden during which a female hostage fell in love with her captor, had voluntary sexual relations with him while a captive, and continued the relationship after he went to prison. Miller, *Terrorism and Hostage Negotiations*, p. 46.

100 **age of ninety-six:** Ibid., pp. 14–36; Tom Mathews, "Seizing Hostages: Scourge of the 70s," *Newsweek*, March 21, 1977, p. 16.

101 **"the greater your power":** Roger Fisher, William Ury, and Bruce Patton, *Getting to Yes*, 2d. ed. (New York: Penguin Books, 1991), pp. 97–106.

101 **to achieve its goals:** Peter H. Kim and Alison R. Fragale, "Choosing the

Path to Bargaining Power: An Empirical Comparison of BATNAs and Contributions in Negotiation," *Journal of Applied Psychology*, Vol. 90 (2005), pp. 373–381 (BATNA was a better measure of bargaining power for small bargaining zones but relative contributions to the relationship mattered more for large bargaining zones).

102 **"simply cannot do without":** Donald J. Trump, *The Art of the Deal* (New York: Random House, 1987), p. 37.

103 **section of Fifth Avenue:** Ibid., pp. 103–104.

103 *than do equivalent gains:* There is a rich literature on the importance of how people think about potential losses versus potential gains. See Daniel Kahneman and Amos Tversky, "Prospect Theory: An Analysis of Decision Risk," *Econometrica*, Vol. 47, No. 2 (1979), pp. 263–291; Paul H. Schurr, "Effects of Gains and Loss Decision Frames on Risky Purchase Negotiations," *Journal of Applied Psychology*, Vol. 72, No. 3 (1987), pp. 351–358; Eric van Dijk and Daan van Knippenberg, "Buying and Selling Exchange Goods: Loss Aversion and the Endowment Effect," *Journal of Economic Psychology*, Vol. 17 (1996), pp. 517–524.

105 **the jury unanimously endorses:** Harry Kalven, Jr., and Hans Zeisel, *The American Jury* (Boston: Little Brown, 1966), pp. 486–91; John Sabini, *Social Psychology*, 2d. ed. (New York: W. W. Norton, 1992), pp. 94–95.

105 **scientists call social proof:** Cialdini, *Influence*, pp. 114–166.

106 **too proud to apply:** Scott Kilman, "Hard-Pressed Ranchers Dream of Marketing Own Brand of Beef," *The Wall Street Journal*, March 26, 1997, p. A1.

109 **of newspaper comic strips:** David M. Herszenhorn, "Widowed Homeowner Foils Trump in Atlantic City," *New York Times*, July 21, 1998, p. B1; Tiffany Danitz, "When Private Land Is Public Property," *Washington Times*, April 6, 1998, p. 14; John Curran, "Elderly Woman Battles Casinos over Her Home," *Los Angeles Times*, February 25, 1996, p. A11.

112 **"up to the President":** Howard Gardner, *Leading Minds: An Anatomy of Leadership* (New York: Basic Books, 1995), pp. 148–149.

112 **coupled with expertise:** Expertise is one of the most well-documented persuasion techniques in the literature on marketing. Elizabeth J. Wilson and Daniel L. Sherrell, "Source Effects in Communication and Persuasion Research: A Meta-Analysis of Effect Size," *Journal of the Academy of Marketing Science*, Vol. 21 (1993), pp. 101–112; Arch G. Woodside and J. William Davenport, Jr., "The Effect of Salesman Similarity and Expertise on Consumer Purchasing Behavior," *Journal of Marketing Research*, Vol. 11 (1974), pp. 198–202.

CHAPTER 7: Step 1: Preparing Your Strategy

117 **Sir Francis Bacon (1597):** Michael Kiernan, ed., *Sir Francis Bacon, The Essays of Counsels, Civill and Morall* (Cambridge, Mass.: Harvard University

Press, 1985), pp. 145–147. The essay from which this quote is taken is called "Of Negotiating" and first appeared in 1597.

117 **Turkish folk saying:** R.G.H. Siu, *Folk Wisdom and Management 3,333 Proverbs* (Washington, D.C.: Manuscript, 1994), p. 30.

119 **American business mergers:** Dr. Gulliver identifies eight distinct stages. Simplified, these stages include: 1) search for an arena, 2) formulation of an agenda, 3) preliminary statements, 4) narrowing of issues, 5) preliminaries to final bargaining, 6) bargaining, 7) agreement and ritual confirmation, and 8) implementation. P. H. Gulliver, *Disputes and Negotiations: A Cross-Cultural Perspective* (New York: Academic Press, 1979), p. 82. I prefer to condense these eight steps into four for pedagogical purposes. Other scholars have identified basically similar stages in the negotiation process. Ann Douglas, *Industrial Peacemaking* (New York: Columbia University Press, 1962), pp. 13–99; Ian Morley and Geoffrey Stephenson, *The Social Psychology of Bargaining* (London: George Allen & Unwin Ltd., 1977), pp. 284–93; Michael E. Holmes, "Phase Structures in Negotiation," in *Communication and Negotiation* (Newbury Park, N.J.: Sage, 1992), pp. 83–105; Camille P. Schuster and Michael J. Copeland, *Global Business: Planning for Sales and Negotiations* (Fort Worth, Tex.: The Dryden Press, Harcourt Brace College, 1996), pp. 27–28.

121 **in this particular transaction?:** The discussion in the text is a variant on the "Dual Concern" model. Peter J. D. Carnevale and Dean G. Pruitt, "Negotiation and Mediation," *Annual Review of Psychology*, Vol. 43 (1992), pp. 539–543.

122 **John D. Rockefeller, Jr.:** Allan Nevins, *Vol. 2, John D. Rockefeller: The Heroic Age of American Enterprise* (New York: Scribners, 1940), pp. 417–422. Ron Chernow, *Titan: The Life of John D. Rockefeller, Sr.* (New York: Random House, 1998), pp. 390–392.

124 **the Depression-scarred 1930s:** Abraham Pais, *Einstein Lived Here* (New York: Clarendon Press, 1994), p. 188. Another account of these negotiations can be found in Dennis Brian, *Einstein: A Life* (New York: John Wiley & Sons, 1996), p. 232.

125 **pockets of everyone involved:** The story comes from Benjamin Franklin himself. L. Jesse Lemisch, ed., Benjamin Franklin, *The Autobiography and Other Writings* (New York: Penguin, 1961), pp. 29–30.

131 **whether you like it or not:** For an excellent summary of academic learning on the role of agents in negotiation, see Robert H. Mnookin, Lawrence E. Susskind, and Pacey C. Foster, *Negotiating on Behalf of Others: Advice to Lawyers, Business Executives, Sports Agents, Diplomats, Politicians, and Everybody Else* (Thousand Oaks, CA: Sage Publications, 1999).

131 **using a good lawyer to help you negotiate deals:** Good lawyers can actually create value in negotiations. Bad ones usually prolong the process and add costs. See Ronald J. Gilson and Robert H. Mnookin, "Disputing Through Agents: Cooperation and Conflict Between Lawyers in Litigation," *Columbia Law Review*, Vol. 94 (1994), pp. 509–578.

132 **longer when they are selling yours:** Steven D. Levitt and Stephen J. Dubner, *Freakonomics: A Rogue Economist Explores the Hidden Side of Everything* (New York: HarperCollins, 2005), pp. 120–131.

133 **ease the negotiation over many hurdles:** For a good summary of various communication methods and their effect on negotiation, see Kathleen L. McGinn and Rachel Croson, "What Do Communication Media Mean for Negotiations? A Question of Social Awareness," in Michele J. Gelfand and Jeanne M. Brett, eds., *The Handbook of Negotiation and Culture* (Stanford, CA: Stanford University Press, 2004), pp. 334–349.

133 **use the narrowest communication pipeline (e-mail) the most:** I have written more extensively on the general issues of electronic negotiations. See G. Richard Shell, "Electronic Bargaining: The Perils of E-Mail and the Promise of Computer-Assisted Negotiations," in Stephen J. Hoch and Howard C. Kunreuther, *Wharton on Making Decisions* (New York: Wiley, 2001), pp. 201–221.

133 **benefits of using e-mail . . . to negotiate our home sale:** For a general discussion of the benefits of electronic negotiation, see Leigh Thompson and Janice Nadler, "Negotiating Via Information Technology: Theory and Application," *Journal of Social Issues*, Vol. 58, No. 1 (Spring 2002), pp. 109–124.

134 **studies of e-mail negotiations have confirmed this problem:** The study described in the text can be found in Michael Morris, Janice Nadler, Terri Kurtzberg, and Leigh Thompson, "Schmooze or Lose: Social Friction and Lubrication in E-mail Negotiations," *Group Dynamics, Theory, Research & Practice*, Vol. 6, No. 1 (May 2002), pp. 89–100. A similar study was done involving law students at different universities, with similar results. Negotiators who shared a getting-to-know-you telephone call before initiating e-mail negotiations were more successful avoiding impasse than those who did not. Janice Nadler, "Legal Negotiation and Communication Technology: How Small Talk Can Facilitate E-mail Dealmaking," *Harvard Negotiation Law Review*, Vol. 9 (2004), pp. 223–245. See also Nicholas Epley and Justin Kruger, "When What You Type Isn't What They Read: The Perseverance of Stereotypes and Expectancies Over E-Mail," *Journal of Experimental Social Psychology*, Vol. 41 (2005), pp. 414–422. For further research regarding the pitfalls of using e-mail to negotiate, see Raymond A. Friedman and Steven C. Currall, "Conflict Escalation: Dispute Exacerbating Elements of E-mail Communications," *Human Relations*, Vol. 56, No. 11 (2003), pp. 1325–1347; Charles E. Naquin and Gaylen D. Paulson, "Online Bargaining and Trust," *Journal of Applied Psychology*, Vol. 88, No. 1 (2003), pp. 113–120 (e-mail negotiators had less trust and had less desire for a repeated transaction than did face-to-face negotiators).

135 **an advantage when using IM:** Research on IM negotiating is just getting started. See Jeffrey Loewenstein, Michael W. Morris, Angnish Chakravarti, Leigh Thompson, and Shirli Kopelman, "At a loss for words: Dominating the conversation and the outcome in negotiation as a function of intricate arguments and communication media," Vol. 98 (2005), pp. 28–38.

CHAPTER 8:   Step 2: Exchanging Information

138   **Sir Francis Bacon (1597):** Michael Kiernan, ed., *Sir Francis Bacon, The Essays of Counsels, Civill and Morall* (Cambridge, Mass.: Harvard University Press, 1985), pp. 145–147. The essay from which this quote is taken is called "Of Negotiating" and first appeared in 1597.

138   **Fulfulde folk saying:** R.G.H. Siu, *Folk Wisdom and Management 3,333 Proverbs* (Washington, D.C.: Manuscript, 1994), p. 24. The Fulfulde people live in Africa, mainly within Nigeria.

139   **discussed in Chapter 4:** As discussed in Chapter 4, fairness and reciprocity are basic building blocks to successful relationships. Paul C. Cozby, "Self-disclosure, Reciprocity, and Liking," *Sociometry*, Vol. 35, No. 1 (1972), pp. 151–160.

140   **"task-oriented" in negotiation:** Camille P. Schuster and Michael J. Copeland, *Global Business: Planning for Sales and Negotiations* (Fort Worth, Tex.: The Dryden Press, Harcourt Brace, 1996), pp. 27–28 (discussing the prevalence outside North America of prenegotiation discussion of nonbusiness matters ranging from personal concerns to social conversation).

140   **single transaction at issue:** Ibid., p. 28 (discussing the importance of relationship formation in negotiations outside North America).

140   **get to meaningful bargaining:** Ibid., pp. 107–112. ("Because relationships are paramount [in Latin America] and getting to the task is not the highest priority, more time is spent at the early part of the process getting to know the other person and deciding on the parameters of the negotiation process.")

140   **rapport between the negotiators:** Bruce Barry and Richard L. Oliver, "Affect in Dyadic Negotiation: A Model and Propositions," *Organizational Behavior and Human Decision Processes*, Vol. 67, No. 2 (1996), pp. 127–143.

141   **also won the contract:** Carl Blumay, *The Dark Side of Power: The Real Armand Hammer* (New York: Simon and Schuster, 1992), pp. 96–97.

141   **the funeral home business:** Connie Bruck, *Master of the Game: Steve Ross and the Creation of Time Warner* (New York: Penguin, 1994), p. 27.

142   **"we know and like":** Robert B. Cialdini, *Influence: The Psychology of Persuasion* (New York: William Morrow, 1993), pp. 167–207.

142   **reflect well on them:** Two early works that helped identify this phenomenon are T. M. Newcomb, *The Acquaintance Process* (New York: Holt, Rinehart, and Winston, 1961), and D. Byrne, *The Attraction Paradigm* (New York: Academic Press, 1971). For a more recent survey and study on how similarity of mood affects liking, see Kenneth D. Locke and Leonard M. Horowitz, "Satisfaction in Interpersonal Interactions as a Foundation of Similarity in Level of Dysphoria," *Journal of Personality and Social Psychology*, Vol. 58, No. 5 (1990), pp. 823–831.

142   **of relatedness and similarity:** M. B. Brewer, "In-Group Bias in the Minimal Group Situation: A Cognitive-Motivational Analysis," *Psychological Bulletin*, Vol. 86 (1979), pp. 307–324; A. H. Ryen and A. Kahn, "Effects of Inter-

group Orientation on Group Attitudes and Proximic Behavior," *Journal of Personality and Social Psychology*, Vol. 31 (1975), pp. 302–310.

143 **in terms of credibility:** See Edward E. Jones and C. Wortman, *Ingratiation: An Attributional Approach* (Morristown, N.J.: General Learning Press, 1973); Edward E. Jones, "Flattery Will Get You Somewhere," *Transaction*, Vol. 2, No. 4 (1965), pp. 20–23; David Drachman, Andre DeCarufel, and Chester A. Insko, "The Extra Credit Effect in Interpersonal Attraction," *Journal of Experimental Social Psychology*, Vol. 14 (1978), pp. 458–465.

143 **partners were not amused:** Dean Takahashi, "It's Dog Eat Dog, So Executives with Loose Lips Get the Muzzle," *The Wall Street Journal*, July 15, 1997, p. B1.

145 **copy and replay TV programs:** This story originally comes from a series that ran in *The New Yorker* magazine. See "Annals of the Law: The Betamax Case I," *The New Yorker*, April 6, 1987. It is retold in Robert M. March, *The Japanese Negotiator: Subtlety and Strategy Beyond Western Logic* (Tokyo: Kodansha International, 1989), pp. 119–123.

148 **engaged in actual transactions:** N. Rackham and J. Carlisle, "The Effective Negotiator—Part 1: The Behavior of Successful Negotiators," *Journal of European Industrial Training*, Vol. 2, No. 6 (1978), pp. 6–11; N. Rackham and J. Carlisle, "The Effective Negotiator—Part 2: Planning for Negotiations," *Journal of European Industrial Training*, Vol. 2, No. 7 (1978), pp. 2–5.

149 **activities by average negotiators:** N. Rackham and J. Carlisle, "The Effective Negotiator—Part I: The Behavior of Successful Negotiators," *Journal of European Industrial Training*, Vol. 2, No. 6 (1978), pp. 6–11.

149 **"probe an opponent's position":** Williams, *Legal Negotiation and Settlement* (St. Paul, Minn.: West Publishing, 1983), pp. 15–46. Williams's research studied practicing lawyers in two major U.S. cities. In addition to discovering the traits of effective negotiators, Williams found that least effective negotiators are either too "trustful" and "obliging" (for cooperative negotiators) or "irritating," "headstrong," and "arrogant" (for competitive negotiators). Ibid.

149 **negotiators in that industry:** Howard Raiffa, *The Art and Science of Negotiation* (Cambridge, Mass.: Harvard University Press, 1982), pp. 120–121.

149 **skill after "verbal clarity":** Chester Karrass, *The Negotiating Game*, rev. ed. (New York: HarperBusiness, 1992), pp. 241–244.

150 **provide them with leverage:** For a formal economic model that expresses this same thought, see Vincent P. Crawford and Joel Sobel, "Strategic Information Transmission," *Econometrica*, Vol. 50, No. 6 (1982), pp. 1431–1451.

151 **50 percent of the time:** Leigh Thompson, *The Mind and Heart of the Negotiator* (Englewood Cliffs, N.J.: Prentice-Hall, 1998), p. 49.

151 **due to bluffs that backfired:** Leigh Thompson, "An Examination of Naive and Experienced Negotiators," *Journal of Personality and Social Psychology*, Vol. 59, No. 1 (1990), pp. 82–90.

153 **"they want the deal":** I got this quote from Harvey Mackay. See Harvey Mackay, *Swim with the Sharks* (New York: Ivy Books, 1988), p. 107.

153 **proceed on that basis:** Research suggests that personalizing the negotiation encounter is especially good advice when you lack leverage. Ian Morley and Geoffrey Stephenson, *The Social Psychology of Bargaining* (London:
George Allen and Unwin, 1977), pp. 138–182. See also James K. Esser, Michael J. Calvillo, Michael R. Scheel, and James L. Walker, "Oligopoly Bargaining: Effects of Agreement Pressure and Opponent Strategies," *Journal
of Applied Social Psychology*, Vol. 20 (1990), pp. 1256–1271; Dean Tjosvold
and Ted L. Houston, "Social Face and Resistance to Compromise in Bargaining," *Journal of Social Psychology*, Vol. 104 (1978), pp. 57–68.

CHAPTER 9: Step 3: Opening and
Making Concessions

156 **Samuel Johnson:** *Roget's International Thesaurus* (New York: Thomas Y.
Crowell, 1946), p. 530.

158 **ready to negotiate:** This story comes from Mark McCormack. See Mark
McCormack, *On Negotiating* (Los Angeles: Dove Books, 1995), p. 129.

158 **Beatles considerably more money:** Bob Woolf, *Friendly Persuasion: How to
Negotiate and Win* (New York: Berkley Books, 1990), pp. 180–181.

159 **to rethink its goals:** Bruce K. MacMurray and Edward J. Lawler, "Level-of-
Aspiration Theory and Initial Stance in Bargaining," *Representative Research
in Social Psychology*, Vol. 16, No. 1 (1986), pp. 35–44.

159 **we anchor and adjust:** Max H. Bazerman, *Judgment in Managerial Decision
Making*, 4th ed. (New York: John Wiley & Sons, 1990), pp. 27–30.

159 **could offset this effect:** James K. Esser, "Agreement Pressure and Opponent Strategies in Oligopoly Bargaining," *Personality and Social Psychology
Bulletin*, Vol. 15, No. 4 (1989), pp. 596–603.

160 **should open optimistically:** Jerome M. Shertkoff and Melinda Conley,
"Opening Offer and Frequency of Concession as Bargaining Strategies,"
Journal of Personality and Social Psychology, Vol. 7, No. 2 (1967), pp. 181–185;
Gary Yukl, "Effects of the Opponent's Initial Offer, Concession Magnitude,
and Concession Frequency on Bargaining Behavior," *Journal of Personality
and Social Psychology*, Vol. 30, No. 3 (1974), pp. 323–335. This research finding, while confirmed repeatedly, could be the product of its experimental
setting. Typically, the subjects in these investigations (usually inexperienced undergraduates in psychology classes) sit in cubicles and, thinking
they are negotiating against another subject, make written or computerized offers and counteroffers for commodities such as used cars or appliances, sending and receiving bare price terms. The experimenters confront
subjects with a set of "programmed" openings and concession-making
strategies by the "other party" and record the subjects' responses and final
deals. Starting very high (or low), conceding slowly, and diminishing the
size of concessions as bargaining proceeds is the best way to bargain in this
artificial setting. Whether it is therefore the best way to handle real people
with real things to buy and sell is a more complicated question.

160 **mediated by a broker:** Mike Allen, William Donohue, and Becky Stewart, "Comparing Hardline and Softline Bargaining Strategies in Zero-Sum Situations Using Meta-Analysis," in M. Afzalur Rahim, ed., *Theory and Research in Conflict Management* (New York: Praeger, 1990), pp. 86–103.

161 **examine the contrast principle:** Robert B. Cialdini, *Influence: The Psychology of Persuasion* (New York: William Morrow, 1984), pp. 11–14, 42–45.

161 **or even to say "yes":** Robert B. Cialdini, Joyce E. Vincent, Stephen K. Lewis, Jose Catalan, Diane Wheeler, and Betty Lee Darby, "Reciprocal Concessions Procedure for Inducing Compliance: The Door-in-the-Face Technique," *Journal of Personality and Social Psychology*, Vol. 31, No. 2 (1975), pp. 206–215. See also Robert Vincent Joule, "Tobacco deprivation: The foot-in-the-door technique versus the low-ball technique," *European Journal of Social Psychology*, Vol. 17 (1987), pp. 361–365.

162 **scare the employer away:** Esser, "Agreement Pressure and Opponent Strategies in Oligopoly Bargaining."

163 **"'what I really deserved'":** Gail DeGeorge, *The Making of Blockbuster* (New York: John Wiley & Sons, 1996), pp. 38–39.

163 **(see Chapter 2) is still appropriate:** Dean G. Pruitt and Steven A. Lewis, "Development of Integrative Solutions in Bilateral Negotiation," *Journal of Personality and Social Psychology*, Vol. 31, No. 4 (1975), pp. 621–633.

163 **automobile dealers of America:** Keith Bradsher, "Sticker Shock: Car Buyers Miss Haggling Ritual," *The New York Times*, June 13, 1996, p. D1.

164 **"deal is through negotiation":** Ibid., p. D23.

164 **to the moderate point:** P. L. Benson, H. H. Kelly, and B. Liebling, "Effects of Extremity of Offers and Concession Rate on the Outcomes of Bargaining," *Journal of Personality and Social Psychology*, Vol. 24 (1983), pp. 73–83. Similar results have been reported elsewhere. See S. S. Komorita and Arline R. Brenner, "Bargaining and Concession Making Under Bilateral Monopoly," *Journal of Personality and Social Psychology*, Vol. 9, No. 1 (1968), pp. 15–20.

164 **who refused to move:** As psychologist W. C. Hamner has expressed it, "Negotiators expect something more than just a mutually rewarding payoff. They also seem to expect a rewarding social exchange, trial by trial. That is, they define bargaining as a give-and-take process and therefore expect it to consist of a series of exchanges, not just one large concession." See W. C. Hamner, "Effects of Bargaining Strategy and Pressure to Reach Agreement in a Stalemated Negotiation," *Journal of Personality and Social Psychology*, Vol. 30 (1974), pp. 458–467; Hamner's sentiments are echoed in a more recent study that highlights the importance of "procedural justice" norms in allocation decisions of all kinds. See Tom R. Tyler and Eugene Griffin, "The Influence of Decision Makers' Goals on Their Concerns About Procedural Justice," *Journal of Applied Social Psychology*, Vol. 21 (1991), pp. 1629–1658.

166 **concession strategy works best:** Seungwoo Kwon and Laurie R. Weingart, "Unilateral Concessions from the Other Party: Concession Behavior, Attributions, and Negotiator Judgment," *Journal of Applied Psychology*, Vol. 89, No.

2 (2004), pp. 263–278. Mara Olekalns, Philip L. Smith, and Therese Walsh, "The Process of Negotiating: Strategy and Timing as Predictors of Outcomes," *Organizational Behavior and Human Decision Processes*, Vol. 68, No. 1 (1996), pp. 68–77; Gary Yukl, "Effects of Situational Variables and Opponent Concessions on a Bargainer's Perception, Aspirations, and Concessions," *Journal of Personality and Social Psychology*, Vol. 29, No. 2 (1974), pp. 227–236.

166 **play it in competitive situations:** Martin Patchen, "Strategies for Eliciting Cooperating from an Adversary," *Journal of Conflict Resolution*, Vol. 31, No. 1 (1987), pp. 164–185.

168 **this phenomenon "concession devaluation":** Negotiation scholars also call this "reactive devaluation." Margaret Neale and Max Bazerman, *Cognition and Rationality in Negotiation* (New York: Free Press, 1991), p. 75; Robert Mnookin, "Why Negotiations Fail: An Exploration of Barriers to the Resolution of Conflict," *Ohio State Journal of Dispute Resolution*, Vol. 8 (1993), pp. 235, 238–247.

168 **"we esteem too lightly":** This saying is attributed to Thomas Paine. *Roget's International Thesaurus* (New York: Thomas Y. Crowell, 1946), p. 555.

168 **interests, priorities, and differences:** Richard E. Walton and Robert B. McKersie, *A Behavioral Theory of Labor Negotiations* (New York: McGraw-Hill, 1965), pp. 126–182.

169 ***"big" (most important) issues:*** Lewis A. Froman, Jr., and Michael D. Cohen, "Compromise and Logroll: Comparing the Efficiency of Two Bargaining Processes," *Behavioral Science*, Vol. 15 (1970), pp. 180–183.

169 **proceeds through "package bargaining":** Pruitt and Lewis, "Development of Integrative Solutions in Bilateral Negotiation"; Elizabeth A. Mannix, Leigh Thompson, and Max H. Bazerman, "Negotiation in Small Groups," *Journal of Applied Psychology*, Vol. 74, No. 3 (1989), pp. 508–517; Gary A. Yukl, Michael P. Malone, Bert Hayslip, and Thomas A. Pamin, "The Effects of Time Pressure and Issue Settlement Order on Integrative Bargaining," *Sociometry*, Vol. 39, No. 3 (1976), pp. 277–281.

169 ***on issues X and Y:*** Gavin Kennedy, John Benson, and John McMillian, *Managing Negotiations* (Englewood Cliffs, N.J.: Prentice-Hall, 1982), pp. 88–98.

172 **than a simple compromise:** Roger Fisher, William Ury, and Bruce Patton, *Getting to Yes*, 2nd ed. (New York: Penguin, 1991). These authors advocate brainstorming as a technique to help in problem-solving situations. Also see Thomas J. D'Zurilla and Arthur Nezu, "A Study of the Generation-of-Alternatives Process in Social Problem Solving," *Cognitive Therapy and Research*, Vol. 4, No. 1 (1980), pp. 67–72 (showing that the best way to find quality solutions is simply to generate as many options as possible).

172 **"good guy/bad guy" routine:** Good examples can be found in several "war story" books about mergers and acquisitions. See Bryan Burrough and John Hellyar, *Barbarians at the Gate: The Fall of RJR Nabisco* (New York: Harper & Row, 1990), pp. 266–269; DeGeorge, *The Making of Blockbuster*, pp. 141–143.

172 **we have met before:** Robert Cialdini has an excellent discussion of the psychological principles that underlie the "good guy/bad guy" routine. See Cialdini, *Influence*, pp. 186–187.

173 **connection with optimistic openings:** John A. Hilty and Peter Carnevale, "Black Hat/White Hat Strategy in Bilateral Negotiation," *Organizational Behavior and Human Decision Processes*, Vol. 55, No. 3 (1993), pp. 444–469.

CHAPTER 10: Step 4: Closing and
Gaining Commitment

175 **English rhyme:** *Roget's International Thesaurus* (New York: Thomas Y. Crowell, 1946), p. 533.

175 **Slovakian folk saying:** R.G.H. Siu, *Folk Wisdom and Management 3,333 Proverbs* (Washington, D.C.: Manuscript, 1994), p. 73.

176 *Barbarians at the Gate:* Bryan Burrough and John Helyar, *Barbarians at the Gate: The Fall of RJR Nabisco* (New York: Harper & Row, 1990).

176 **"be in this deal":** Ibid., p. 203. The authors note that Kravis denied saying "We have to be in on this deal. And we will be in this deal."

177 **tense but optimistic:** The story of the fateful events of November 30, 1988 can be found in *Barbarians at the Gate*, pp. 474–502.

178 **"Absolutely not," says Kravis:** Ibid., p. 481.

178 **"one person to another":** Michael Lynn, "Scarcity Effects on Value: A Quantitative Review of the Commodity Theory Literature," *Psychology and Marketing*, Vol. 8, No. 1 (Spring 1991), p. 52.

178 **we missed an opportunity:** Graham Loomes and Robert Sugden, "Regret Theory: An Alternative Theory of Rational Choice Under Uncertainty," *The Economic Journal*, Vol. 92 (1982), pp. 805–824.

180 **imposed by stiff competition:** Chester Karrass, *The Negotiating Game*, rev. ed. (New York: HarperBusiness, 1992), pp. 20–23.

181 **trademark of his style:** David Johnson, "In Taj deal Trump used an old tactic," *The Philadelphia Inquirer*, November 18, 1990, p. D1.

181 **a family in New Orleans:** Gail DeGeorge, *The Making of Blockbuster* (New York: John Wiley & Sons, 1996), pp. 73–74.

182 **to win the contest:** Burrough and Helyar, *Barbarians at the Gate*, pp. 482–483.

182 **Psychologists call it overcommitment:** Howard Garland, "Throwing Good Money After Bad: The Effect of Sunk Costs on the Decision to Escalate Commitment to an Ongoing Project," *Journal of Applied Psychology*, Vol. 75, No. 6 (1990), pp. 728–731.

186 **lack of balance at the beginning:** One well-known professional negotiator, Bob Woolf, maintains that he never splits the difference. Instead, he treats the offer to split as an admission. The other party has told him, in effect, that it can do the deal at a point halfway between the last two offers. Interview, "How to Negotiate Practically Anything," *Inc.*, February 1989, p. 10.

187 **out of the Korean War:** Jeffrey Z. Rubin and Bert R. Brown, *The Social Psychology of Bargaining and Negotiation* (New York: Academic Press, 1975), p. 96. The story was originally reported in the press. See UPI, "2 Sides Sit Silently 4½ Hours at Korean Truce Meeting," *Philadelphia Evening Bulletin,* April 11, 1969, p. 10. I take my spelling of General Yi's name, which appears in several different forms in news reports, from the *New York Times.* See "U.S., at Meeting in Korea, Protests Downing of Plane," *New York Times,* April 18, 1969, p. A1.

188 **return to the table:** William Ury has an entire book on this subject. See William Ury, *Getting Past No* (New York: Bantam, 1991), pp. 105–129.

189 **up between the parties:** Murrary Chass, "The National Pastime's True Most Valuable Player," *The New York Times,* November 28, 1996, p. B23.

189 **can work in private:** Moving the parties to a private location where they can work on an agreement without having to answer to constituents is especially useful in international relations. See Clyde Haberman, "How the Oslo Connection Led to the Mideast Peace," *The New York Times,* September 5, 1993, p. A1.

189 **then wait for reciprocation:** This process has been confirmed experimentally. See S. S. Komorita and James K. Esser, "Frequency of Reciprocated Concessions in Bargaining," *Journal of Personality and Social Psychology,* Vol. 32, No. 4 (1975), pp. 699–705.

189 **Initiatives in Tension Reduction:** Charles E. Osgood, *An Alternative to War or Surrender* (Urbana, Ill.: University of Illinois Press, 1962), pp. 85–134.

190 **Sinai Peninsula to Egypt:** Howard Raiffa provides an excellent discussion of the Camp David accords as an example of assisted negotiation. See Howard Raiffa, *The Art and Science of Negotiation* (Cambridge, Mass.: Harvard University Press, 1982), p. 205.

190 **compared with available alternatives:** William P. Bottom and Amy Studt, "Framing Effects and the Distributive Aspect of Integrative Bargaining," *Organizational Behavior and Human Decision Processes,* Vol. 56, No. 3 (1993), pp. 459–474.

191 **backed out of the deal:** Patrick McGeehan, "Morgan Stanley, Dean Witter Have Big Breakup Fee," *The Wall Street Journal,* February 18, 1997, p. B12.

191 **that $8.3 million figure:** Bob Woolf, *Friendly Persuasion: How to Negotiate and Win* (New York: Berkley Books, 1990), pp. 19–22.

CHAPTER 11: Bargaining with the Devil Without
Losing Your Soul: Ethics in Negotiation

196 **Anacharsis (600 B.C.):** *Roget's International Thesaurus* (New York: Thomas Y. Crowell, 1946), p. 548.

196 **O'Loughlin, Allstate Insurance Company:** Mr. O'Loughlin was a senior vice president at Allstate Insurance Company at the time he was quoted as saying this. See Bruce Horovitz, "When Should an Executive Lie?," *Industry Week,* November 16, 1981, p. 87.

196 **a Philadelphia newspaper columnist:** Darrell Sifford, "Mastering the Fine Art of Negotiation," *Philadelphia Inquirer,* June 30, 1991, p. 11.

198 **life in every culture:** Sissela Bok calls white lies "the most common and the most trivial forms that duplicity can take." Sissela Bok, *Lying: Moral Choice in Public and Private Life* (New York: Vintage, 1978), p. 60. Some interesting research on "everyday" lying is reported in two articles. See Bella M. DePaulo, Deborah A. Kashy, Susan E. Kirkendol, Melissa M. Wyer, and Jennifer A. Epstein, "Lying in Everyday Life," *Journal of Personality and Social Psychology,* Vol. 70, No. 5 (1996), pp. 979–995; Deborah A. Kashy and Bella M. DePaulo, "Who Lies?," *Journal of Personality and Social Psychology,* Vol. 70, No. 5 (1996), pp. 1037–1051. Curiously, the strongest predictor of whether a person was likely to lie a lot was whether he or she had high-quality same-sex relationships. As the researchers put it, "People who described their same-sex relationships as warm, enduring, and satisfying told fewer lies overall, and especially fewer self-centered lies, than people who described their same-sex relationships in less glowing terms.

198 **return for concrete concessions:** Robert J. Robinson, Roy J. Lewicki, and Eileen M. Donohue, "Extending and Testing a Five Factor Model of Ethical and Unethical Bargaining Tactics: Introducing the SINS Scale," *Journal of Organizational Behavior* (1998).

199 **a major motivational objective:** Gerald R. Williams, *Legal Negotiation and Settlement* (St. Paul, Minn.: West Publishing, 1983), p. 19.

199 **interviews are "persistent liars":** Bruce Horowitz, "When Should an Executive Lie?," *Industry Week,* November 16, 1981, pp. 81–87.

199 **"engage in ethical behavior":** James J. White, "The Pros and Cons of 'Getting to Yes,'" *Journal of Legal Education,* Vol. 34 (1984), pp. 115–124, quote on p. 118. Business ethicist and economist Robert H. Frank of Cornell University echoes White's analysis when he says, "The art of bargaining, as most of us eventually learn, is in large part the art of sending misleading messages about [reservation prices]." See Robert H. Frank, *Passions Within Reason* (New York: W. W. Norton, 1988), p. 165.

200 **traits of a skilled negotiator:** Chester Karrass, *The Negotiating Game,* rev. ed. (New York: HarperBusiness, 1992), pp. 242–243; Howard Raiffa, *The Art and Science of Negotiation* (Cambridge, Mass.: Harvard University Press, 1982), pp. 120–121.

201 **regulate the negotiation process:** Much of the following discussion comes from an article I wrote in 1991. See G. Richard Shell, "When Is It Legal to Lie in Negotiations?," *Sloan Management Review,* Vol. 32 (1991), pp. 93–101.

201 **negotiation of commercial agreements:** The Uniform Commercial Code states that the general duty of good faith applies only to the performance and enforcement of agreements, not their negotiation. See *Uniform Commercial Code* § 1-203. See also *Restatement (Second) of Contracts* § 205 (1981), comment c ("Bad faith in negotiation" is not "within the scope of this Section"). Ibid., § 205, comment c.

201 **"'bad faith' in negotiations":** *Feldman* v. *Allegheny Intn'l, Inc.*, 850 F. 2d 1217, 1223 (7th Cir., 1988).

201 **relies (6) causing damages:** W. Page Keeton, Dan B. Dobbs, Robert E. Keeton, and David G. Owen, *Prosser and Keeton on the Law of Torts* (St. Paul, Minn.: West Publishing, 1984), p. 728.

204 **infestation in her home:** *Miles* v. *McSwegin*, 388 N.E. 2d 1367 (Ohio, 1979).

204 **negotiating to purchase it:** *Zaschak* v. *Traverse Corp.*, 333 N.W. 2d 191 (Mich. Appl., 1983).

204 **preferring the term "bluffs":** Robert A. Wenke, *The Art of Negotiation for Lawyers* (New York: Law Distributors, 1985), p. 33. For a summary of research on ethical attitudes about bluffing and other traditional "competitive bargaining" behavior, see Roy J. Lewicki, Joseph A. Litterer, John W. Minton, and David M. Saunders, *Negotiation*, 2nd ed. (Burr Ridge, Ill.: Irwin, 1994), pp. 392–398.

205 **to their expressed preferences:** John G. Cross, *The Economics of Bargaining* (New York: Basic Books, 1969), pp. 166–179 (exaggerated demands make it possible to engage in cooperative process of mutual concession making); P. H. Gulliver, *Disputes and Negotiation: A Cross-Cultural Perspective* (New York: Academic Press, 1979), pp. 135–141 (exaggerated demands set legitimate boundaries of dispute); Thomas Schelling, *The Strategy of Conflict* (New York: Oxford University Press, 1963), pp. 22–28 (strength of commitment is key to success in using misleading statements about reservation price to capture larger share of bargaining surplus).

205 **to a third person:** American Bar Association, *Model Rules of Professional Conduct*, Rule 4.1(a) official comment (1983).

205 **legal case from Massachusetts:** *Kabatchnick* v. *Hanover-Elm Bldg. Corp.*, 103 N.E. 2d 692 (Mass., 1952).

205 **later that same day:** *Beavers* v. *Lamplighters Realty, Inc.*, 556 P. 2d 1328 (Okla. Appl., 1976).

206 **"state of his digestion":** *Edgington* v. *Fitzmaurice*, L. R. 29 Ch. Div. 359 (1885).

207 **intention was "material":** A particularly vivid example of this sort of conduct was litigated in *Markov* v. *ABC Transfer & Storage Co.*, 457 P. 2d 535 (Wash., 1969). See also *Gibraltar Savings* v. *LDBrinkman Corp.*, 860 F. 2d 1275 (5th Cir., 1988) (debtor's promise to creditor to keep holding company solvent when plans were under way to dissolve holding company deemed fraudulent, resulting in $6 million verdict).

207 **from his largest customer:** *Alio* v. *Saponaro*, 520 N.Y.S. 2d 245 (A.D., 1987).

207 **to sell their discoveries:** *Smith* v. *Snap-on Tools Corp.*, 833 F. 2d 578 (5th Cir., 1988) (no liability when inventor made a gift of invention to the company); *Smith* v. *Dravo Corp.*, 203 F. 2d 369 (7th Cir., 1953) (liability when inventor intended negotiations to lead to sale of trade secret).

208 **the final written contract:** *Turner* v. *Johnson & Johnson*, 809 F. 2d 90 (1st Cir., 1986).

209 **approach others as equals:** See Geoffrey M. Peter, "The Use of Lies in Negotiation," *Ohio State Law Journal*, Vol. 48, No. 1 (1987), pp. 1–50.

210   **"much money or power":** Albert Z. Carr, "Is Business Bluffing Ethical?,"
      Harvard Business Review, Vol. 46 (1968), pp. 143–153. One modern fol-
      lower of the Poker School might be former California real estate mogul
      and successful negotiation entrepreneur Roger Dawson, who teaches peo-
      ple to become "Power Negotiators." Dawson specializes in teaching "gam-
      bits," telling people that one of the secrets of success is "to think of
      negotiating as a game." See Roger Dawson, *Roger Dawson's Secrets of Power
      Negotiating* (Hawthorne, N.J.: Career Press, 1995), p. 94.

210   **person successfully deceived them:** Carr, "Is Business Bluffing Ethical?,"
      p. 145.

212   **conduct is therefore unethical:** Immanuel Kant, *Foundations of the Meta-
      physics of Morals,* L. W. Beck, trans. (New York: Liberal Arts Press, 1959).

213   **bluffs about bottom lines:** J. Gregory Dees and Peter C. Cramton, "Shrewd
      Bargaining on the Moral Frontier: Toward a Theory of Morality in Prac-
      tice," *Business Ethics Quarterly,* Vol. 1, No. 2 (1991), pp. 135–167. Also see
      Alan Strudler, "On the Ethics of Deception in Negotiation," *Business Ethics
      Quarterly,* Vol. 5, No. 4 (1995), pp. 805–822.

213   **as an ethical option:** Scholars have hypothesized that a corrupt work envi-
      ronment can lead otherwise good people to engage in unethical conduct.
      Daniel J. Brass, Kenneth D. Butterfield, and Bruce C. Skaggs, "Relation-
      ships and Unethical Behavior: A Social Network Perspective," *Academy of
      Management Review,* Vol. 23 (1998), pp. 14–31. In addition, there is empiri-
      cal support for the idea that people tend to orient toward goals supported
      by the institutions in which they live and work. Tim Kasser, "Aspirations
      and Well-being in a Prison Setting," *Journal of Applied Social Psychology,* Vol.
      26 (1996), pp. 1367–1377.

217   **daughter a used car:** Dale Singer, "I've Kicked the Tires. Now I'll Kick My-
      self," *The New York Times,* February 2, 1997, p. F14.

218   **a hidden psychological premise:** Robert B. Cialdini, John T. Cacioppo,
      Rodney Bassett, and John A. Miller, "Low-Ball Procedure for Producing
      Compliance: Commitment Then Cost," *Journal of Personality and Social Psy-
      chology,* Vol. 36, No. 5 (1978), pp. 463–476. Under the lowball procedure,
      a salesman induces a customer to make an active decision to buy one spe-
      cific car by offering an extremely good price. The salesman then uses one
      of several devices to remove the low price, including "checking with the
      boss," who overrules the salesman's offer. Other techniques include low-
      ering the trade-in allowance, threatening to leave out standard features
      such as the radio or air-conditioning, and so on. Consumer groups have
      identified and condemned the practice for decades. See, for example, *Con-
      sumer Reports,* Vol. 39 (May 1974), p. 368.

219   **real estate market: 1997:** Tracey Rozan, "A Hot Market Leads to Cold-
      Blooded Dealing," *The New York Times,* May 25, 1997, Sec. 9, p. 1.

220   **"with the latter's demands":** Frank J. Monteverde, Richard Paschke, and
      James T. Tedeschi, "The Effectiveness of Honesty and Deceit as Influence
      Tactics," *Sociometry,* Vol. 37, No. 4 (1974), pp. 583–591. A similar study

found that "the disadvantaged player in a bargaining game lied more often than his more powerful opponent and gained better bargaining outcomes as a consequence." See C. S. Fischer, "The Effect of Threats in an Incomplete Information Game," *Sociometry*, Vol. 32 (1969), pp. 301–314.

220 **"using less ethical tactics":** Roy J. Lewicki, Joseph A. Litterer, John W. Minton, and David M. Saunders, *Negotiation*, 2d ed. (Burr Ridge, Ill.: Irwin, 1994), p. 402.

221 **"willing to use them":** Ibid., p. 401. People who expect a short-term relationship are more likely to see ethically questionable behavior as acceptable than are those who foresee a long-term relationship. They are also more likely to anticipate unethical conduct from others and to use questionable tactics as a defense strategy themselves.

221 **lies have been told:** Peter J. DePaulo and Bella M. DePaulo, "Can Deception by Salespersons and Customers Be Detected Through Nonverbal Behavioral Cues?," *Journal of Applied Social Psychology*, Vol. 19, No. 18 (1989), pp. 1552–1577.

221 **"to interpret their speeches":** Michael Kiernan, ed., *Sir Francis Bacon, The Essays of Counsels, Civill and Morall* (Cambridge, Mass.: Harvard University Press, 1985), pp. 145–147.

221 **draw a firm conclusion:** Recent studies on lie detecting have suggested that only specialists, such as Secret Service personnel, are good at detecting liars. See, for example, Paul Ekman and Maureen O'Sullivan, "Who Can Catch a Liar?" *American Psychologist*, Vol. 46 (1991), pp. 913–920. Other researchers claim that average people can outperform chance, at least when it comes to telling that "something fishy is going on." Bella M. DePaulo and Robert Rosenthal, "Telling Lies," *Journal of Personality and Social Psychology*, Vol. 37, No. 10 (1979), pp. 1713–1722; Richard A. Maier and Paul J. Lavrakas, "Lying Behavior and Evaluation of Lies," *Perceptual and Motor Skills*, Vol. 42 (1976), pp. 575–581. Even these studies reveal that people are not very good at determining what people are covering up—only that they are covering *something* up.

224 **"Red Herring" technique:** Dawson, *Roger Dawson's Secrets of Power Negotiating*, pp. 94–100.

224 **Sony's new movie division:** Nancy Griffin and Kim Masters, *Hit and Run: How Jon Peters and Peter Guber Took Sony for a Ride in Hollywood* (New York: Simon & Schuster, 1996), pp. 233–251.

225 **to obtain their release:** Actually, the timing turned out not to matter. Steve Ross refused to give Guber and Peters a release, sued Sony for $1 billion for inducing a breach of contract between Warner and Guber-Peters Entertainment, and won a handsome settlement.

CHAPTER 12: Conclusion: On Becoming an
Effective Negotiator

229 **Pashto folk saying:** R.G.H. Siu, *Folk Wisdom and Management 3,333 Proverbs* (Washington, D.C.: Manuscript, 1994), p. 81. The Pashto language is spoken in a remote part of Pakistan and originated in Central Asia.

229 **Robert Louis Stevenson:** *Roget's International Thesaurus* (New York: Thomas Y. Crowell, 1946), p. 546.

233 **agents for others' interests:** James A. Breaugh and Richard J. Klimoski, "Social Forces in Negotiation Simulations," *Personality and Social Psychology Bulletin*, Vol. 7, No. 2 (1981), pp. 290–295 (finding that people bargained harder on behalf of a group of which they were a part than if they were merely "hired guns" who acted as bargaining agents). In general, agents tend to assert goals more aggressively than do people bargaining on their own behalf. See Max H. Bazerman, Margaret A. Neale, Kathleen L. Valley, Edward J. Zajac, and Yong Min Kim, "The Effect of Agents and Mediators on Negotiation Outcomes," *Organizational Behavior and Human Decision Processes*, Vol. 53, No. 1 (1992), pp. 55–73.

233 **people are watching them:** Peter J. D. Carnevale, Dean G. Pruitt, and Scott D. Britton, "Looking Tough: The Negotiator Under Constituent Surveillance," *Personality and Social Psychology Bulletin*, Vol. 5, No. 1 (1979), pp. 118–121.

233 **she made a request:** The studies were led by Harvard University's Ellen Langer. See Ellen Langer, Arthur Blank, and Benzion Chanowitz, "The Mindlessness of Ostensibly Thoughtful Action: The Role of Placebic Information in Interpersonal Interaction," *Journal of Personality and Social Psychology*, Vol. 36, No. 6 (1978), pp. 635–642. An account of this work can be found in Robert B. Cialdini, *Influence: The Psychology of Persuasion* (New York: William Morrow, 1984), pp. 4–5.

APPENDIX A: A Note on Your Personal
Negotiation Style

242 **almost as far as do organized courses on negotiation:** J. Z. Rubin and R. B. Brown, *The Social Psychology of Bargaining and Negotiation* (New York: Academic Press, 1975); R. C. Bordone, "Teaching Interpersonal Skills for Negotiation and for Life," *Negotiation Journal* 16, No. 4 (2000), pp. 377–385; R. S. Fortgang, "Taking stock: An analysis of negotiation pedagogy across four professional fields," *Negotiation Journal* 16, No. 4 (2000), pp. 325–338. A related, more modern line of psychological pedagogy on negotiation deals with cognitive errors to which people of all races, genders, and interpersonal orientations are prone. Led by Max Bazerman (building on foundations laid by Daniel Kahneman and Amos Tversky), negotiation

teachers have learned to instruct their students about systematic biases in human cognition that can cloud negotiator judgment. The experimental evidence for such phenomena as "fixed pie" biases, gain-loss framing, availability, endowment effects, escalation of commitment, and overconfidence is strong, and classroom demonstrations of many of these biases are relatively easy to conduct. The pedagogical goal is to help people learn to recognize cognitive biases, overcome them in appropriate situations, and become more effective negotiators as a result. Like materials on gender, race, or culture, materials on cognitive psychology complement rather than substitute for content related to bargaining styles. The biases are not predispositions toward handling negotiation situations so much as they are hardwired quirks in the human information-processing system that affects many forms of decision making. D. Kahneman and A. Tversky, "Prospect Theory: An Analysis of Decision Under Risk," *Econometrica*, Vol. 47 (1979), pp.136–291; D. Kahneman, D. P. Slovic and A. Tversky, *Judgment Under Uncertainty: Heuristics and Biases* (Cambridge: Cambridge University Press, 1982).

242 **bargaining styles can play crucial roles in negotiation:** R. W. Gilkey and L. Greenhalgh, "The Role of Personality in Successful Negotiating," *Negotiation Journal*, Vol. 2, No. 3 (1986), pp. 245–256.

248 **"thief thinks everybody steals":** R. G. H. Siu, *Folk Wisdom and Management: 3,333 Proverbs* (Washington, D.C.: Manuscript, 1994), p. 13.

248 **assume that others are cooperative:** H. H. Kelly and A. Stahelski, "Social Interaction Basis of Cooperators' and Competitors' Beliefs About Others," *Journal of Personality and Social Psychology*, Vol. 16 (1970), pp. 66–91; James K. Esser and S. S. Komorita, "Reciprocity and Concession Making in Bargaining," *Journal of Personality and Social Psychology*, Vol. 31, No. 5 (1975), pp. 864–872.

249 **you end up making a deal:** Donald J. Trump, *The Art of the Deal* (New York: Random House, 1987), p. 88.

250 **(TKI), which I recommended in the first edition:** R. H. Kilmann and K. W. Thomas, "Developing a Forced-Choice Measure of Conflict-Handling Behavior: The 'Mode' Instrument," *Educational and Psychological Measurement*, Vol. 37 (1977), pp. 309–325. There is some doubt about the construct validity of the TKI. See M. A. Konovsky, F. Jaster, and M. A. McDonald, "Using Parametric Statistics to Explore the Construct Validity of the Thomas-Kilmann Conflict Mode Instrument," *Management Communication Quarterly*, Vol. 3, No. 2 (1989), pp. 268–290; B. Kabanoff, "Predictive Validity of the MODE Conflict Instrument," *Journal of Applied Psychology*, Vol. 72, No. 1 (1987), pp. 160–163. These concerns may also apply to the Bargaining Styles Assessment Tool, on which no research has been conducted to assess validity.

250 **Blake and Mouton in the mid-1960s:** R. R. Blake and J. S. Mouton, *The Managerial Grid* (Houston: Gulf Publications, 1964).

Selected Bibliography

Alston, Jon P. *The Intelligent Businessman's Guide to Japan.* New York: Charles E. Tuttle, 1990.

Axelrod, Robert. *The Evolution of Cooperation.* New York: Basic Books, 1984.

Babcock, Linda, and Sara Laschever. *Women Don't Ask: Negotiation and the Gender Divide.* Princeton, N.J.: Princeton University Press, 2003.

Bazerman, Max. *Judgement in Managerial Decision-Making,* 4th ed. New York: John Wiley & Sons, 1998.

———, and Margaret A. Neale. *Negotiating Rationally.* New York: Free Press, 1992.

Blau, Peter M. *Exchange and Power in Social Life.* New York: John Wiley & Sons, 1964.

Bok, Sissela. *Lying: Moral Choice in Public and Private Life.* New York: Vintage, 1978.

Byrne, D. *The Attraction Paradigm.* New York: Academic Press, 1971.

Carnegie, Dale. *How to Win Friends and Influence People,* rev. ed. New York: Pocket Books, 1981.

Cialdini, Robert B. *Influence: The Psychology of Persuasion.* New York: William Morrow, 1984.

Cohen, Herb. *You Can Negotiate Anything.* New York: Lyle Stuart, 1980.

Cross, John G. *The Economics of Bargaining.* New York: Basic Books, 1969.

Dawson, Roger. *Roger Dawson's Secrets of Power Negotiating.* Hawthorne, N.J.: Career Press, 1995.

Douglas, Ann. *Industrial Peacemaking.* New York: Columbia University Press, 1962.

Fisher, Roger, and Daniel Shapiro. *Beyond Reason: Using Emotions When You Negotiate.* New York: Viking, 2006.

Fisher, Roger, and Scott Brown. *Getting Together: Building a Relationship That Gets to Yes.* New York: Houghton Mifflin, 1988.

Fisher, Roger, William Ury, and Bruce Patton. *Getting to Yes,* 2d. ed. New York: Penguin, 1991.

Frank, Robert H. *Passions Within Reason.* New York: Norton, 1988.

Freund, James C. *Anatomy of a Merger.* New York: Academic Press, 1975.

———. *The Acquisition Mating Dance.* Clifton, N.J.: Prentice-Hall, 1987.

———. *Smart Negotiating.* New York: Simon & Schuster, 1992.

Gardner, Howard. *Leading Minds: An Anatomy of Leadership.* New York: Basic Books, 1995.

Gulliver, P. H. *Disputes and Negotiations: A Cross-Cultural Perspective.* New York: Academic Press, 1979.

Jones, Edward E., and C. Wortman. *Ingratiation: An Attributional Approach.* Morristown, N.J.: General Learning Press, 1973.

Karrass, Chester L. *The Negotiating Game,* rev. ed. New York: HarperBusiness, 1992.

Kennedy, Gavin, John Benson, and John McMillian. *Managing Negotiations.* Englewood Cliffs, N.J.: Prentice-Hall, 1982.

Kolb, Deborah, and Judith Williams. *Everyday Negotiations: Navigating the Hidden Agendas in Bargaining.* New York: Jossey-Bass, 2003.

Kramer, Roderick M., and David M. Messick. *Negotiation as a Social Process.* Thousand Oaks, Calif.: SAGE Publications, 1995.

Kramer, Roderick M., and Tom R. Tyler. *Trust in Organizations: Frontiers of Theory and Research.* Thousand Oaks, Calif.: SAGE Publications, 1996.

Lax, David A., and James K. Sebenius. *The Manager as Negotiator: Bargaining for Cooperation and Competitive Gain.* New York: The Free Press, 1986.

Lewicki, Roy J., et al. *Negotiation,* 2d. ed. Burr Ridge, Ill.: Irwin, 1994.

Locke, E., and G. Latham. *A Theory of Goal Setting and Task Performance.* Englewood Cliffs, N.J.: Prentice-Hall, 1990.

McCormack, Mark H. *On Negotiating.* Los Angeles: Dove Books, 1995.

March, Robert M. *The Japanese Negotiator: Subtlety and Strategy Beyond Western Logic.* Tokyo: Kodansha International, 1989.

Menkel-Meadow, Carrie, and Michael Wheeler eds. *What's Fair: Ethics for Negotiators.* San Francisco: Jossey-Bass, 2004.

Miller, Abraham H. *Terrorism and Hostage Negotiations.* Boulder, Colo.: Westview Press, 1980.

Mnookin, Robert, Lawrence Susskind, and Pacey C. Foster. *Negotiating on Behalf of Others.* Whitehall, N.J.: Sage, 1999.

Mnookin, Robert, Scott Peppet, and Andrew S. Tulumello. *Beyond Winning: Negotiating to Create Value in Deals and Disputes.* Cambridge, Mass.: Harvard University Press, 2004.

Morley, Ian, and Geoffrey Stephenson. *The Social Psychology of Bargaining.* London: George Allen & Unwin Ltd., 1977.

Murnighan, J. Keith. *The Dynamics of Bargaining Games.* Englewood Cliffs, N.J.: Prentice-Hall, 1991.

Neale, Margaret, and Max Bazerman. *Cognition and Rationality in Negotiation.* New York: The Free Press, 1991.

Newcomb, T. M. *The Acquaintance Process.* New York: Holt, Rinehart, and Winston, 1961.

Nierenberg, Gerard I. *Fundamentals of Negotiating.* New York: Hawthorn/Dutton, 1973.

Nixon, Peter. *Mastering Business in Asia: Negotiation.* New York: Wiley, 2005.

Osgood, Charles E. *An Alternative to War or Surrender.* Urbana, Ill.: University of Illinois Press, 1962.

Pruitt, Dean. *Negotiation Behavior.* New York: Academic Press, 1981.

———, and Jeffrey Z. Rubin. *Social Conflict: Escalation, Stalemate, and Settlement.* New York: Random House, 1986.

Rahim, M. Afzalur, ed. *Theory and Research in Conflict Management.* New York: Praeger, 1990.

Raiffa, Howard. *The Art and Science of Negotiation.* Boston: Harvard University Press, 1982.

Rosenberg, Morris. *Conceiving the Self.* New York: Basic Books, 1979.

Roth, Alvin E., ed. *Game-Theoretic Models of Behavior.* Cambridge: Cambridge University Press, 1985.

Rubin, Jeffrey Z., and B. R. Brown. *The Psychology of Bargaining and Negotiation.* New York: Academic Press, 1975.

Schelling, Thomas C. *The Strategy of Conflict.* London: Oxford University Press, 1960.

Schuster, Camille P., and Michael J. Copeland. *Global Business: Planning for Sales and Negotiations.* Fort Worth, Tex.: The Dryden Press, HarcourtBrace College, 1996.

Shapiro, Ronald, and Mark Jankowski. *The Power of Nice.* New York: Wiley, 2001.

———. *Bullies, Tyrants, and Impossible People: How to Beat Them without Joining Them.* New York: Crown Business, 2005.

Singer, Linda. *Settling Disputes: Conflict Resolution in Business, Families, and the Legal System.* Boulder, Colo.: Westview Press, 1990.

Stark, Peter B. *It's Negotiable.* Amsterdam, The Netherlands: Pfeiffer & Company, 1994.

Susskind, Lawrence, and Jeffrey Cruikshank. *Breaking the Impasse: Consensual Approaches to Resolving·Public Disputes.* New York: Basic Books, 1987.

Thaler, Richard H. *The Winner's Curse: Paradoxes and Anomalies of Economic Life.* New York: The Free Press, 1992.

Thompson, Leigh. *The Mind and Heart of the Negotiator.* Upper Saddle River, N. J.: Prentice-Hall, 1998.

———. *Negotiation (Frontiers of Social Psychology).* New York: Taylor & Francis, 2005.

Trump, Donald J. *The Art of the Deal.* New York: Random House, 1987.

Ury, William. *Getting Past No.* New York: Bantam, 1991.

Walton, Richard E., and Robert B. McKersie. *A Behavioral Theory of Labor Negotiations.* New York: McGraw-Hill, 1965.

Wenke, Robert A. *The Art of Negotiation for Lawyers.* New York: Law Distributors, 1985.

Williams, Gerald R. *Legal Negotiation and Settlement.* St. Paul, Minn.: West Publishing, 1983.

Woolf, Bob. *Friendly Persuasion: How to Negotiate and Win.* New York: Berkley Books, 1990.

Zartman, I. William. *The Negotiation Process: Theories and Application.* Beverly Hills, Calif.: SAGE Publications, 1978.

◄ For Further Information ►

WHARTON EXECUTIVE NEGOTIATION WORKSHOP: Bargaining for Advantage
   The Wharton School
   255 South 38th Street, Suite 202
   Philadelphia, PA 19104-6359
   (800) 255-3932 (U.S. and Canada)
   (215) 898-1776 (worldwide)
   (215) 898-2064 (fax)
   execed@wharton.upenn.edu (e-mail)
   http://executiveeducation.wharton.upenn.edu (World Wide Web)

Index

FOR THE BEST IN PAPERBACKS, LOOK FOR THE 🐧

In every corner of the world, on every subject under the sun, Penguin represents quality and variety—the very best in publishing today.

For complete information about books available from Penguin—including Penguin Classics, Penguin Compass, and Puffins—and how to order them, write to us at the appropriate address below. Please note that for copyright reasons the selection of books varies from country to country.

In the United States: Please write to *Penguin Group (USA), P.O. Box 12289 Dept. B, Newark, New Jersey 07101-5289* or call 1-800-788-6262.

In the United Kingdom: Please write to *Dept. EP, Penguin Books Ltd, Bath Road, Harmondsworth, West Drayton, Middlesex UB7 0DA.*

In Canada: Please write to *Penguin Books Canada Ltd, 90 Eglinton Avenue East, Suite 700, Toronto, Ontario M4P 2Y3.*

In Australia: Please write to *Penguin Books Australia Ltd, P.O. Box 257, Ringwood, Victoria 3134.*

In New Zealand: Please write to *Penguin Books (NZ) Ltd, Private Bag 102902, North Shore Mail Centre, Auckland 10.*

In India: Please write to *Penguin Books India Pvt Ltd, 11 Panchsheel Shopping Centre, Panchsheel Park, New Delhi 110 017.*

In the Netherlands: Please write to *Penguin Books Netherlands bv, Postbus 3507, NL-1001 AH Amsterdam.*

In Germany: Please write to *Penguin Books Deutschland GmbH, Metzlerstrasse 26, 60594 Frankfurt am Main.*

In Spain: Please write to *Penguin Books S. A., Bravo Murillo 19, 1° B, 28015 Madrid.*

In Italy: Please write to *Penguin Italia s.r.l., Via Benedetto Croce 2, 20094 Corsico, Milano.*

In France: Please write to *Penguin France, Le Carré Wilson, 62 rue Benjamin Baillaud, 31500 Toulouse.*

In Japan: Please write to *Penguin Books Japan Ltd, Kaneko Building, 2-3-25 Koraku, Bunkyo-Ku, Tokyo 112.*

In South Africa: Please write to *Penguin Books South Africa (Pty) Ltd, Private Bag X14, Parkview, 2122 Johannesburg.*